DARWIN - CHRISTMAS EVE - 1974

SURVIVING
TRACY

SURVIVORS TELL THEIR OWN STORIES OF COURAGE AND SURVIVAL AGAINST THE MOST DEVASTATING CYCLONE IN AUSTRALIA'S HISTORY

Editing: Tabitha Ormiston-Smith
Copyright © 2015 Patti Roberts
Pattiroberts7@gmail.com
All rights reserved.

Paradox Promotions
Covers & Formatting
http://bit.ly/paradoxcovers

ISBN-13: 978-1519790200

ISBN-10: 1519790201

DEDICATION

To all those souls who lost their lives to Tracy.

May you forever rest in peace.

Ramon Williams, photographer and journalist with Worldwide Photos.

The briefing officer told us to prepare for the worst scenes imaginable.

"If you have read Orwell's 1984, that will give you an idea of what to expect."

CONTENTS

A NOTE FROM THE EDITOR

My first real knowledge of the devastation that was Cyclone Tracy came about in 1977 or 1978, when I was involved in the reconstruction of the community buildings on Mornington Island, which had been hit by the outer edge of the cyclone. I had, of course, heard about it on the news, and one knew that Darwin had been very, very hard hit, but one didn't quite realise the extent of the devastation, and of the effect on people's lives. My own experience of disasters had been relatively mild; growing up in Lismore, NSW, I was accustomed to the annual floods; our house was a comfort point for rescue workers, and during the worst of it we'd have them coming in shifts for a hot shower, coffee and hot soup. They'd warm up and dry off and get some food and off they'd go. To me it meant a little excitement, and feeling one was somehow worthwhile. Displaced people would be taken to shelter in church halls on the high ground, and we all used to go through our wardrobes to help answer the calls for clothing and blankets and so on, and I thought of Tracy as something rather similar to that – tragic for the individuals affected, even devastating, but hardly anyone ever died, and people's houses were still there when the water went down.

Reading through the accounts in this book, I realised that I had had no idea, not the faintest clue, of what it was really like. To emerge from hiding after a night of terror and find one's house gone, just gone. To listen to the shrieking of the house being torn to pieces. The house - that icon, common to every human culture, of comfort and safety – just torn to pieces. No one could ever be quite the same again after such an experience. Indeed, this is borne out by many of the accounts; so many people in this book close their accounts with the remark that they still don't handle high winds well.

This collection brought me to tears at times. There are so many accounts of personal heroism, of incredible courage, of selflessness and an indomitable spirit. Over and over one reads of people who faced the total devastation of their world and were not laid low. People whose first thought on realising their own survival was to help others. People who set aside their own troubles to go to the aid of their neighbours.

There are darker images as well. I was shocked to learn that even in a disaster of this magnitude, there were looters, and I don't think I will ever lose the image of a small boy, his world gone, crouching on a schoolroom floor clutching his puppy, all that remained to him, and a faceless, booted soldier tearing the puppy from his grasp and shooting it before his eyes.

But the one thing that above all emerges for me, reading this collection, is the essential fineness of the ordinary person. The cheerfulness and good humour with which so many people greeted the ruin of their world, the alacrity with which people set aside their grief and shock and went to help others, make one proud to be a member of our species. It is a message of hope in darkness.

Tabitha Ormiston-Smith.

SANTA NEVER MADE IT INTO DARWIN.

CHRISTMAS 1974

Real stories from those who survived to tell the tale.

Special acknowledgements

To all those who opened their hearts and came to the rescue of so many in need that Christmas day, and the days and months that followed. We are forever grateful.
To the Red Cross and Salvation Army for your endless hours of support.
To all those who remained behind, to the men and women who arrived in the hundreds with support and provisions to help us rebuild our homes and shattered lives.

Many thanks to all those who supplied cherished family photographs.

CHAPTER 1 – PATTI ROBERTS

I, for one, will never forget that Christmas. I know I am not alone.

To a child of 14, hearing the news of a cyclone heralded the possibility of an awfully big adventure.

Growing up in the sleepy township of Darwin, where cyclone warnings were as common as thunderstorms, meant life was pretty much uneventful and boring for most at the tender age of fourteen, where everyone else's life was far more exciting than your own mundane existence.

So yes, give me an adventure, please.

When I learned that yet another cyclone was heading our way, I remember a conversation I had with my little sister as we stood in the back yard beside our little vegetable patch, a garden inspired by our scary grade 7 primary teacher who was called, not affectionately, Stilla the Gorilla. He has passed now, so if Mr Stilla (dressed in his white shirt and matching white shorts) is looking down on me as I write this, I hope he does not think too ill of me.

You know the saying, be careful what you wish for? I've thought a great deal about those words since Tracy.

"I wish it would hit," my 14-year-old self had said. "Nothing exciting ever happens in Darwin...." Those were the words I remember saying to Fay, my little sister. The words are almost as clear in my mind now as though I'd said them just yesterday.

Above, the clouds loomed, dark and heavy, whispering conspiratorially, as if they were planning on granting me my frivolous wish.

Who knew that only days later, I would be lying under the bed with my little sister, as the relentless wind, the foreboding sound of which I hope never to hear again, tore our home apart piece by piece.

Who knew this, that what pursues the eye of the cyclone is far more vicious than what comes before?

I certainly didn't.

The wind pounded and shook the houses until the nails, nuts and bolts holding the house together eventually rattled loose, and one by one, sheets of the corrugated tin roof began flapping until they let go and flew away. The whistling wind began filling the house through cracks and holes until the pressure literally exploded the house, blowing it apart at the seams.

During the second stage of the cyclone, the part that follows the eerie stillness of the eye, when you think the worst is over and you confidently think you can go back to bed, the sound of chaos and destruction is amplified beyond comprehension. Within minutes of the eye passing over us, Cyclone Tracy had morphed into an apocalyptic monster from hell.

I remember bolting out of bed and running across the bedroom towards the door as though a monster was chasing me, then calling out, "God, somebody help me!"

On hearing my plea, my father jumped out of his own bed - just as a house pillar came crashing through the roof and impaled his pillow. To this day, I believe I saved my father's life.

My older sister, Susan, reached me first and grabbed hold of me. When our father arrived, he told us to get under our beds. I remember climbing under my bed, but the rest is a blank until I climbed out from beneath it at daybreak. I think the mind blocks out things that are just too horrifying to remember.

The first thought on my mind was for my mother, who had spent the entire night alone with our cat, in her bedroom on the ground floor. Afterwards, she told us how she thought we were all dead when she heard the upstairs part of the house being blown and torn apart.

As a kid, I never thought about how my Mum coped with those torturous thoughts alone. As an adult, though, with a child of my own, I can only imagine how helpless and alone she must have felt, with the agonizing belief that her children were dead.

By morning our home, apart from three bedrooms, was gone.

We were lucky, but most of Darwin was flattened to the ground and unrecognisable.

As the wind subsided and the sun began to rise, people began calling out to neighbours. "You all okay?"

"Yes, we're fine."

And we were fine. We were alive.

The old Chinese couple across the street had lost their entire home, everything was destroyed. The old man found his wife the next morning, naked but alive, inside their refrigerator.

Our neighbour three houses down, however, was not so lucky, and was struck and killed by a piece of flying corrugated iron when she went outside to fetch her dog after the eye of the cyclone had passed over.

Christmas day was a soggy event. Our gifts, what was left of them, were found beneath our lounge room carpet, along with one very water-logged Christmas tree.

What food could be salvaged had to be eaten straight away before it perished. We had a BBQ breakfast, lunch and dinner that day.

That night when I went to bed, although I don't recall in which part of the house that was, I realized for the first time how quiet a place was without the usual hum of a city powered by electricity.

Two to three days later, I can't be sure, I was evacuated, along with my mother, Audrey Dunn, my big sister, Susan, and my little sister, Fay, to Brisbane.

On the aircraft, seven of us were seated in three seats.

After landing in Brisbane and being 'accounted for', we were given clean clothing and housed in little cottages at Wacol.

Wacol was also the place where a boy, another

evacuee from Darwin, French kissed me for the first time. I was horrified. I thought it was the most disgusting thing ever.

Our father, Albert "Digger" Dunn, stayed behind in Darwin with our Persian cat, Kuchi, to rebuild our home. Unlike many pets in Darwin, Kuchi both survived the cyclone and escaped a bullet. It wasn't until sometime afterward that I learned that many pets had been shot after the cyclone, in an attempt to stop the spread of disease.

Kuchi, however, went on to live a very happy life, and if I remember correctly, died in her sleep in 1984.

We remained in Wacol until our return to Darwin in February 1975. I remember how grateful and triumphant I felt when I learned that we would be returning to Darwin in time to begin the new school year back at Darwin High.

I've read a lot about Cyclone Tracy over the years, and I have briefly accounted for much of what I have learned below.

***

In the late afternoon of the 24th of December 1974, Darwin was cloaked by clouds and rain squalls, and wind gusts began to intensify.

There were no doubts by this stage that Darwin was in for one hell of a storm, and power would most likely be lost for a few hours. By 10 p.m. on Christmas Eve, the winds were beginning to cause physical damage to Darwin. By midnight most of the power was out, and the damage was becoming serious. As Cyclone Tracy made her way across the city, crossing the coast near Fannie Bay at around

3.30am on Christmas morning, Tracy indiscriminately clawed and howled her way through Darwin, completely annihilating some homes, while leaving others untouched.

Wind gusts were officially estimated at up to 230 km/h—the Bureau's anemometer at Darwin Airport reached 217 km/h before it was destroyed by flying debris.

Darwin had become a war zone overnight.

Greeted by a scene of unimaginable destruction, how many must have wondered if they were the only survivors that Christmas morning, as they crawled from the rubble that had once been their homes?

But while some came together to help, others took to the streets and looted anything they could lay their hands on.

Many of those who lost their lives were killed by flying debris or crushed beneath their homes. Records identified 66 – 77 (records vary) names of individuals who perished as a result of Tracy - 53 on land and 13 at sea. The number of lives that were actually lost, on land and sea, will never be known.

145 people were seriously injured; more than 500 received minor injuries.

About 70% of houses suffered serious structural failure, while others were completely destroyed.

In the immediate aftermath of the cyclone, evacuation of the majority of the population became essential, given that there was no running water, no sanitation, no electricity, little shelter and a high risk of disease outbreaks. Like any war zone, Darwin was on the brink of total collapse.

Photograph by Ramon Williams

After the cyclone, an airlift evacuated over 30,000 people, which is the biggest airlift in Australia's history. Thousands of others left by car.

The total damage bill topped 1 billion dollars, a colossal sum in 1974.

To this day, Cyclone Tracy is among the most destructive cyclones ever recorded in Australian history. Let us hope that it stays that way.

Did the cyclone change me? I can't really be sure. I still love a good thunderstorm, and rain on a tin roof.

Today, I am an author living in Cairns, Far North Queensland. In my heart however, I will always consider Darwin as my home town.

On September the 14th 2015, I became the proud grandmother to Jacob Roberts, and in March 2016, I will hold him for the first time.

Living in Cairns, I still experience my fair share of cyclones, and we have certainly dodged a few bullets as far as cyclones go. I don't go crazy and stock the shelves until they buckle, or fill the bathtub and numerous containers with water. I do stay aware, though, by following the warnings and updates, always mindful that Tracy might have an evil twin out there somewhere, just waiting to attack. Patti Roberts.

CHAPTER 2 - ANDY STUMP

I was twenty-one and a wanderer. I left Cairns mid-1974 after living and working there for several months, and travelled south through Victoria and South Australia and across to Western Australia, before heading north and arriving in Darwin in about August 1974. I would have stopped somewhere if a job had come up, but it seems I was destined to meet with disaster a few months later. I don't recall how, but I got a job that came with a tiny flat at Carpentaria College at Nightcliff, working on the grounds and buildings of the then Anglican residential facility. I heard the cyclone warnings and thought, 'we are in for a bad storm', and the only preparation I remember doing was to tie up some young banana palms with sticks and string.

I have no idea of times through the night, but I did go to bed for maybe an hour or two before spending most of the ordeal sitting on a chair in a doorway with two blankets over me. It wasn't much fun on my own, but I realised I couldn't go anywhere. I missed the 'light show' under my blankets, but the noise was very frightening, especially hearing the brick walls falling in the two-storey building

adjoining my little refuge, which survived mostly intact. I was very grateful to be in one piece in the morning, and camped around my flat with several others before driving out several days later in my battered Holden station wagon. Andy Stump.

Andy lived and worked in Victoria and Queensland after Tracy. In 1978 he met Yvonne in Adelaide, and his travels were over. They have four daughters, two sons, and a granddaughter and three grandsons, so life is busy.

RINGS WATCHES & GIFTS

Photograph by Ramon Williams

Photograph by Ramon Williams

CHAPTER 3 - BETH CATS

My name is Beth Cats. My husband Corry and nine month old baby daughter Amanda (Mandy) and I survived Cyclone Tracy. We lived on the corner of Henbury Avenue and Gsell Street, Wanguri.

It is true when people say things come in threes. Toward the end of 1974 we had an earth tremor, then Cyclone Selma around the beginning of December and then the big one, Cyclone Tracy on Christmas Eve.

When Cyclone Selma came through, all we got was a lot of wind and rain, so when Cyclone Tracy arrived I think we had become a bit complacent and thought it would be the same. Christmas Eve I went out to the airport about 4 p.m. to collect a Christmas cake my sister had sent up from Perth. A beautiful cake which we never got to eat. We had a building company, and that evening we had invited some of our workers and their families over for a Christmas party. At about 7 p.m. I even drove up to Kentucky Fried

Chicken in Nightcliff to pick up a party box of chicken. It was windy and rainy, but I thought it was just like last time.

As our friends Ann and Bob Dixon and their four children, Evelyn, Robert, Spencer and Anthony, who lived in Alawa, were coming over to spend Christmas with us, we arranged for them to come over after Midnight Mass and sleep over, to save coming out in the wind and rain on Christmas morning – they were cooking the turkey. They arrived around 9.00 p.m., all in a flap (with the cooked turkey) saying a cyclone was coming. Sure, have a drink – it's Christmas.

Some people left to secure their own places, and we had one family of four decide to stay, plus we had a young lad, Ted, from New Zealand, who worked for us and who had been living with us for a couple of months.

Ann started taping up the kitchen windows; we were not panicking, but thought we had better go outside and tie down our 21 foot boat. My husband, Corry, put one foot outside and decided maybe not, it was now too windy. The water was being blown in under the window tracks and also the closed sliding was bowing in with water coming in from the sides. We were starting to get worried now.

Our daughter Mandy was asleep in her cot, and we thought we would bring the cot out into the passage; it was a safe place to be. The guys had to take her door off as the cot was too wide to fit through the doorway – the style was louvre doors throughout, back then.

As we had fairly open ground across the road from us (Dripstone High School is there now), the guys decided to put our mattress up against the dining room window, then turn the dining table on its side to hold it there. They had just backed away to assess what they had done when a huge piece of debris hit the front of the house. The whole front of the house just disintegrated, the roof blew off and all that remained were the large exposed beams which had been cyclone bolted when built. Once the front wall had gone, there was nothing to hold the beams, so they began flicking around like matchwood, and these beams were seven metres long and they were still tied to the rest of the house with cyclone bolts. With all the flicking around, the beams started to shake the remainder of the house to bits.

We now had to bolt to the bathroom. Luckily the guys brought in the louvre door from our daughter's room and rested one end on the vanity and the other end on the towel rail, with six adults and seven children crammed in under it. Young Ted sat in the Roman bath with a crash helmet on, just in case. As things got worse outside, the roof over the bathroom went, and as the ceiling fell in the guys would arrange a section over the louvre door as they held it down. It was very scary, and all the children were so good. Holding baby Mandy, I had a pillow under her on my lap and one on top of her, just in case anything fell on us.

Sometime before midnight, our neighbours' half-built house started to fall apart, with bricks and debris falling into our swimming pool. We had no calm of the eye; the wind blew all night and we ended up sitting in several inches of water.

Anthony Dixon, who was 3 years and 4 months old, remembers "being scared, but thought it was cool having a sleepover at Aunty Beth's and that the adults were sleeping under blankets in the hallway. I remember I could stretch my feet up against the other side of the hallway."

Evelyn Dixon, who was 9 years 9 months, remembers Ted wanted to go to the toilet. We were already sitting waist deep in water, but as he said that, an icecream container flew in the bathroom window. He did what he had to do in the icecream container in the shower, then threw it back out the bathroom window, and due to the wind being so strong it blew back over all of us. I also remember Spencer being very cold, so Dad (Bob) took off his shirt to keep him warm, and in the morning Dad was badly wind burned. I remember we were all huddled in the car, and the other lady in the bathroom with us that night was dying for a cigarette, she was going through match after match trying to light one but had no luck; everything was saturated. I also remember us all praying the Our Father and Hail Mary all night long, and Uncle Corry sitting by the bathroom door and us all pushing against him when the wind was trying to blow the door in."

As daylight arrived the winds started to die down, and the guys started to move and have a look outside. There was no roof left, and only partial walls here and there. We couldn't believe our house was gone. The wind had blown down the passage, and the end house wall, spanning two bedrooms, was laid out flat on the ground. Our bedroom only had partial internal walls standing, our bed base had all the springs exposed – I remember clambering over it at some point.

Corry surveyed what was left of our house and thought he would never get another building job in Darwin. Then he looked across the road and didn't feel so bad. Down the street were a row of elevated government houses, and all that was left of them were the concrete piers and steel beams going across the piers. While the guys were exploring outside, we knew there was only one flush of the toilet, so we let all the children, then the women use the toilet and we had our one flush.

I then remembered I had left my engagement and wedding rings on a little weatherman sitting on the fridge. I climbed over mess and debris to get to what was left of the kitchen, trod in the soggy turkey and found the fridge and freezer both open, stuff everywhere and no rings to be found. Bob was complaining that Ann hadn't let him pick at the turkey on the way to our house and now it was gone.

For some reason I had put the Christmas cake, still in its box, and also what was left of the box of Kentucky Fried Chicken, in the linen cupboard. When I opened the linen cupboard doors (louvred) to get the cake and chicken out, there were thousands of tiny pebbles embedded in the chicken and also the cake. Both were completely inedible.

Our neighbours next door in Gsell Street, Jacqui and Terry Bryan and their seven-year-old twin daughters Tammy and Tracey, were in the middle of building their two storey house, and were living in a caravan in an open-ended shed. Their caravan was moving backward and forward, and was about to take off when our 21 foot boat wedged it against the steel uprights of the shed, and they huddled under the caravan table. Pretty terrifying for them. When Corry came out and saw where the boat was, he was horrified, and hurried over to see if they were alright, and apologise. Terry climbed out thanking us for the boat, saying it had saved their lives. Terry and Jacqui helped several people with injuries out of the rain, to under what was left of the bottom level of their house, until medical help came.

One of the families that were with us the in the bathroom (I can't remember their names) found their Fairlane, which had been parked out the front of our house with the handbrake on, at the end of Henbury Avenue, where it had been blown by the strong winds.

The guys went across the road and helped others who were calling out, and found three people stuffed into a 44 gallon incinerator drum. They had been blown out of their house. They were in the yard and found an incinerator and wedged themselves in, and then could not get out without help. There were several broken limbs.

Around mid-morning, Emergency Services came past and commandeered our four wheel drive. We found it the next day in Vanderlin Drive, with a flat tyre. When a vehicle the Emergency Services had taken ran out of fuel or had a flat tyre, they just left it where it was and looked for another vehicle to drive around in.

Having our other vehicle still not too badly damaged, we all decided to drive to friends Robyn and Ron Bowen's house in Floyd Court, Coconut Grove. Corry had built their house earlier in 1974. I managed to grab a few nappies and clothes for our baby from a broken chest of drawers in her bedroom, and scrounged around and found some of our own clothes strewn around the place. There was no formula or bottles to be found, so Mandy had to drink out of a cup, which she was already doing before the cyclone.

It was scary driving on the road and footpaths, trying not get a flat tyre and dodging debris and steel power lines which were lying on the ground all twisted everywhere. When we arrived at the Bowens' house there were several other people already there. They had lost half their roof, and everyone helped tarp that section with tarps from a friend's camping shop. Anything left in the shop was given to Emergency services and handed out to other people in need.

Christmas lunch consisted of a slice of ham and a spoonful of baked beans. Later, with so many people around, we had to find somewhere to sleep Christmas night. Ann and Bob Dixon had a real estate office in Stuart Park which had not been too damaged, and we slept on the floor in the office with only a pillow. During the night when water dripped on us, we were so tired we just rolled over to get out of it.

As we had hardly any nappies we had to wash more frequently. There was water to wash but not enough to rinse. As we had nowhere to go, we rotated to any friends where we could hang the nappies under their houses to dry. Corry went into Darwin to register us with the authorities as requested, so they knew who was still in Darwin. He also found a chemist open and the owners were giving out formula, disposable nappies and anything else people needed. It all became a blur over the next couple of days; we were all just trying to cope with having nothing – some did it better than others.

There was no electricity, no water and no cash

available to anyone.

On Thursday, there were rumours starting to get around about diseases, and there were too many people waiting at the airport to be airlifted out, so our guys decided to send the girls and kids by car to Alice Springs. We travelled in two cars, the Dixon family and their four children in one car, Robyn and her two children, Clinton and Dana, and Mandy and me in the other car. It was decided that Bob Dixon (the only male – he drew the short straw) went with his family to make sure we all stayed safe. We drove non-stop through to Alice Springs, only stopping for food and fuel. We had very little money, and wherever we stopped people were wonderful and filled out vouchers for the food and fuel - we never had to pay for anything. All except for 'Threeways' (at the turn off from Northern Territory to Queensland) – the only place we had to find money for fuel.

We arrived in Alice Springs about 3 p.m. on Friday 28th December, and came across a roadblock. A lovely guy asked if we were from Darwin, and we were so tired we just burst into tears. We were directed to the high school, where we were warmly welcomed and settled in the assembly hall. There were volunteers everywhere helping out and not long after arriving, someone came around to get our details, and details of one relative to whom a telegram would be sent. That one relative was to inform anyone else in the family. All the telegram said was 'All Safe'. That would have been a relief to my mother; my father had died in March 1974, two weeks after our daughter Mandy was born. My mum and aunt had been to visit us in Darwin just a couple of months before Cyclone Tracy, so when my brother rang up my sister on Christmas morning to say Darwin had been devastated by a cyclone, she was beside herself not knowing whether we were alive or not.

After staying at the high school for an hour or so, we were directed to the YWCA, who looked after us all very well. We three women had all started menstruating; we figured it was the shock. I had had on the same clothes for three days, so on arriving in Alice Springs, I threw them in the incinerator. The only thing I had left to wear was the long dress I had worn on Christmas Eve, peasant style with a frill on the bottom, which by then had a tear in it. I still have this dress packed away, and also the sleeping-bag outfit Mandy had on that night.

We were asked if we knew anyone in Alice Springs, and I remembered a friend I had worked with in Darwin when we first arrived in 1972. All I had was a name – no other details. Well they tracked down my friend Vivian Kells, who came around and took us back to her house. Vivian was very generous, and told us to ring our families. It was so hard to talk to my mother on the phone when all I wanted to do was cry. I had to keep it together so as not to upset her, and I think it was the same for her.

That morning we were also taken to another assembly centre, where all our details were taken and we were asked if we had any money. Of course with no banks or any personal items, we really had nothing. We were given money depending on how many children we had – I think I was given $25. We were then told there was a convoy of around two thousand cars on their to Alice Springs from

Darwin, and that we had to leave Alice Springs as soon as possible, so we were put on a chartered flight to Adelaide at about 1 p.m. that day. Bob Dixon stayed behind to help out, and then returned to Darwin to see what he could do. The airline hostesses were just wonderful, they cut up all the food they had and passed it around. Even the pilots insisted on sending their food around. To keep the children happy, the flight attendants took every child up to the cockpit one at a time to see the captain and see how the plane flew – they even took baby Mandy up to see the captain.

The flight was very comfortable, and when we landed in Adelaide, before we could move, a doctor came on board to make sure everyone was okay, and as we got off the plane, there was a volunteer allotted to help each person or family. Once inside the terminal we were again sat down and our details taken. I think I was given another $50. While I was doing this, my volunteer took Mandy from me, and she came back in clean clothes, very well looked after. A section of the Adelaide terminal was set aside for the people from Darwin, and there was a clothes section and a children's section, it was just so wonderful. I had given my daughter a small pillow to cuddle from an early age, which had been lost, and when she became restless at the airport, I asked if there was a teddy in the collection. I was told that unfortunately they had no teddies left, but they had a small pillow – perfect!

What the airlines were doing was that when a plane arrived in Adelaide, wherever it was heading they filled any empty seats with people from Darwin. Mandy and I probably had to wait about three hours before boarding a flight to Perth. By this time we were very tired. When the plane arrived in Perth around 11 p.m., the plane stayed out on the tarmac and we were bussed into a large hangar. Again we were sat down and asked more questions, and again Mandy was taken from me and came back all freshened up and with new nappy on. The wanted to give me more money, but I insisted I would be okay with my family. This was Saturday night, and I was told a social worker would come round to my mother's place the next day to see us. All I wanted to do was get out of the hangar. I think I was the first one out. My volunteer was carrying Mandy for me, and when we came out there was a big area cordoned off. When I saw the massive crowd of people behind the ropes, it all became too much for me, and my legs started to buckle. I could see my mother run from one area, other family members coming from everywhere. The poor volunteer lady was trying to hold me up until my family arrived.

It was so good to be with my mum. And yes, like we were told, a social worker arrived on Sunday to see if we needed anything. My uncle was a brigadier in the Salvation Army, and came around and took us to a big warehouse where there were so many donated clothes all in different sections to choose from. So very moving – my uncle was on the news that night pushing Mandy around in a pram while Mum and I were inside.

After a few days, as there were no materials or anything in Darwin to do any work with, Corry and young Ted decided to drive down to Perth. On Christmas Eve, we had been working on a job in Fannie Bay and the work vehicle (a Falcon station wagon) was involved in an accident and hit a lamp post, which cut the power to the whole of Parap. The car was damaged and missing parts of the body – but it survived the drive to Perth. Again everyone on the west coast was wonderful, with vouchers for fuel and food etc., all except 'Sandfire', where the guys had to scrounge a few dollars to pay for fuel and food.

Corry and Ted arrived in Perth about a week after Mandy and I arrived. Before leaving Darwin, Corry thought he would go back to our house and find some clothes for me, which he did – except that most of them were maternity clothes. He also found my sewing machine, which he brought to Perth to get checked out. I took it to a service agent and the fellow asked about insurance. I couldn't tell him anything about insurance, so he fixed my machine and said if I found there was insurance, we could send him some money, and if not, it was on him. Wonderful people. We had not been long in our house and found out we only had mortgage insurance – no contents insurance.

Corry and Ted were only in Perth for about three weeks before they set off back to Darwin. The morning they were leaving I rang a talk-back show on the radio and talked to host 'Yorkie'. I asked if they could play the song 'Santa Never made it to Darwin' by Bill and Boyd. When Yorkie found out I had gone through Cyclone Tracy, we talked for about twenty minutes on the radio. He wanted to know all about it, and asked many questions. Friends must have recognized my voice, and we had lots of phone calls to find out how we were.

Wherever we went shopping people were marvellous and gave me discounts on everything. When Corry and Ted arrived back in Darwin they stayed with another friend, Max Thomson, and his two teenage children in Rapid Creek. A lot of Max's house was damaged and Corry, being a builder, set about rebuilding the house. The house had to be inspected to see if it was suitable for a baby to live in before we were allowed back into Darwin. We flew back on 6 February. I had several suitcases to take on the plane (all we had) and was charged $85 excess baggage.

We visited what was left of our house in Wanguri and rummaged around in the debris looking for anything to salvage. We rescued the base of our bed, the springs exposed. There was not a lot to find, although where the television was smashed in small pieces, I found a pottery vase that had sat on the TV with not a scratch or mark on it. It was the vase I had received for my 24th birthday, the

November before the cyclone. I also found my engagement ring, but not my wedding ring.

The army then came through and bulldozed what was left.

While we lived at Max Thomson's house it was rebuilt around us; while one room was repaired or replaced we would move into another room. There was no electricity in Darwin until June. We lived with generators for all those months. The generator we would have on to cook meals and then switch it over to have lights so that we could see what we were eating. One of the bedrooms had only part of its roof and no ceiling, so we would wake up itching from the dust and debris being blown in on us. Mandy learned to walk, had her first birthday and was loved by all who lived in the house. We lived with Max until December '75, when we bought a shell of house in Tiwi, which Corry had started to build before the cyclone. The owners had decided not to come back to Darwin. While we rebuilt this house, we had a government caravan to live in. We sort of lived in the front part of the house and cooked and slept in the caravan.

We eventually rebuilt our house in Henbury Ave, Wanguri and moved in in May 1976; by this time I was three months pregnant again. Every time I was in the garden planting etc, I would just dig that little bit extra, in case I found my wedding ring, but I never did.

We lived and enjoyed life in Darwin until October 1988 when we moved to Cairns where we have our own business, hopefully to retire soon. Our daughter and son both live in Cairns with their families and between them, we have six beautiful grandchildren whom we see almost every day. Life is good and the weather slightly cooler than Darwin, and we love the reef and mountains in Cairns.

Above: Beth and Corry Cats - 2015

Photograph by Ramon Williams

CHAPTER 4 - JAN BERRY

A personal account of Cyclone Tracey Christmas Day 1974
by Jan Berry(née Clarke)

Where are the other sixteen people from the party at
127 Mitchell St on Christmas Eve of 1974?

It is strange to think that sixteen other people went
through an identical physical experience with me, yet we
would probably all tell the tale in a different way.

I and my friend Michael had just spent six weeks
coming from New South Wales, going through the magical
outback, off the beaten track and up through the beautiful
Flinders Ranges, and then on up to the mystical Olgas. To
this day I think they were the most awe-inspiring sight I
have ever seen, and there was a serenity about the place.
From Alice Springs, on to Darwin in a dune buggy which
Michael had built!

Michael and I arrived in Darwin about the second

week in December of 1974. After a couple of days of staying with his good friends, I got a share house with some other people. Over the next couple of weeks I remember hearing the weather reports and what you should do if a cyclone came through the area, but being only twenty and naïve, I took no notice whatsoever! I got work at the Don Hotel in the heart of Darwin, and did shift work.

On the night of Christmas Eve I finished at midnight. I knew there was a cyclone, but thought it would be just like a big storm. An acquaintance (I am sorry I don't remember your name) offered to walk me home. There was also a party going on at our place and I knew it would still be in progress.

I remember when I walked outside being absolutely shocked at the ferocity of the raging elements. I don't remember a lot about the walk except that at times we were bent double against the wind, and there was much torrential rain, and power lines were down on the ground.

I was at 127 Mitchell St (I am pretty sure that was the number), and it was nearly a kilometre from the heart of town.

When we finally arrived at the house it was to find the party still half-heartedly going. It was now too late for anyone to leave, with the fierce weather conditions. We sat around in the lounge room wondering what we should do. I don't think anyone had a clue what we were supposed to do, or where we should go to be safe. We were all young, and obviously not natives of the area or we would have known to go downstairs into the laundry. The house was typical of houses at the time, being up on a platform, with stairs on the outside and a laundry underneath the house.

So we sat. And we waited. Suddenly we heard all the louvres along the entire side of the house explode, one after the other. It was like the wind was ripping along the side of the house with a big stick held out, like a child does when he runs along side a picket fence with a stick!

We waited some more. I don't remember anyone speaking very much. Probably couldn't be heard over the roar of the wind anyway. That is one of the things that I remember most vividly about the cyclone. The tremendous roar of the wind. It was so terrifying . It was a primeval roar. It went into the depths of your being. It was like a monster. I have never heard anything like it in the forty years since, and I hope I never do again!

We were all sitting huddled together, but in our own separate worlds. Most of these people I had never seen before in my life, but I think of them from time to time as the years pass, and wonder about them.

Things were starting to happen. I don't know the time, but I think it must have been about 1:30 going on for 2 a.m. on Christmas Day of 1974. The roof in the lounge room started to peel off. The lounge room was the first big room in the house next to the kitchen. Well, I thought, okay. We can do without the roof. We huddled some more, but then the walls started to fall in on us. We decided that we needed to move! We retreated to the next bedroom. I remember crawling over the broken glass of the louvres and getting cut knees. You couldn't stand up to walk.

We went to the next bedroom, and I often have wondered did it really happen in stages as I personally remember it, or did the roof go off in one hit. I remember it as the roof being torn off room by room. We weren't long in this room and the roof started to go, and soon after that the walls started to come in on us.

On to the third and final bedroom we crawled. Sure enough the roof lifted off, and this would have meant that the entire roof had peeled off now. Once again the walls started collapsing, and then it got really scary! The wind started to pick up objects, and was hurling them off the naked platform of the house. In the next few moments, for the first time in my life I really thought about death. I quickly decided, though, that I was only twenty and there was no way I was going to die! I do remember thinking, though, that there would probably be people dying in this cyclone tonight, as it was so ferocious.

We knew then that we had to get down off this platform, as we would be the next objects to be hurled off the edge. If only we had decided that in the beginning. We started to crawl over the broken glass and make our way down the passage and on to the stairs. The stairs were on the outside of the house. We crawled and clung to the stairs and railing, and started to make our way slowly down the stairs. There were seventeen of us. I remember when I was just a few steps from the bottom, the wind picked me up and hurled me through the air like a rag doll. I was lucky that there was a house pylon in the way, as it stopped my outward progress. Who knows where I might have ended up if the pylon hadn't stopped me in my flight. I only received a cut on my nose. We made it to the laundry at last.

We did a head count. There were supposed to be seventeen of us. We were one short! Oh no! I and another guy decided to go back up the stairs and look for the missing person. I don't remember anything much about the trip up and back, but I do remember with vivid clarity that we found the missing man up on the platform of the house, just sitting in a chair! How he wasn't blown off I will never know. I don't know if he was in a state of shock, or had been drinking, or what. We got him back down the stairs without any difficulty.

We then waited for the next couple of hours or so till dawn. There were no serious injuries, and I felt we were all very lucky.

The wind had died right down by dawn. I will always remember, when it became light enough to see, looking out for the first time. I just could not believe what I saw. It was a sea of total devastation as far as the eye could see. There were no roads; they were all covered in debris. It was just destruction in every direction no matter where you looked. I thought at that moment that there would be deaths and many injuries.

I have often wondered over the years what happened to the other sixteen people. We spent one night together and shared the experience of a lifetime, never to see each other again.

I thought as I had had a year's nursing experience, that I should go to the hospital and see if I could be of any help, so I said farewell to everyone and set off in the general direction of the hospital, picking my way through and over the rubble, as there was no road to walk on.

I will always remember being so shocked, when I was walking across the hospital car park, at seeing a man crossing the car park towards the hospital, and he was carrying a woman and she had very badly sliced feet. I have often wondered how she has been, over the years.

As I had only had limited nursing experience, I was just really talking to people or holding a bandage in place. There must have been local flooding in the hospital, as I remember there being lots of water on the floor, and it was a pink colour from the blood. As there was not a lot I could do, I left after a few hours, and went back to our house. I began searching through the debris, looking for any of my things. I found my beautiful down sleeping bag down the back yard with a big gash in it. At some point I stitched it up, and it is still in use forty years later!

My friend Michael somehow or other found me, and he and his friends were all okay. I don't think their house had much damage, as they were in a different suburb.

They were evacuating people, but I did not want to leave and go back south, as I had only just arrived in the Northern Territory. I was lucky enough to secure work on one of the prawn boats working out of the Gulf of Carpentaria, based in Darwin. I worked as a cook and deck hand for the next eight months.

I returned for the 40th anniversary, and could not believe what a beautiful city Darwin had become. I think the landscaping is superb, and it is a wonderful, interesting place. Two of our children were living there, so I went to visit them.

It is still like living in a sauna, though! Jan Berry.

Below: Photographs by Ramon Williams.

CHAPTER 5 - IAN PHILIP CORK

Photo above: Our house before the Cyclone.

I joined the Northern Territory Police in September 1969 as a raw recruit, and had two months' training before graduating as a fully-fledged Constable (what a joke!). In common with other recruits, I had to travel to Darwin on my own for the course, and my wife Shirley, and children Sandra, Elaine and Leanne were brought to Darwin just before the graduation ceremony, and I was posted to Darwin. The Police paid for our accommodation and we rented a flat in Nightcliff, almost on the sea front. After the required waiting period we were allocated a house at No.2, Wonggu Court, Ludmilla North.

This suburb had the RAAF base flight path on one side and the aboriginal reserve at Bagot on the other. The block was totally devoid of vegetation, but there was a house and it was ours. We took the house in the middle of the dry season, and the ground was as hard as a brick. I can remember trying to dig a hole to plant shrubs with a screwdriver. When it finally rained and the ground got softened up, we used to go round to a friend's place and trim paspalum sprigs from around his trees. This was the way you got a lawn going in Darwin. Once the paspalum took, it spread very quickly. Down south paspalum is regarded as a weed, but it was used as lawn in Darwin. It didn't grow tall as it does in the south, neither did it get ergot. Its main advantage was that it could withstand the dry season, which couch grass could not, and it would bounce back very quickly as soon as it rained.

Across the other side of the road from us lived an Italian family, Guido and Pasqua Buccigrossi. We used to get on well with them, but there were some communication difficulties. Pasqua used to talk to Shirley about "pelled tomatoes", and it took Shirley some time to work out that she meant peeled tomatoes. For some reason our girls used to call her "Mitta Patqua". Guido was a bricklayer by trade, and after we bought the house he arranged for the underneath to be concreted. This made it much more useful, and we often used to sit under the house to keep cool. Guido was also going to construct a barbecue for us, but Cyclone Tracy put paid to that idea. When we had cyclone threats I used to tell Guido that he should secure all items that might blow around. After Tracy hit, he said to me: "You used keep telling me about cyclone and put things away. I not know what is cyclone. Now I know what is cyclone!" Another family just down the road took the injunction to tie down loose items seriously – they tied their rubbish bins to their fence. Only trouble was Tracy took their fence as well as their rubbish bins.

I spent two years in the Police Force before deciding it was not for me. I joined the PMG's Department (as it was then) as an exempt technician, not being a qualified technician, as I only had my training as an Amateur Radio Operator. Only in Darwin would I have been offered such a job, as they were short of staff.

We had received some money for some shares in the family sheep and cattle property that my father had given to us some years previously. From memory I think we got $30,000, which was quite a sum of money back then. After we tithed this sum we invested $10,000, bought a new vehicle, a Toyota Corona, for $3,500 (which represented about a year's wages at that time), and decided to purchase the house we were living in. In those days, after you had been living in a Government house for a year you could apply to purchase that house, or you would be offered another vacant house, which would have been lived in previously. We were advised that the Government intended to charge us $23,230, with a deposit of $1,000 and monthly repayments of $123 at a set interest rate of six-and-a-quarter percent for the term of the loan, the first payment being due in October of 1974.

We were told that we had to insure the property for at least $14,000, which confused me. I could not understand why the Government was going to charge us $23,230 but only require us to insure for $14,000 (later I discovered that $14,000 represented the value of the house, the rest the value of the land). I was working just across the road from

Royal Insurance Company, so I went in and insured the house for $25,000. When he heard what I had done, a neighbour did the same and was later grateful to us for the information. We had previously never had our contents insured and I decided that if I had to insure the house, I might as well insure what was in it, so I plucked a figure of $6,000 out of the air and insured the contents for that amount.

We spent a total of about $4,000 on the house, including getting Guido to concrete underneath, having a roof constructed over the set of stairs leading to the living room, and having the previously open veranda enclosed. The veranda was a small area facing the street, adjacent to the kitchen. We often used to sit out there during a storm and watch the lightning. The floor of the veranda was composed of boards with spacing to allow the rain to pass through (much in the style of decking) and we had plywood laid down first with linoleum over the top. This made a little office cum radio room for me.

I always thought that the Department of the Northern Territory houses were very badly constructed and would fly to pieces in a cyclone. The houses all had exposed eaves, and I went around our house with triple grips securing the ceiling joists to the rafters and battens. I also did a deal with the same neighbour for some paint to paint the outside. Previously the house had been clad in unpainted fibro cement sheeting, which looked pretty tacky. By the time I had finished, it was looking quite smart.

Four months after we had bought the house, it was destroyed during Cyclone Tracy, and a number of people commented later as to how unfortunate we had been. However, I really saw it as God's provision in response to our faithfulness in tithing the money we had received from sale of the property. Royal Insurance paid out $25,000 for the house and $6,000 for the contents (although we gave them a list of what we had saved from the cyclone, the company said that we were underinsured and paid the full amount). I think that the insurance companies received such a lot of bad publicity following their intransigence in arguing the toss with policy holders during the Brisbane floods earlier that year that they decided to pay up and not argue after Tracy. The Government received their $14,000 and we received the rest - $11,000. So we actually turned an investment of around $4,000 into $11,000 in four months, which is a pretty good rate of return. However, it is not a method of making money that I would recommend to anyone.

Cyclone Tracy formally came into existence at 10.00 a.m. on 21 December 1974, when it lay well to Darwin's north. On Tuesday 24 December, Tracy rounded Cape Fourcroy, Bathurst Island's western tip, and then moved along an east-south-easterly course towards Darwin. That afternoon we were warned that it was coming, and allowed to go home early to prepare. However, we had already had a couple of cyclone warnings that season and they had amounted to nothing, so we were not overly worried. Nevertheless, I did pass on my customary warning to Guido. By early evening, however, we knew that we were going to cop it. Ray Wilkie, who later was the forecaster on Channel Ten in Brisbane, was the senior forecaster for the

Weather Bureau in Darwin at the time. He was reputed to have said that the cyclone would pass without hitting Darwin. Years later, in his Brisbane days, I remembered that. His predictions didn't improve either - if he said that the current rain period was over, you could bet your bottom dollar that there would be floods.

Shirley had done some cooking preparations, having recalled that a cyclone left Townsville, I think it was, without power. Although it was Christmas Eve, she decided to cook the Christmas chickens early, so that if the power failed we would at least have something to eat. Standard preparations included filling the bath with water, although they didn't tell us that if the ceiling fell into the bath, the water would not be drinkable anyhow. The ABC announced that they would be on the air for the duration to keep people informed. Quite early in the evening there was a big flash in the sky as two major power lines came together, blacking out the whole of the town, including 8DR. There was an emergency ABC radio transmitter some miles south of Darwin, which had a transmitting tower concealed in the ground. The studios were in a bunker at Civil Defence Headquarters (the ones we had to test on Tuesday nights when I worked for the former PMG's Department) and the idea was that, in an emergency, the tower would rise up out of the ground and the studios at Civil Defence could be used to keep the population in the picture. We always used to say that if there ever was an emergency, this system wouldn't work - and it didn't.

Cyclones take quite some hours to build up to full power, and we had plenty of time to prepare ourselves. We filled the bath with water and put the lounge suite up against a wall cupboard, which had all the Christmas presents inside. We put the dining room table over the lounge suite to give us some sort of shelter in case the situation became too hairy. It was probably just as well that the power failed early on, as we couldn't see too clearly what was happening. As the storm built up in intensity we could look out through the windows and see bits of debris, mostly corrugated iron roofing, sailing past. We heard a few bumps on the roof and a few leaks started in the ceiling.

I can remember saying jokingly that I would soon have to put an umbrella up. Around midnight the eye of the cyclone passed over us, and all became quiet. The kids told me that the manhole in their bedroom ceiling had gone, so I climbed up on a chair to look and found to my astonishment that I could see sky above. We went outside and noticed that the whole roof had gone. Later on I discovered how effective my triple grips had been. Most people just lost the roofs of their houses. With ours, the storm took the roof and the attached ceiling joists as well,as can be seen in some of the photos I took later. Because I had painted the barge boards blue, we could track down large chunks of our roof, with ceiling joists attached, a couple of streets away. I have always thought that Cyclone Tracy did not do a great deal of damage of itself - most of the damage was caused by NTA houses coming to pieces and flying through the air.

During the period of the eye of the cyclone, we all went down into the street to see how neighbours were faring. There was some damage, but not too extensive. A number of us decided to congregate in the Ablong's house, just across the road. It was of brick construction and appeared to be safer than our Northern Territory Administration home, and it appeared to have been relatively undamaged. There were the five of our family, four of the Ablong family, two Raes from the house next door to the Ablongs and six Stringers from a few houses away. (At that time Col Stringer owned "Stringers Fishing and Outdoor World". He later became a noted evangelist and writer.) As I mentioned, it takes some hours for a cyclone to build up in intensity as it approaches. When the eye goes over all is quiet, then the cyclone hits from the other direction, but at full force within a very short space of time. I was last under their table with my backside sticking out. I heard glass doors cracking behind me and decided that it was time to seek a safer spot. So I went and stood in the shower. The roof went, the shower ceiling came down on top of me and there I was with water running down my neck holding the ceiling up. I cannot recall ever having felt so cold. I really thought I was going to die alone. Nevertheless I felt at peace with God. I felt that, if my time had come, I was ready.

The others under the table, meanwhile, were lying in water, and Shirley was trying to hold a settee down to stop it being blown away, when a beam came in through the window and held the settee down for them. By daylight the storm had passed and we could go outside to see what had happened, only to be confronted by a scene of devastation. It seemed as though the second phase of the cyclone did far more damage than the first phase, although this may have been because the house structure had been severely weakened during the first onslaught.

All the front part of our house had gone, including the kitchen, our new veranda, (including its floor coverings), and the living/dining room. If we had stayed in the shelter of our own house we would have been stuck out in the open, as the two doors out of the living room both opened out in the direction the wind was coming from, and we could not have opened either of them against the force of that wind. The lounge suite, which was supposed to have been our protection, was in the neighbour's pool. Our freezer (containing a kilo of prawns, which made a horrible smell later on) and many of our possessions were all scattered around the park next door to our house. The table was still in position, but would not have afforded us any protection, as we would have been out in the open with all the walls and ceiling gone. The chickens Shirley had saved for our Christmas lunch were full of shards of glass, and inedible. Our car, which was parked under the house, escaped relatively unscathed except for where a wall had come down along the side of the car, causing some damage. However, it was well and truly driveable.

A furniture pantechnicon parked in Tudawali Street, which led into Wonggu Court, had been blown over onto its side and Wonggu Court itself was littered with debris to the extent that it was impassable to traffic. The only way we could drive out was through the park. There were power lines down everywhere - even the power poles had been blown down. Our rotary clothes hoist had all its arms pointing in one direction, and the banana palms had all been blown off at ground level. We heard rumours that the cyclone was coming back in our direction and we were advised to seek shelter in the school at Ludmilla, so we decided to drive down there while we could. A number of folk had the same idea, and we ended up spending two nights there. The morning after Tracy we drove back to the house in somewhat of a dazed state. We wandered around picking things up and putting them down again with no sense of purpose. Back at the school we just sat, and I can clearly remember thinking that if someone put a gun to my head and told me that they would pull the trigger if I didn't stand up, I would have difficulty deciding if it was worth it. At one stage the call went out for someone with first-aid experience to help, but I just sat there, even though I was well qualified in first aid, and had been an ambulance driver for some years. It was a very strange feeling, and I don't think that anyone who hasn't been through such an experience can fully understand the after-effects.

By the Friday night telephone communications were restored, and residents were permitted to make free calls to relatives. Shirley was permitted to make one call of no more than three minutes' duration to my parents to let them know we were alive and well. They had been very worried, as they had just been sitting down to Christmas dinner when they heard the news. They had been expecting a Christmas phone call from us and because they had heard nothing. I found out later that they were convinced we had died in the cyclone.

Alan Stretton, a retired general, was appointed to take charge of the situation, and it was a wise choice in my opinion. He determined to get everyone possible out of Darwin and bring in people who hadn't been in the cyclone to deal with the problems. I know that, for myself, I would probably have been useless, and I don't think I would have been alone in that. The RAAF was brought in to conduct the evacuations, with women and children being first in line. On the Friday morning it was the turn of Shirley and the girls, and they were taken to the airport on the back of a truck. I have always thought Shirley had a wistful look about her and I can still picture the look on her face as they drove away, wondering when we would meet again. Later that day I drove down to the airport with the intention of enquiring whether they had got out safely. However, men were not being allowed past the airport gate, and I could not get any information. I assumed that they were well and truly gone, but I later learned that they spent all day on the tarmac. Shirley told me that a plane would come in and nobody would know where it was going, so people would gather their belongings and trudge out to the plane. If it was bound for the wrong destination for them, they would trudge back and repeat the process when the next plane came in. In addition, preference was being given to women with very young children and those who had been injured. She must have had a trying day, spending the day with three children with very little shade in Darwin's hot sun. The last commercial plane left before it got too dark for them to operate, possibly due to there being none of the normal airport lighting, and they were not on it, but a few hours later some RAAF Hercules aircraft came in, as they were capable of operating under the prevailing conditions, and it was around midnight when Shirley and the girls were finally put on one bound for Brisbane. In the meantime, the girls lay down on the warm tarmac and slept. Earlier they had been grateful to have been supplied with sandwiches provided by the Salvation Army, flown in on the last commercial plane of the day. In Brisbane, Shirley and the children were picked up by my brother-in-law, Rex, who drove up from the Gold Coast for them.

Although we were not hurt physically in the cyclone, psychologically it was a very different story. Trauma counselling was unheard of at the time. Maybe if that had been available, things would have been different. I drove around Darwin afterwards, but I could not take many photos - it was too distressing. I have a souvenir booklet, which I later bought in Canberra, but I never looked at it. I could not watch programs about Tracy on the television. Sometimes I could talk about Tracy, but at others it all became too much. Even now, years later, writing this has aroused strong emotions. (However, since joining the Cyclone Tracy Survivors Group, it has become easier.) I mentioned this to Shirley some years later, and she said she had had the benefit of talking about the experience many times, and had got it out of her system. She said that, because I had not, I was still holding onto it. However, recently we sat down together to share afternoon tea and we both ended up in tears. I guess that Cyclone Tracy is something that neither of us will really get over. We have forgotten just how loud the wind was, even though it was almost unbearably loud at the time. Nowadays, while we are living on the Gold Coast, mention on weather reports of cyclones in our vicinity will still arouse great apprehension in me. None of the bad experiences I have ever had in my life measures up to Tracy.

When I drove around Darwin after the cyclone I found it extremely difficult to get my bearings. I could recognise the main roads, of course, but so much had changed. The street signs had all blown away. Most of the leaves had been blown off the trees, so that I could now quite clearly see the tail fins of the aeroplanes at Darwin airport, whereas previously we had not been able to see anything at the airport. All the birds had either left town of their own accord or had been blown away (although they were reputed to have returned within six hours). I went to try to find out how some friends of ours had fared and I was unable to locate their house, because all the landmarks I would have used to navigate were no longer there.

Tracy went over Darwin in an S-shaped configuration, and I later heard it said that if someone had been trying to work out the best way to destroy the city, that way would have been it. A phenomenon known as "explosive deepening" began, whereby the eye shrank rapidly, causing an enormous and progressive increase in the ferocity of the wind, which reached a speed of over 300 km/hr. Nobody knew the actual wind speed, because the anemometer got blown away before the worst of the storm. It is also probable that tornadoes developed around the periphery of the eye, as a refrigerator was reputed to have been embedded about 15 metres up in a water tower. (Cyclones are not supposed to have an upward spiralling effect.) While we got a temporary respite when the eye went over us, in the northern suburbs they did not get that - all they had was a ninety degree wind shift. Consequently, suburbs such as Nightcliff fared much worse than we did. Some people had their whole houses blown away and were left clinging to the floor boards. In some streets, row after row of houses were left totally destroyed. One fellow in a wheelchair had to be abandoned at the top of his steps, and spent the rest of the time trying to shield himself from flying debris with a garbage can lid. One lady was holding her child in her arm and had her arm cut off by flying corrugated iron. The official death toll was 65 – 49 on land and 16 at sea. However, nobody knows the true cyclone toll. There was reputed to have been a colony of hippies down on Mindil Beach, I think it was, and they were never heard of again. Likewise, probably many people were lost when they took their boats out to sea. Darwin was the sort of place people came to in order to get lost from officialdom and the like – but they didn't intend to get lost that way!

Although our house was damaged to the extent of being written off, our experience was not particularly traumatic compared with those of others. One family we heard of were in their house when it got blown off its stilts on to the ground, with them in it. I reckon that would have been a hairy experience. At one house in Fannie Bay (Darwin's poshest suburb, next to Fannie Bay Gaol), the occupants were sheltering under a table and they heard swish, swish noises above them. They looked and saw that sheets of corrugated iron from the Gaol were flying in through one window and out through another.

After Shirley and the kids were taken to the airport, I drove off to look for petrol. Because there was no power, none of the petrol bowsers would work (long gone were the days when you could take the front off a petrol bowser and pump it by hand). However, at one service station they had rigged up a generator to power the pumps. For some reason the generator and the pump motors were incompatible, and one pump motor was burned out. So they had to attach the generator to one bowser, fill up five cars, move over to the other bowser and fill another five cars, then wait for three quarters of an hour for the motors to cool down before repeating the process. I think it took me about four hours to get a fill of petrol, but at least I was doing something, and I started to feel like living again.

From there I went home and started collecting some salvageable items, mainly linen. I pulled the power wires out of the house and strung up a clothes line under the house, and managed to get a number of sheets and towels dry. I also managed to find many important papers, including our marriage certificate. Although there had been about six inches of rain these papers were relatively undamaged, which was a blessing. Because it was the Wet Season, the weather was extremely hot and humid. I had a couple of shirts, and I would wear one and wash the other out in the swimming pool at an adjacent house – No. 5 Mawalan Court. (The pool was, of course, full of debris and the water wasn't the best, but beggars can't be choosers. Shirley washed her hair in water from the pool, but that doesn't say anything about her!) I would then dry that shirt under the house and wear the other one until it got saturated with sweat, and then repeat the process. Some enterprising folk had managed to get hold of petrol generators, but they were mainly used to power portable refrigerators to keep the beer cold - you have to get your priorities right, don't you?

I had a huge wooden box (it must have been at least 4 feet all round) that had originally housed a transmitting valve for ABD6, where I had previously worked. I had kept it with no particular view in mind, just thought it would be useful for something. However, it was just right for such a situation, and I managed to fill it with sheets, towels and the like. I then tried to roll it over into the store under our house, but it wouldn't fit through the door. So I decided to roll it over to a neighbour's house. Why I thought it would fit through his door when it wouldn't fit through ours I don't know. So I covered it with a sheet of plastic and left it at his house. Later I discovered that I had left it just where it copped the most water coming off the roof when it rained. Very much later, when I had been in Canberra for a while, a senior officer from the Attorney-General's Department (I was working in that Department at the time) went to Darwin to oversee the recovery of such items as belonged to people from the Department. I told him about my box and he said that he would arrange for it to be flown to Canberra, but when I told him how big the box was, he decided to have it sent down by road freight.

A good deal of time passed with no sign of the box, and eventually I got fed up with waiting and rang the freight company, only to find out that they had no idea what had happened to it. I made some enquiries and found it was sitting in a warehouse in Sydney somewhere. Arrangements were made for it to be sent to Canberra, and some six months after I had left it, we finally got it. Bear in mind that it had been out in all the weather during the whole time, and we thought that everything inside would have been useless. A few of the linen items had a bit of mould on them and the stem of a glass cakestand was broken. Apart from that everything was fine. There was a book called "The Spirit of Christ" in the box, and Shirley was sure that He had had a hand in its preservation. In addition, the authorities went around a number of Darwin houses salvaging any items of use, and we received a few more bits and pieces from that source, but nothing much of any great value.

Lionel Murphy, who was the Attorney-General at the time, came to Darwin and called a meeting of Departmental staff. At the meeting he told us that we could leave Darwin and turn up at any capital city in Australia and be given a position, which was of some comfort. I decided that, seeing that Shirley and the kids were gone and we had no home, there was no prospect of our family's being re-united in the foreseeable future. So I determined that the best thing to do was for me to leave Darwin too, in common with many others. Darwin had a population of around 49,000, of which 5,500 were away from the city at the time,8 before the cyclone and only about 10,000 afterwards. Many people just got in their cars and drove south on Christmas Day with no money or fuel - they just had to get out of the place. People who hadn't been there during Tracy found this hard to understand, but I could.

As well as the items in the box, I managed to salvage quite a lot of our possessions, which I loaded into the car, leaving only the driver's seat empty. On the Saturday or the Sunday (my memory is somewhat hazy as to the date. I thought it was the Saturday, but I am recorded in the Red Cross list of evacuees as being in Katherine on Sunday 29th December), I hit the road out of Darwin and spent the night in Katherine, where evacuees were being billeted. The next night I spent at a motel in Camooweal and adjusted my clock the wrong way (half an hour forward instead of backward). Consequently I got up very early the next morning and wondered why nobody was about. Quite early that day I got to Mt Isa, where I was given some emergency cash by Welfare, which I used to buy some underpants of all things - I probably just couldn't think of anything better to buy. We were also allowed to sign vouchers to obtain petrol along the way. I discovered that all vehicles from Darwin were being checked for roadworthiness before being allowed to leave Mt Isa. Why this was I have no idea. Surely if a vehicle had made it to Mt Isa, it would make it the rest of the way. I waited in line for about four hours and the sky got blacker and blacker with approaching rain. I decided I wasn't going to sit in the line any longer, and determined to leave Mt Isa and run the risk of there being a road block on the way - there wasn't. The road out of Mt Isa that I chose was a tarmac road heading due south to Boulia. From there it headed east to Winton on gravel road. All the way the clouds were building up, and by the time I got to Boulia the weather was very threatening. As I left Boulia the rain started, and I ran onto the gravel road. The car slipped and slid for a while and then ran out of the rain, giving me a clear run to Winton.

Darkness fell when I was about halfway along this road, and there were mice everywhere on it. At one stage my car headlights picked up something white on the road, so I slowed down only to discover that there were cattle all over the road, all of them dark except for one white one. If it had not been there, I would almost certainly have ploughed right into them, particularly as I was getting very tired by this time and was nowhere near as alert as I should have been. I spent the night in a motel in Winton and left early the next morning before breakfast, and was back onto dirt road when the rain started again. I decided that I was not going to make it, so I turned round and went back to Winton, got back into my bed and slept for a while. After I woke I was chatting to the owner of the motel and said that I didn't think I would be able to get through. He tried to call the police for me to find out if the road was passable, but apparently the police in Winton were good at not being found in case of need. However, he persuaded me to give it a go, so I had some breakfast and tried again. There was only light rain, which soon petered out and I was able to make it to the tarmac without any problems. Later I learned that soon after I had got through a semi-trailer had become bogged on the road, blocking it for all traffic for days. I should have spent another night on the road, but I was on the homeward stretch and nothing was going to stop me. I finally arrived at 55 The Promenade, Isle of Capri, at around two in the morning and woke Shirley up, but I was too overcome with emotion to speak for a while. She saw someone sitting on the end of her bed and thought it was someone trying to tell her that I had been involved in an accident or something. We had a joyful reunion, I can tell you. I drove about 1,000 miles that day, which is the longest drive I have ever made. Of course I should not have been driving for that length of time, but there was a major incentive to finish my journey.

My mother's reaction to my homecoming was very different to Shirley's. She seemed quite hostile (although she later denied this), which we found very hurtful. Some years later I had to undertake a unit of Psychology as part of a course I was undertaking. I came across the "Uncle Harry" principle. They didn't call it that, but this is how it works: Uncle Harry is seriously ill and expected to die very soon. The family adjust to his imminent death, but Uncle Harry makes a miraculous recovery and returns home, expecting to be greeted with great joy. However the family are very hostile because they had adjusted to his expected death, and he hadn't done the right thing by recovering. Uncle Harry finds his family's attitude very hurtful. Then I understood why my mother had reacted in the way she did. The situation was probably exacerbated by the fact that she already had a full house before the five of us turned up.

After a couple of days I rang the Attorney-General's Department in Canberra and told them where I was. They offered to find me a position in Brisbane or Canberra, and I decided on Canberra as it was the home of the Commonwealth Public Service, and opportunities for advancement were much better there than they would have been in Brisbane. While I was on the Gold Coast I had the damage to the car repaired, ready for the drive to Canberra. I set off on my own, arriving on the long weekend in January, and went to a hostel where the Department had booked accommodation for me. That night I froze in spite of having five blankets on the bed. The next day I went shopping for electric blankets without success - you don't find electric blankets in Canberra shops in January.

I also registered with Welfare for emergency accommodation, and was allocated a house at 16 Geeves Court in Charnwood. Under normal circumstances it would have taken three years to obtain government housing in Canberra, but ours was allocated in three days! We later discovered that the house had been vacant for six months - Shirley reckoned it had been kept especially for us. So I rang Shirley up and told her to book a plane ticket for the next day, Sunday. Then I rang Welfare to enquire about furniture, and they told me that they wouldn't be able to arrange anything before Monday. When I told them that Shirley and the children were coming down on the Sunday (this being Saturday), Welfare wanted me to delay the family's arrival. However, I told them that I could not do that as Shirley had already bought the tickets (not knowing whether she actually had or not). So Welfare decided to put the family up in a motel for the night. The motel turned out to be Noah's Town House, one of the top motels in Canberra, right in the heart of the city and quite close to the hostel where I was staying. I thought that Welfare's offer of a night in a motel included me - it didn't. However, that motel did have an offer going whereby an extra member of a family could stay for $1 - and that was me. So I got a night's accommodation in a luxury motel, including a hot breakfast, for $1, which I thought was a pretty good deal.

The next day Welfare arranged for delivery of furniture from the old Hotel Canberra, which had recently been demolished. So we got five of the old hotel-style beds with their clusters of springs, a kitchen table and chairs, five bedside cupboards and some of the old suitcase stands, as well as eiderdowns. We could have had sheets and towels as well, but we had stocked up on these while we were on the Gold Coast recuperating, so we had enough linen. The furniture was supplied on a needs basis, that is to say that when we no longer needed it, we were supposed to return it. In the end we were told we could keep what we wanted. Most of it we sent back, but we kept the dining chairs, only getting rid of them in 2003, and a couple of bedside tables, one of which we still have.

We only needed a refrigerator and a washing machine, neither of which Welfare supplied, so we went shopping out to Fyshwick and bought a refrigerator from Les Kilbey for $269. It was marked down, having fallen off a truck (no it was not stolen, it had literally fallen off a truck and had an almost undetectable dent). We looked at washing machines and saw one we liked, but didn't have the money to buy it. We asked Les Kilbey if he would put it aside for us, but when he found out that we didn't have a washing machine, he said he would send it out with the refrigerator and we could pay when we had the money. I remarked on his generosity and he replied that he had been in business for fifteen years and had never had anyone take advantage of him. I wonder if such faith in humanity would be exhibited today. Naturally we paid for it as soon as we could. So we were set up with all we needed and I went back to work.

The Department found a place for me in their city office working for a senior officer who had been seconded to deal with some issues with the Legal Aid Office and the Department's accounting system. He needed an offsider, and I was it. The Department couldn't put me into a non-existent position, so they put me into a position of Clerk Class 5, which had not been filled for some time. As I was only a Clerk Class 2/3, I could only be placed into the position temporarily and the Department paid me at a Class 4 rate on a part-performance basis. After some time, when my boss thought I had learned the job well enough, they advertised the position and I was promoted to it. One person appealed my promotion, as he was quite entitled to do, and I think he thought he should have had it because he was already a Clerk Class 4. However, my boss made sure that the appeal was not successful, and my promotion was confirmed.

The rented house in Charnwood was costing us $17 per week and the insurance company was paying us six month's loss of rent, which bought us in more than the $17 a week, and we wondered if it was worth buying a house, as we could have continued to rent the Charnwood house. However, we went looking, without much success initially. We had determined that $35,000 was as much as we could afford to pay for a house and told various real estate agents what our limit was, and they would take us to houses costing $37,000, or which faced west or something equally ridiculous. We had almost given up when we were going for a walk one afternoon and came across a house with a real estate agent sitting outside. I think the house must have been on display or something. Anyhow, we got chatting to him and told him what we were looking for. He said he would come and pick us up at the weekend and show us some houses. We weren't real keen in view of our previous experiences, but agreed, although we were pretty much ambivalent as to whether he showed up or not. However, he was as good as his word.

He took us around a number of houses and we ended up at 25 Bennet Street in Spence. He showed us a new house costing $34,500, which was just inside our limit. In Canberra the price of a new house was set by the builder with the government, so there was no bargaining. That was the price and that was it. The house was about two weeks away from completion, and we were quite impressed and decided to buy it. He rang me up the next day and told me that the house was ours, but there were problems. One was that someone else wanted the house and had contacted the builder, who had told him he could have it, but the agent had been to the solicitor and the house was ours. The second problem was that he had misquoted the price, which was actually $34,900, not $34,500. We thought he was making up the story about the other buyer to cover for his mistake about the price. However we were talking to the painter some days later and he confirmed the story.

The procedure for buying the house was that we had to apply to the Commissioner for Housing for a loan, which normally took weeks to approve, and had to be for a specific house. If the house was sold during the approval process, you had to start all over again with an application for another house. Nowadays, of course, you can get pre-approval from lenders for a loan of a set amount before you go looking at a specific house, and don't have to go through all that process. In our case, someone from the Commissioner's office rang me up within a couple of days to say that the loan had been approved and they wanted to settle immediately. I had to tell them that we were not in a position to do so, as the house wasn't finished. We couldn't believe the speed at which the process was happening. Later we discovered that the Commission had $6 million they were trying to get rid of before the end of the financial year, this being the middle of June. They preferred to spend all the money, but were prepared to commit it on the basis of imminent settlement if it was not possible to spend it. So we got our loan. On 1 July the rules for eligibility for Commissioner for Housing (government) loans were changed, and we would then not have been eligible.

So, once again we were into the mortgage business, with repayments of $105.75 per month on a loan of $15,000. It appeared that we were going to be able to pay the mortgage without too many problems on my salary - Shirl was not working at the time. However, I had quite forgotten about the mortgage on the Darwin house. The NT Government had placed a six-month moratorium on mortgage repayments, and wrote to me after the six months had expired asking me to resume paying my $120 per month. I had not realised that it was not possible to pay off part of a mortgage, and I thought the NT Government would just take the repayments out of the $14,000 the insurance company had paid them - but things didn't work like that. The NT Government put the $14,000 into an account where it earned 1% less than the rate of interest they were charging us, and we were expected to keep paying the mortgage until the amount we paid and the $14,000 made up the total of the loan.

This was a disaster, as I couldn't afford to pay off two loans, and we didn't know what we were going to do. We still had the block of land in Darwin, but it was held under a Darwin Town Area Lease and we were not able to sell it for five years. Once again, God came to our rescue. The NT Government decided that for residents who had been in Darwin at the time of the Cyclone, they would not enforce the five-year rule, and we were free to sell. Col and Jan Stringer (friends who had shared the Ablong house with us during Tracy) knew someone who wanted to buy our block, and they negotiated for us. So we managed to sell the block, pay off the NT Government and still had $1,000 left which we used to buy carpet for the Bennet Street house.

Life returned to some semblance of normality for our family, but we have never returned to Darwin, although one of our daughters went back to Darwin some years later for a visit and went to our old house, which had been rebuilt, for a look. We are now living at Bonogin on the mostly sunny Gold Coast. Shirley would like to go back for a visit – not to live – but for me there is a small part of me that says I would like to go and see how the place looks now. On the other hand, a much larger part of me whispers to me that I would not be able to cope. Who knows – maybe time will tell.

Ian Philip Cork.

Below: Front of our house after Tracy, showing freezer in the Park, refrigerator upstairs and the lounge we had intended to shelter under!! Bottom: Rear of our house - master bedroom.

Above: Corner of Tudawali and Daniels Streets, Ludmilla.

Above: Tudawali Street.
Next page: The famous pool. (Photographs by Ian Philip Cork)

Ian and his wife, Shirley, now live at Bonogin in the Gold Coast Hinterland. Ian is a semi-retired massage therapist and Shirley is a semi-retired naturopath. They have three children, all grown-up girls who live on the Gold Coast.

CHAPTER 6 – DARYL & ANNETTE LEHMANN

My wife Annette and I arrived in Darwin from Adelaide in September 1974, recently married, young, naïve but with a sense of adventure. We travelled up to Alice Springs on the Old Ghan and then by car to Darwin in our brand new Torana (after waiting two days in Alice due to the derailment of the freight train bringing our car). We settled in to Darwin well, moving into an elevated house on Lee Point Road, which was the edge of Darwin's residential development in those days, and both working, I at the Department of Education and Annette at Bell Photographers. I joined the local footy umpires, we quickly made many friends, and life was good.

Little did we know of the adventure that was to come. By mid-December we had witnessed an earth tremor, and Cyclone Selma had passed across the Top End. It added to the excitement of being in our new home, but we were glad that our first experience of a cyclone was only mild.

Annette's Mum and Dad, Irene and George, arrived from Adelaide on 23rd December, to spend Christmas with the newlyweds and to see the Top End for the first time. After they had settled in we took them to the lovely new shopping centre at Casuarina, and they were suitably impressed. Little did they know that this was the only Top End attraction they were going to see.

On Christmas Eve, Annette and I both went to work as normal, but we were aware that another cyclone was brewing close to Darwin. I remember leaving work at 5.30 p.m. after the obligatory Christmas Eve drinks, and thinking how windy it was. I was feeling very buoyant with a few drinks under my belt and my wallet fat with my Christmas pay inside (there were cash salary payments in those days), but I was keen to get home to Annette and the in-laws, and hear the latest on this cyclone that was hanging around the Top End.

After tea that evening, the winds were increasing and the rain started to get very heavy. The latest cyclone warning was that Tracy (I now took notice of the name seriously for the first time) was going to have some effect on Darwin, but was expected to pass across the top of the Tiwi Islands. Nevertheless, we made preparations by making sure everything was secure downstairs and the car was safely under the house. It was now dark and the rain was teeming down, with the odd bolt of lightning and accompanying thunder. We couldn't believe it when the "bin boys" came along collecting rubbish in the driving rain and wind. The frogs were going off in the huge stormwater pipes over the road, which were part of the about-to-be-developed suburb of Wulagi. We watched the trees in the new suburb bending 45 degrees in the wind, and were astounded by the ever-increasing lightning and the occasional bolt hitting the ground in the scrub opposite.

The latest warning on the radio (we were now glued to the local ABC broadcast) was saying that Tracy now might be veering towards Darwin. We weren't overly worried, being new to Darwin and thinking it would be no worse than an Adelaide southerly buster. In some ways I found it quite exciting, and I was in awe of all the rain, wind, lightning and thunder. My sense of invincibility was heightened by the fact that George and I had cracked a Darwin stubby and I was full of Dutch Courage.

We felt safe in the house and had prepared quite well, or so we thought. After finishing the Darwin stubby I poured us all a port as a nightcap, thinking we would sleep better. We sat in front of the lounge window watching the ever-increasing rain, wind and lightning outside. We could now hear debris being tossed around outside, and the odd branch breaking off a tree. We were hoping it wouldn't get much worse, but were still not unduly worried. About 11 p.m. I heard a flapping sound on the roof and realised that some of the roof sheeting had come loose. We could also now hear metal objects flying around. About 12.30 a.m. we could hear that more sheeting had come loose on our roof, and the house was rocking in the wind. However, we still felt safe in the house, and stayed put.

Photograph by Ramon Williams

About 1 a.m. the house was moving quite badly. The wind was buffeting the house from the North, blowing straight into the verandah area. I now know this was placing unbelievable pressure on this semi-enclosed area. Without warning, the cornice on that side fell off and the verandah wall cracked vertically from floor to ceiling. The two parts of the wall rocked back and forth, and we could hear more iron being torn from the roof. The noise from the wind and the sound of objects being tossed around was deafening.

We now knew we had to leave the house, but how? And where would we go?

We decided to at least get downstairs somehow, and go from there. We decided to go down the front stairs, as the wind was hitting the other side of the house and the back stairs. We inched our way down the stairs, hanging on to the hand rail for dear life. The force of the wind was overwhelming and debris was flying all around us. We finally made it, and sheltered briefly under the carport before deciding the only place to shelter was in the downstairs storeroom. By this time the power was gone and it was pitch black. We had a small torch with us, but nothing else. The next two or three hours were terrifying. We could hear our house being destroyed and the sound of roofing iron flying about, and then all our possessions sliding and screeching across the polished wood floors. This told us that the roof AND our walls had gone, and that only the floorboards were left. It was then that I remembered I had left my wallet with all my Christmas pay on our bed. BUGGER. I also remembered we were watching over our neighbours' house, and hoped it would be ok. WRONG! My other thought was, "Why did our house have to be the one to be destroyed?" Crazy thoughts, but I was glad we were at least all safe.

I was beginning to wonder if the wind would ever stop, but another hour went by before it started to abate. I shone the torch around and noticed a big crack down the besser brick wall of the storeroom, and a gap in the floorboards. I realised that all the floorboards from the storeroom to the back of the house were gone, and we were very close to being fully exposed to the elements. Anyway, at least the worst was over, I thought. But no, the wind suddenly started picking up again and ended up blowing in the opposite direction. The eye of the cyclone, or at least part of it, had been over us. We bunkered down again, sitting in six inches of water and listening to the screeching, howling and all the deafening noises all over again. Our next concern was a new sound. The bang, bang, banging of the floorboards above us told us they were working loose and could soon expose us fully to the elements and debris flying around. The besser brick wall with the crack in it was moving, as well.

We wondered when this would all end and what our fate would be. Just before daylight, the winds finally started easing and we started to think the worst was over and we had survived. Once it was daylight, I climbed onto a box and looked out through the gap between the floorboards and the storeroom wall. The scene I saw will never leave me, and thoughts of it make me cold to this day. It was a scene of utter devastation as far as the eye could see. There was no foliage on any tree, only a few trunks. The houses throughout the whole area were completely destroyed. Power poles were bent over sideways. Cars, whitegoods, furniture and other possessions were strewn everywhere. It really was like a nuclear bomb had hit Darwin. There were no signs of life, and I immediately wondered how many casualties there might have been.

Eventually we all went outside, and other people started appearing. Miraculously, our car had survived, but nothing else. We had only the clothes on our back, no food, money or transport. People were wandering around looking at their houses and the destruction.

Our next thought was what to do next. After realising the totality of the destruction, and that we were on our own and no one was coming to save us, we decided to try and clear our driveway of debris so we could get the car out. We achieved this after two hours of back-breaking work. This included literally dragging the end wall of the house off the driveway. It was evident that once the roof had gone, the wall of the house had just fallen down, basically intact.

We backed the car out and proceeded to drive slowly down Lee Point Road, clearing our way as we went. It was now that others told us Casuarina High School (now CSC) was basically intact and could provide shelter for the time being. We picked our way down Parer Drive, and eventually got to the high school late in the day. It was decided that we would all sleep in the classrooms that night. The other issue was food. Fridges and freezers were raided, and then someone had the brainwave about going off to Casuarina Shopping Centre and getting what we could from there. The result of this was a monster barbecue in the grounds of the high school. Annette and Irene ended up spending the night in a classroom, and George and I slept in the car. We were worried about security, as we had one of the few cars around with a tank full of petrol.

After a bad night's sleep, Boxing Day greeted us with no news from the outside world. We were unaware of any communications at this stage, and to make matters worse Irene was feeling quite ill. After speaking to a couple of other people with cars, we decided that we would try and head south. We knew if we could get to Adelaide River or Katherine we could get medical help, food, clothing and so on. We didn't know how towns down the track had fared, but we knew things weren't going to happen quickly in Darwin, so in the end it was an easy decision to leave. We slowly worked our way out of Darwin, still shell-shocked at what we had been through, and amazed at the devastation as we left. What was even more amazing was that by the time we got past Noonamah the damage lessened, and a few more kilometres down the road there was none. We realised then how we had worn the full brunt of Cyclone Tracy. Talking to people now, they wonder why Tracy did so much damage compared to others of similar or higher intensity. One line of thought is the length of time Tracy hovered over Darwin before it moved on. It lasted longer than many cyclones that I am aware of, and this certainly would have exacerbated the destruction.

Ask Ian Butterworth if he agrees with me. I worked with Butters for many years, and I am sure he would have an opinion.

The next chapter in this story involves the trip south to Adelaide. We left Darwin with only the clothes on our back, no money and no way to access any, but we needn't have worried. At every town and roadside stop people were waiting for us with food, clothing, petrol – whatever we needed we were given. In Tennant Creek for example they had set up the Community Hall as a supermarket. There were aisles of trestle tables full of clothes, food and other items. We weren't allowed to leave without a full wardrobe of clothes and suitcases or bags to hold them. A lady at the door gave us a hamper full of freshly made sandwiches, cakes and cordial. The local servo gave us petrol for the next stage of our trip.

One of our overnight stops was at Barrow Creek. They cooked up a big barbecue for all the Darwin Refugees, as we were called, all washed down with any beverage we wanted. Accommodation was in the big stone building at the back of the pub. It consisted of rooms with a hallway down the middle, and although it was hot, we were very comfortable. We went to sleep quickly after our meal, only to be awoken at 2 a.m. by someone screaming out 'SNAKE, SNAKE!' A six foot brown snake had wandered in to see who was occupying his normally vacant hideaway. There was no going to sleep after that, so we decided to head off to Alice.

We crawled along at 60 km/hr, being worried about animals on the road, and arrived in Alice Springs at daybreak. The town was abuzz. We were treated like royalty. Accommodation, food, clothing, petrol, tyres etcetera. Everyone was so helpful. Obviously all the refugees were keen to continue on south, so buses, planes and freight vehicles were all offered as alternatives. It must be remembered that the Stuart Highway was still dirt south of Kulgera, so it was a long and difficult drive. After much consideration, Annette and Irene decided to take the bus, and George and I decided to drive the Torana through to Adelaide. With a full tank of petrol, again provided by the locals, and the mandatory food and clothing, we headed off. The road was rough, but we took it easy and shared the driving. We were thoroughly sick of the dirt after day one, but on day two we got some great news. The local authorities had agreed to let us drive through the Woomera Rocket Range, which was substantially shorter and best of all, bitumen. We were rapt. The only proviso was that we had to ring through on the roadside phones every five kilometres. We made Adelaide safely, as did the girls.

The story doesn't end here. I returned to Darwin early in the New Year, and Annette came back two weeks later. We lived in twelve separate places over the next eighteen months, including the partially demolished Kurringal Flats, a fifteen foot caravan, the MV Patris (a Greek cruise ship commandeered by Commonwealth Hostels and moored at the now demolished Iron Ore Wharf), and a demountable in Knight Street, with floorboards from a demolished elevated house as our outdoor area. The camaraderie was strong, and no one complained. In the early days after Tracy, daily visits to the ice works and Darwin High School hall for food were part of the routine. Working in partially wrecked offices with no ceilings or windows was the norm, but nothing compared to all those commencing the clean up and rebuild. The sound of light aircraft flying around Darwin spraying to prevent disease was common. They were hard times, but we were well looked after and the social life was good. There were plenty of parties and barbecues, and sport had recommenced. Concerts were organised and there were always the R and R fairs for respite.

They were character-defining times, and strong bonds were created with others who had been through Cyclone Tracy, and with those who were helping us rebuild the place. It can't have been all bad, as we are still here, as are our three adult children who all grew up in Darwin and Jabiru. After thirty-six years the memories are still vivid, and every 24 December is a special time for Annette and me, the newlyweds from Adelaide who survived Cyclone Tracy. Daryl Lehmann.

Photograph by Ramón Williams

Photograph by Reason Williams

CHAPTER 7 - SUE GULLEFER

I had finished work around 3 p.m. on 24 December 1974. The cyclone warnings had been around for a few days, but as usual, we all thought it would pass us by. "Just another cock-eyed Bob" was the feeling. My husband, Brian, and our two children lived in The Narrows. A big family Christmas was to be at our house next day, so I set about the preparations - all the while the cyclone alerts were broadcast with monotonous regularity. It really wasn't even that windy - a gently swirling breeze with a misty spray of rain.

No need to worry. At around 8 p.m., my sister raced into our house in a mild state of panic - the RAAF personnel and their families were being told to go to shelter, and aircraft were being moved to Tindal. We could hear the drone of the planes' engines. The wind had picked up and it was beginning to rain quite solidly. Hmm, I thought - this one could be a problem! So I filled our bathtub, just in case, and packed up a few precious things like photo albums. Around 10.30, we went to bed with the radio on. At about midnight, the wind was howling, and there were frightening bangs and crashes along with a constant roaring - like a freight train coming. The radio was still going but it was impossible to hear it over the screaming noise from the cyclone.

We feared the worst as we rushed to pick up our two children (aged five and six) from their beds, and we all huddled together in the centre of the house, hanging onto each other tightly as the storm outside screamed and lashed the building. The family cat joined us, mewing and pacing back and forth over us all. We believe we actually felt the brick walls pulsating with the fury of the storm. Our son asked if we were going to die, and Brian said, "No, but if we do we will be together." Scary. I remember the sound of the toilet bowl being sucked out - it was like the roar of a waterfall.

My nerves had caused me to want to 'go' frequently. When the eye passed over, it was so still. People were out hammering and calling out to one another. We picked up debris and re-stacked what we could, knowing the wind was soon to return from the opposite direction. It was wasted effort - everything was flattened by next morning. An eerie, greenish light gave us visibility for about 30 minutes, but we could still hear the sounds of the Northern Suburbs being destroyed.

Almost as quickly as the wind had stopped, it started again - even stronger. Amazingly, our house survived, and just as dawn broke, the wind dropped dramatically and we

Photograph by Ramon Williams

felt we could safely venture outside. It was still pouring with rain, but the sight was shocking! Devastation! Twisted and broken remnants of people's homes and lives. No trees left - just some bits without any foliage - we could see through the wreckage of our rear neighbours house.

Houses all around us were broken and some totally destroyed, although The Narrows was probably one of the few suburbs which still had many ground level brick houses in a fair condition - especially in the lowest area. Our daughter had eventually drifted off to sleep, but when she awoke, she asked if Father Christmas had come, and then burst into tears asking, "where is everyone going to live?" The bath tub I had filled with 'clean drinking water' was black with mashed foliage and about ten years of ceiling dust etc. The manhole cover had been sucked out, and it had all spewed into the tub below.

We considered ourselves to be very lucky, unlike the majority of Darwin people, including my parents (Stuart Park), sister and family (Berrimah), most of my in-laws (Millner and Alawa) as well as other family members and many friends whose homes were destroyed. All of our lives were changed forever.

Although none of our family or close friends had suffered any significant *physical* injuries, the *emotional* damage was not to become evident until much later.

Other events that followed were also horrendous, but that is another story for another day. In a sense, Tracy of 1974 was just the beginning.

Sue Gullefer.

CHAPTER 8 – JAN HARRIS

9 Symes Street Nakara.

On December 24th 1974, warnings of an impending cyclone were being broadcast constantly during the day, with instructions on how to prepare our properties in case of an emergency.

Having two young children, one aged four years and a five-month-old baby, I shopped for extra supplies, even though we had lots of food ready for Christmas celebrations.

Our very good friend Graham Wallace waited until we had put the children to bed, and brought the bike we had for Michelle, which had been stored with them at their home in Nightcliff, so we could put it together. This was around 8.30 p.m. We were to spend Christmas day with the Wallace family.

The wind and rain had picked up quite considerably. We filled the bath with water, packed wall hangings, ornaments etc. into the linen press, filled a thermos with boiled water, and all the preparations we were being told to do via the radio broadcast warnings. We did leave the presents under the Christmas tree in case our daughter woke early.

10 p.m. saw Bill (my husband) and me mopping out the lounge room, as the rain was coming through the sills of the louvres. We now rolled up the floor rugs, placing them on the lounge.

After we had been lying down for a short time, the noise from the wind became so intense that we decided to get dressed. Luckily I thought to put my wedding and engagement rings back on, as I don't usually wear them around the house. We woke our two children and headed into the toilet; this was supposedly the safest room in the house. Bill managed to grab the torch and a kitchen chair for him to sit on nursing Michelle; I sat on the loo nursing Bradley, our dog. Cindy was with us, also.

The sound of smashing louvres was followed by the wind sucking the rear wall of the toilet away, snapping the cistern at the pipe. Now the ceiling was flapping and we had electrical cords around us; one cord was around my neck. The panic we felt, thinking we would be electrocuted! But the power had been off for some time.

We could see Vicki and Jim Shean's house next door; it looked like a pack of cards. We thought they must have died, and we would be next.

It was time to move. Bill managed to climb over to our

outside stairs, and raced down to check if we could shelter in the shed under the house. I don't know how I managed to hold the two children while this happened. Bill appeared, and managed to help us all to the shed. This must have been while the eye was above us, or it would have been impossible.

Once we were huddled in the shed, the cyclone returned with more fury. The floor boards lifted like a concertina and the besser blocks from the back wall started to cave in on top of us - we had to move!

Our car was parked under the house. It was our last option. The windows on the driver's side of the car were smashed, so we were able to climb through and sit on the floor behind the front seats. We were sitting on broken glass, and from my shopping that day I had left a packet of soap powder on the floor, which was now floating soap suds!!

The sound of tin scraping along the car body and timber hitting the windscreen was petrifying. At one stage Michelle, our four-year-old daughter, had become so cold and stiff that I thought we had lost her. From the floor of the car we could see the cement pillars of our house, and we were terrified they would also collapse and crush the car. There seemed to be an eerie glow in the sky, so we could see some of what was happening around us.

Morning arrived, with a policeman at the window of our car checking to see we were alive and telling us to stay put and he would be back. We never saw him again. This was around 6 a.m. Looking out from our safe spot we saw the bath that had been filled with water sitting at the bottom of our stairs. We had moved at the right time, or the bath would have landed on us.

Next door, at number 11 Symes Street, Pauline and Merv Haines had survived with their three teenage children literally holding the bathroom walls around them. We all emerged, checking on each other.

By this stage Bradley was way overdue for a feed. Bill, checking around the rubble in our front yard, amazingly found in the mud the thermos we had filled still intact, an unopened tin of formula and a cool drink bottle. No sterilisation, but a makeshift bottle was made up, Merv found food Pauline had cooked for Christmas and the Volkswagen kombi van became our breakfast restaurant as we ate cold turkey and I'm not sure what else.

We now made our way down to the fire station which was at the end of our street, not easy walking as the area was like a rubbish tip; nothing was recognisable. Part of the ceiling in the passageway had collapsed, leaving just enough still intact to crawl under to reach the rooms. Many of us from the area had made our way to the station, causing the building to be overcrowded. Toilets were blocked, and rumours were flying around that the storm was coming back; the panic was overwhelming.

We had lost our dog when the toilet collapsed, but she had found her way home, my cousin Tom Waterhouse who worked out at the airport with Qantas found his way to our area and Cindy guided him to us at the fire station. I am not sure what time this was, as so many hours had passed. It was so good to see him.

We were now told we would be moved to Nakara

primary school. Tom said he would return to Qantas and try to round up baby bottles and some nappies that they handed out on long flights, and he would see us at the school when he could.

Nakara Primary was a brand-new school due to open after Christmas, so many people were there and by now all the toilets were blocked here as well. With no water to flush them the situation was dire, and our men rounded up shovels and proceeded to dig makeshift trenches on the oval Tarps were found from somewhere and so the task of using this style of toileting had to be overcome!

Desks were laid down to use for beds; otherwise the floor was next best. A makeshift kitchen was soon set up by some of the ladies, everyone rallying with whatever we could find. Portable barbecues were found and used.

Bill is not sure to this day how he managed to make his way to Berrimah, where he worked with Bushfire Council & Forestry Department. He took control of the water truck, and was then sent to flush out toilets, also the makeshift morgues, one being the Casuarina post office which was at the corner of Symes Street. Bodies from our area were taken there, not something he will ever forget.

The second day after Tracy, Bill had the truck next to our school and we managed to stand under the hose for a short wash. By this time we were very smelly. I didn't see much of Bill those days at the school, as he was kept busy delivering water.

Unfortunately Bill had taken Cindy our dog out to Berrimah thinking she would be okay, as she had been to work with him before. As he drove out Cindy followed, and some workmates saw the police pick her up and she was shot. We never found out where she was taken.

Tom did bring baby bottles and some supplies to Nakara, which helped lots of the little ones. Michelle slipped over on the cement at the school, cutting the back of her head. I'm not sure what we put on the cut; we were all terrified of disease. Some medical staff did arrive about day two, and all of us were injected against typhoid.

We had found some containers and lots of bottles of Pine O Cleen, which was poured neat into these containers for us to walk through every time we entered the classrooms. Possibly not good for our skin, but a measure we could adopt to cut down on disease.

Nakara Primary had been forgotten as far as buses to the airport went, until on day three. Tom and his friend (later to be his wife) Leonie Murphy arrived at the school with some clothes for me to change into. It didn't matter what size, so long as they were clean, and they saw us onto the bus. Tom then met me at the airport to help, as Bradley now had a raging temperature. Nursing staff sponged Brad down, which was all they could do. Tom found out the Hercules was going to Perth, so ushered us to that line.

Our families in Perth didn't know, until our names were recorded for that flight, that we were alive.

My sister was in constant contact with the Red Cross in Perth, and finally had a call to say we were on our way. When we arrived the Red Cross took Bradley from me to bath him, and Michelle was with me as I registered. I felt a tap on my shoulder, turned around and saw my brother-in law and my sister - I think that was when I fell apart!

FRANCIS ST

Photograph by Ramon Williams

Bradley was checked out by a doctor that night, and two days later was in Princess Margaret Hospital with a throat infection. Michelle ended up with an ear infection, and was treated at home.

Bill was still in Darwin, and at that stage he had not found the keys to our car. We hadn't thought to grab them on the night. It was a few days later, when he had time to start rummaging through our pile of rubble, that he shifted a piece of wall to find the keys lying underneath - how lucky! He managed to salvage a few things, packing them into our trailer, which had remained in the yard. Michelle's bike had remained upstairs, as the front floor boards hadn't lifted and the ceiling had caved in on top of a lounge chair and the bike, forming a protection. The bike was well used by Michelle, and handed down to Brad when he was old enough to ride.

He started his long journey to Perth car windows taped with plastic, the assistance along the way with food, drinks and places to sleep plus fuel vouchers were amazing.

One of our very best friends, Roger Burke, who had lived with us at times in Darwin and also worked with Bill, was holidaying in WA when Tracy struck. He contacted me once I was at my parents place, found out at what point Bill was and flew to Derby to meet him and help with the drive to Perth. What a great friend to have.

After a couple of weeks Bill was able to work on loan to the Forestry Department in WA. The only problem was, they decided to place us in Collie, three hours from Perth.

We had a forestry house to go to unfurnished. We had to hire furniture, and thanks to our wonderful family and friends, were given household items to use. The Salvation Army, bless them, supplied us with bedding, clothes and many other items. Our stay in Collie was just six weeks, as Bill was recalled to Darwin to work. I went back to my parents in Perth, as there was nowhere for us to live in Darwin and I certainly wasn't ready to take two small children there.

Bill spent the next five months in Darwin, until he managed to procure a job with The Bush Fires Board of WA.

I joined the Cyclone Tracy action group in Perth, but the group didn't last very long, so just a couple of meetings were held.

We were sent to Kalgoorlie when Bill returned; seven hours from Perth and this was just for six months. Finally we headed back to the home we had purchased in the suburbs, so after fourteen months tried to put our lives back together.

We have succeeded, and have just returned from a family Christmas in Darwin to celebrate 40 years on, knowing how great it is to be alive. Jan Harris.

CHAPTER 9 – DEB HENDRY

Deb Hendry (née Walker) - This 'Walker Family' story. Cyclone Tracy Memories (the night from hell) - Michelle Walker Roberts (aged 20), Deb Walker Hendry (aged 14) and Jannine Walker Hardy (aged 12).

It was Christmas Eve 1974, and Michelle's 21st birthday would be on Christmas Day. Luckily, we had had the party the weekend before. Our interstate relatives staying with us that night were Nanna, Pop, and an uncle, with our family being Mum, Dad, us three girls and our three pets. Our home was in Ambon Street, Wagaman. We were all in for more than we bargained for, and a night to remember.

As daylight faded and the rain and winds picked up, Dad decided to take heed of the warnings, and started to tie all the loose objects down. When he came in, his eyes were red raw from the wind and salt water that he was getting pounded with. Around 9 p.m. our elevated house began to

leak, mainly through the louvres, which were bowing, and could not keep the water out. We moved the Christmas tree and presents further away, but after half an hour the water was all over the floor, so the pressies went up on the table. Later that night, Jannine opened the back door to get the mop to mop the floors. Dad panicked and told her to leave the mop, as it was too dangerous outside.

By 11 p.m. all power was off, and just after midnight we could hear the sounds of screaming metal, nails separating from the roof and other items hitting our house. We were all lumped together in the hallway just near the entrance to the bathroom. Mum and Michelle were panicking and having some sort of shouting match, thankfully not much was heard by anyone and God knows what was said, except that they were both hysterical. Dad told them to hold it together and not panic. Next thing our neighbours were shouting and banging on the back door. Dad let them in and found that their house had exploded, God knows how they made it to our place with minimal injuries. Not long after that, the men decided that everyone should evacuate downstairs to the cement block storeroom, as it seemed more secure.

We had to go down the stairs on our bums, one at a time, everyone close together. Dad was the last to go down, and he looked in their bedroom, which was the room near the stairs, and saw their bed being sucked up, spiralling out of what had been their bedroom; the roof had gone. Dad, being a collector, had several large drums, and all the leftover booze from the 21st, pots, pans and goodness knows what else packed in the storeroom, which was not a big area. We all squeezed into it, sat huddled together on these items and tried to stay dry, but we got drenched anyway!. For safety, we put the pots on our heads. We have never been so cold. No-one could talk above the screaming sound of wind, flying roof tin and other debris. We did not get the 'eye' that others talk about, so it was relentless until around 6.30 a.m. Apparently there was thunder and lightning, but we don't recall seeing any. Remembering it was Michelle's 21st Birthday and Christmas Day, we sung Happy Birthday and the odd carol to take our minds off what was happening around us.

When the wind eased and dawn broke, Dad attempted to open the door, but there was a big steel post against the door that had to be moved. When we went outside the store room, many of the besser blocks were coming apart at the mortar, and we don't know how much longer we could have endured the battering. We were so frightened, and were amazed that we actually came through it alive and physically unscathed.

Our emotions are hard to describe. We were scared of what we would find, and that we might be the only survivors, and at the same time feeling guilty, but grateful to be alive. Luckily, we were spared from seeing anything other than our neighbours and friends dazed and just sitting in their cars, and the total devastation for miles. From our house we could see the ocean and the water tank several kilometers away at Nightcliff / Rapid Creek, which we had not been able to see before. A short time later, a person came to tell us to go to Wagaman Primary School, as Tracy was coming back. Upon arriving, we found people already there, and more arrived after us - many had various injuries. Later, we were invited to go to the 'farm' at Noonamah. Getting there was an adventure in itself; it took hours to get to, as the debris choked roads. Mum drove, while Dad and others walked beside the car to clear a path. We had only the clothes we stood up in, and odd shoes that we found. We bathed all together in the Elizabeth River once a day. When the mass evacuation of women and children started, Deb drove out to Karratha in one of our cars with an uncle, aunty, cousin and our dog Lassie, as he would have been shot if he stayed, due to the fear of spreading disease.

The rest of us were evacuated to Perth.

It was amazing landing in Port Hedland, where the Salvos and Red Cross workers gave out packages to everyone; in them were disposable knickers, toothbrush and toothpaste. What a wonderful gesture, and we have been grateful and supportive of these groups ever since.

This uninvited experience that we all shared changed the old Darwin as we knew it, a lifestyle we loved and our lives forever. Forty years on, so many survivors are still struggling, but sharing our stories in an effort to heal our individual emotional and physical scars.

Michelle now lives on the Gold Coast and is self-employed in their family business. Jannine and Deb still live in Darwin and work for the Northern Territory Public Service. Jannine at the Bakewell Primary School, and Deb for the Department of Lands and Planning.

They still own the house that they lost on the 'night

from hell', an experience that they will never forget and that they share with so many other Territorians.

Left: Deb, Michelle (middle) & Jannine on the right.

Below: Our grandparents family home (40 years later), where we Walker survivors (13 in total) were evacuated to and lived after Cyclone Tracy. Including our grandparents who were up for Michelle's 21st on Christmas.

Photograph by Ramon Williams

CHAPTER 10 – IAN HERON

I am 52 now, and although four decades have passed, my memories are still as vivid and recountable as if it were yesterday.

Christmas Eve, Darwin NT 1974. Being only twelve years old at that time, I was so excited by the prospect of hopefully receiving my very first pushbike. I can still see it now, after all these years, a second-hand Malvern Star Dragster, with sissy bar, and long saddle seat, three gears and faded red in colour. A honker horn to top it off.

I had wanted a bike for ages, as most of the other kids in my suburb (Ludmilla), back then, had one.

I woke up that morning and peeked into our shed, to try and get a sneak look at the supposed bike. NOTHING. I was devastated. I mean, how could my parents forget just how much I wanted that bike?

I had been good, and had done all my chores without

questions or whining, for months. Still, I hoped that it was stashed elsewhere, as they (my Mum), knew just how sneaky I could be.

Back then a bicycle, was a huge status symbol, and greatly sought after by boys and girls alike. I returned inside and said to my sister, Kylie, "To HELL with Christmas, Santa is not real anyway," and in doing so crushed her heart, as she was only six at the time, and still believed in Santa.

The day went on as usual for a busy young kid on school holidays. I went fishing, with huge dark clouds looming above, gusty winds, and a few heavy showers occasionally, down at Ludmilla Creek, behind where the Kullaluk Community now stands, on Dick Ward Drive, not returning until very late in the afternoon, with a haul of mud crabs and a few small barramundi, bream and whiting. I gave most of which I gave to a family who lived on the Bagot Community, save for 2 huge crabs, that I cooked on the coals there in Bagot, and ate.

Photos courtesy of the internet. My mates, or bunjis, David and his younger brother Mark, who lived in the next street over, Attawomba St, as well as a few other kids, also bunjis, from the Bagot community, also hung around with us mob. Some of us had a few cents, so we decided to throw in together and buy a packet of smokes to share from the Ampol servo on Bagot Rd, next to where McDonald's now stands, and off we all went.. I had also pinched six Carlton Draught beers from my stepfather's carton to take with us. Hey, it was Christmas Eve, so I thought, why should the adults have all the fun?

When I got home, my mother was happy and in a good mood, (partly due to the box of Coolabah Rose in the fridge), and also, because they were headed out that night to a Christmas party at a local inner city hotel, with friends as I recall. So off they went in her little yellow Datsun sedan.

Car pictured is not the original.

Before they headed off, I was told that I was in charge, and that both of us had to be in bed by 9 p.m., or no Christmas presents. Yeah right, I thought. What presents?

It's Christmas Eve, and you want me in bed by 9... Dream on.

I made dinner for my sister and me (rice a riso with bacon), and settled back to watch our black and white TV. There were only two TV stations in Darwin back then, ABC and NTD8.

At around 10.30-ish, the wind and rain had begun to really pick up, and somewhere after 11 p.m., I think, we lost TV reception, and then our power went out, so off to bed I went, extremely annoyed.

I can recall the constant Cyclone Warnings and the siren noise on the TV during the early part of my viewing, and to this day I shiver whenever I hear it. The old warning siren is what I am talking about.But over the preceding days and weeks, Darwin residents had been bombarded with many false warnings, so they were just ignored as rubbish by many. How stupid we all were. Complacency was everywhere that month.

By 2 a.m., it was becoming very clear to me that something was most definitely not right.

The wind was screeching by now, and the rain was so loud as it slammed into our house, then suddenly a loud crash came from our dining room. I heard our budgie screech, so I went out to investigate, and to my total disbelief a huge length of timber had become airborne and had smashed its way through the brick wall and pierced his cage. I think he died right there from fright, as there were no visible wounds that I could see. Our dog Tan Tan, a pedigree Doberman, had puppies, and all were in the laundry. I went over and patted her, as she had become very nervous, and was now shaking and howling. I went to open the back door, but she stood in front of me and emitted a low growl, so I backed off and went to see if my sister was awake. She was, and crying, asking me where Mummy was. I told her that Mummy was out at a party and would be home soon, and told her to go back to sleep as I returned to my room.

I don't remember just when my stepfather returned home, I think it might have been around 3 a.m. or so, but he did, and he was alone. My mum's Datsun had broken down, along the Stuart Highway, near the Parap intersection.

He had walked home in the Cyclone, to make sure us two kids were alive and safe, then he went back out and tried to start his Volkswagen ute, but it wouldn't start, as the engine's electrics were flooded by water, so he waited until the eye had arrived, and people had emerged from their houses to see what was happening, and try and do running repairs if possible.. He got a push start I think, from the bloke next door, a TV reporter from Channel 8, and headed off to locate my mother again..

Not the actual UTE, but same model.

He never found her at all that night; it seems she had been rescued by some strangers that were driving around, so he again tried to return to us. Along the way, he helped some people that had lost their house and a family member had passed away, so he took them to Ludmilla School I believe, although I could be wrong as to where he took them.. When he finally arrived back, around 4 a.m., he grabbed both my sister and me and shoved us under my single bed, placing other protective mattresses and a wardrobe over us, and left again, looking for my mum. The noise seemed never to end, and as someone's roof was lifted and smashed nearby, the sheet iron made the most horrible sounds as it dragged along the bitumen, like a million fingernails all being scratched down a huge blackboard at the same time, but a thousand times louder. I also remember the smell of foetid, brackish water that had filled our house up to the skirting boards as we lay on the floor under my bed, but the stench several days later will never leave my nostrils, and it permeated all over Darwin. Rotting meat, mouldy bedding and clothes, unwashed bodies, and the smell of salty rotting mud everywhere.

I did not see my stepfather again until around 7 a.m., but I still remember the look on his face, and it haunts me to this very day. My step father was a builder/brick layer, and by no means a coward or wimp. And most definitely one of the toughest men I have even known, but to see a grown man cry back then just threw me for six. He had not located my mother, and thought the worst had happened, as her car was not where he had last seen it.

By now the cyclone had passed, and people were slowly coming outside to survey the damage and check on neighbours. I can still feel the utter shock and sense terror of what I saw as I emerged from my house. My whole world had just completely vanished, GONE! I was numb with fear and apprehension, and in total awe of the scene of total destruction that now lay before me. It was still raining a little, and the stillness of the town was disconcerting. Where was everything that I remembered? I could look out across Bagot and see the RAAF base, well what remained of it, as there were only stumps where once houses and hangars had been. Where had all the trees gone? There was rubbish and debris as far as the eye could see, and that was for miles. As I walked around looking at other houses, I could see Coconut Grove and a little of Nightcliff, and I think the top of the screen from the drivein, to my right, and Kurringal Flats in Fannie Bay to the left, all the long grass was flattened level with the ground, or twisted into strange shapes, as were the trees, or what little remained of them. Power poles were bent over. The total lack of noise scared me; no birds, cars, people talking, dogs barking, none of the typical every day noises we all take for granted. NOTHING.. Just a stony silence.

Not the Christmas gift, but very close to it.

I went back inside, and was handed one of my few Christmas presents by my step father, a tiny transistor radio, and an oblong battery, 'Still no bloody bike, though,' was all I could think. This may seem selfish and disrespectful, but shock had replaced what little feelings that remained.

I inserted the battery and turned the radio on. Nothing but static.

My stepfather, had become frantic by now, and was beside himself with worry for my mother, who was still out there somewhere. Was she alive or dead? We had no way of knowing.

I found a packet of Mum's smokes (Rothmans Filters), and lit one. My stepfather looked at me, and said nothing. I returned to my radio, and at thirty minute intervals to preserve the battery, kept checking for a signal or a voice. I cannot remember exactly what time it was, but sometime before 12 p.m. I think, finally a crackle came from the tiny speaker. A voice from the bowels of Darwin, it was the local ABC radio service, with an emergency broadcast to all Darwin residents, saying to remain indoors and to stay away from fallen power lines, and that shelters would be made availableas soon as possible. Do not drink the tap water, boil all water if possible. Do not use your toilets, as the sewage system had been destroyed. Do not eat the contents from your refrigerators. Eat only canned or dry foods. Gather up all medical supplies, identification, and valuables, and lock up your pets. Keep off the roads as much as possible.

During this broadcast, lots of people from my street had gathered around my tiny little radio crying, and I felt so damn important and needed, for perhaps the first time in my short life, and when the broadcast had finished I was given a huge round of applause, and a pat on the back, and many hugs. God, I felt so proud.

Out the front of our house in Ludmilla, a red and white

fire hydrant stood, without a handle, so I found a shifter in my step fathers truck, went over to it and turned the handle's stem. There was nothing but a few rusty dribbles and loud gurgles and burps at first, but then a gushing torrent rushed out from it. So those of us present, had a bogey (bath), and washed the few rags that we called clothes.

By now a slow but steady procession of people, cars, motor bikes and one bloke with a wheelbarrow with two kids in it, was making its way along our street. Some were injured, most were crying and in shock.

But nobody spoke a word. A beat-up car pulled up out front, no windscreen, and badly dented, and a small, frail figure emerged from the back seat. It was my mum, covered in mud, soaked to the bone, and ghostly white. Her dress had been ripped and torn in places, and one breast was totally exposed, as the shoulder strap had broken. Bras were something that were very much optional in the 70's. All those present lowered their gaze as she made her way over to me. She hugged me so hard that I thought I would suffocate. Her arms were shaking, and badly scratched from the flying grit and leaves, and her voice was just a whisper, but the only thing she asked me for, and I will never forget this... "DID I HAVE A CIGGY". Then she broke down and collapsed in our front yard.

She has told me a couple of times, just what she experienced that night, all alone in her tiny car, and of her rescue, in the early hours of Christmas day, but I have sworn never to make it public, as it is my mother's story of Cyclone Tracy, not mine, and in fact it contains some very harrowing details of seeing death, and the dead, first hand, and now I am in tears as I write this. So, enough. One day she may wish to share her story of survival, and of her own nightmarish ordeal, but I will never push her to reveal it. Nor will I ever make it public, while she is alive. I have made a solemn promise to her.

So there we were on Christmas Day late in the afternoon. We climbed into my stepfather's ute, and headed towards Nightcliff, via Bagot Road. Some people had cleared a few streets to make getting about possible. Everywhere we looked and went, the scale of the damage was total, nothing familiar was recognised but for a few landmarks scattered amongst the ruins of what remained, and the water tower in Nightcliff/Rapid Creek. There were cars overturned, houses completely gone, and just vacant blocks remained. How could anyone have survived this?

When we arrived at the Nightcliff foreshore, the sea was relatively calm, but so very dirty, and we got out of the ute and just walked around in shock and horror as we looked upon the devastated houses, and shops that used to be along Aralliea Street. There used to be a little shop on the corner; it had been damaged badly. The landscape was so dramatically rearranged that it was very difficult to distinguish one vacant block from the rest.. Where were all the coconuts and mangos? The leaves had been totally stripped, as had all but the toughest vegetation.

Anything that had been painted now looked so bizarre, after being sand-blasted by the ferocious winds whipping up the sand from the beach.

We couldn't drive much further from Nightcliff that

day, so we returned to Ludmilla, deciding to have a quick look at Fannie Bay if possible, before we went home, and as we approached Kurringal Flats, I noticed something that has, and will remain forever etched into my memory for eternity. The top two stories had been totally obliterated, giving the effect of rows of skulls; the places where windows had once been had now been replaced with what, to me, resembled eye sockets. I wondered how all the people that lived there had fared during the cyclone, and how many had been killed.

The block facing us, what we all now know as Dick Ward Drive, also faces Ross Smith Avenue, and was the block my mother and sister and I once lived in on the ground floor, only 18 months or so prior. My favourite tree, a huge Tamarind, had just been ripped from its roots and now dangled from a rooftop. Parap was badly damaged, and my old school resembled a rubbish tip, the bike sheds had been smashed beyond recognition, as had many of the class rooms. The whole town didn't seem to exist anymore.

We turned around and went back home, stunned by what we had witnessed that day, and to try to eat and sleep, my mum put her double bed in the lounge room, and the four of us cuddled up in the only dry room in our house, with our all dogs sleeping in bed with us. Needless to say nobody got much sleep that Christmas night. Boxing day came, and we continued to clean up our place, and help as many of our neighbours as we could. My stepfather, being a builder, had many tools, and a generator, so he began cutting timber off the nearby damaged houses, so the residents could get safer access inside. This became the norm that day: cut, drag, hammer, cut, drag, hammer.

I and some others set about scrounging around the streets for sheet iron that could be salvaged and reused to put temporary patches on roofs to keep the rain out, and seeing as there was so much sheet metal lying around, it was an easy task, although my hands became so badly cut and scratched from the iron that my mother became worried about infection, and decided that we all had better make our way to Darwin High School the next day for any assistance that was available. I can still feel and smell the medication as it was injected, and we all had sore arms for weeks afterwards.

While we were at Darwin High School, I became very aware of just how many displaced people there were, and how much everybody chipped in to help. Money was scattered all over the place, as there was no need for it, nor was there anywhere to spend it, or anything to buy. Not that anyone would ever accept it anyway.

The smell of fresh food cooking, was a blessing, and all the many hundreds of people chatting seemed overly loud after the total silence of the past couple of days. We made our way through the throngs of refugees, as we were by now being called, and we were asked to sign a register, so the authorities knew how many people had survived, and in case friends and family members came looking. Red Cross seemed to just pop up from all corners, as did the Salvos, and other churches and faiths. A medical centre had been set up for the injured and those needing attention.

Crime was never an issue, as people had bugger all to steal, but if anybody was caught stealing or looting, they were swiftly and harshly dealt with. I remember passing a house or shop, with a sign nailed to it with hand-painted writing, saying LOOTERS WILL BE SHOT. Many years later, a photo emerged with that very sign, and a bloke standing guard with a gun.

Mothers needed food for young babies, and I remember one lady had no breast milk, so an indigenous stranger who was nursing her own baby offered to feed her baby, and I watched in horror as the baby drank with gusto, and at that time, being so young, I thought YUK, how could she, but in later years, understood the gravity of what the stranger had offered. I get choked up thinking of her generosity today.

So day after day, people came together and gathered at many of the open schools that had been set up to house and feed and care for us mob of bedraggled and grateful citizens, as I always called us, for I did not understand why we were being called refugees, and the mere mention of that word today evokes memories of those trying times. Refugees to me, back then, were people from Vietnam, escaping the war, not us Aussies, that had called Darwin home for most, if not all of our lives, like me.

Pets had become a problem, and as I later found out in a not so very nice way, the authorities had begun shooting them on sight to prevent spreading disease and predation on the dead, plus there wasn't anyone to care for many of them. This angered me greatly, as my own dog Tan Tan had been destroyed, and for many years I hated the police whenever I had dealings with them. Which was often, as I grew older.

I can smile now, as I remember one particular police officer, who was known far and wide as Crasher Krowler, for reasons that escape me now. But he was always chasing me for shoplifting, or wagging school, when I later returned to Darwin, post-evac, and mostly for riding my motor bike on the roads, with no rego or licence, and sometimes no helmet. He just never gave up, and neither did I.

Poor bugger, I am sure he had many sleepless nights trying to figure out a way to snare me, but for the most part he never did. Sorry, Crasher. 'Maybe next time,' I would yell, as I flew past at breakneck speeds, offering up a not-so-polite one-fingered salute. He did catch me on one occasion that has stuck firmly in my memory, and the way he dealt with me back then still makes me grin. After a very loud and angry confrontation with Crasher, he grabbed me and kicked me so hard up my backside that I could not ride my motor bike for a week, but I continued as normal when it got better. I still rode, and he still chased me. This went on for years..

It is now the day before New Year's Eve. My sister and I had been placed on the evacuation list, like most of the kids after Cyclone Tracy. There were no schools to go to, as they were being used as shelters and food/medical outposts, as mentioned above. Our names had been drawn and we were at the old Darwin Aerodrome, as it was then known, for to call it an airport would cause much laughter and teasing by today's standards, but it was all we had. My sister and I were given baggage tags that had our names, city of destination, and the names of the people that would

be collecting us at journey's end. In our case, Brisbane, later to be flown to Cairns, to stay with an aunt. So here we were, two little kids, looking so lost, and very nervous at going on a huge Jumbo for the first time in our lives. We had very little actual baggage to take, as the airlines needed the room for us refugees, and we were bundled onto the jet and literally squashed together like sardines.

We had to stop over in Sydney to refuel, and were asked to leave the jet while this was done. We were all offered food, drinks, and seats in the lounge areas of Sydney airport, with strict instructions not to leave the room, as refuelling wouldn't take very long. Well coming from Darwin, and having never seen an escalator before, you can guess what happened. I just had to ride it, and decided to drag my sister along for the ride also, over and over, up, then down and then back up again. I never did hear the loudspeaker calling and calling our names because of all the fun I was having, so time just slipped away, until a very big and scary-looking security guard finally saw us and came over to get us. By this time our plane had left without us, and we both had to wait for another connecting flight, hours later.

All the while we had a very stressed aunt in Brisbane, waiting for two no-shows. We eventually got a ride, and arrived in Brisbane more than five hours late. A concerned taxi driver noticed us, and saw our ID tags with our names and suburban address – School Road, The Gap, Brisbane QLD- written on it, and took us there at no cost. She was in fact, on her way back to the Brisbane airport to collect us both for the second time.

My aunt was not amused, to say the least. Her neighbours next door heard the taxi driver knocking and knocking on the door of her house, and came over. They already knew we were arriving, and took us both inside and gave us a bath, because we stank from being cooped up and not showering for over a day, and a big feed of salad and cold roast lamb, and we scoffed it down with great delight, and then they put us to bed in their huge king-sized bed, with soft pillows and a doona.. I had never seen a doona before, coming from Darwin; they are never needed there.

I burst out laughing when I saw it.

At around 5 a.m., my not-so-happy aunt returned home very upset, until it was explained to her that we both had arrived, and were safe and well, and asleep, and decided to let us remain there until later that morning.

When we did finally manage to drag our sorry backsides out of that comfortable bed, we got a huge lecture, and a scolding that I will never forget, and as we sat there watching her turn red and get angrier by the minute, the TV was on, and a news broadcast was showing Darwin, and lo and behold, there I was on telly! A reporter was asking those being airlifted out what and how they felt about the Cyclone. I was so excited when I was asked that all I managed to blurt out was YOU BLOODY BEAUTY... NO BLOODY SCHOOL, and then I cracked up laughing.

My aunt nearly crapped in her knickers I think, when she heard me say that on TV, and so began her misfortune of having me stay there. The men in the room all looked away, but deep down I knew they were all laughing along with me.

I stayed with my aunt in Brisbane for six months, attending The Gap State School, (Pictured below), and I hated every second of it. What school in any right state of mind wouldn't let kids walk or play on the grass? Plus I was made to wear not only a uniform, but, and you won't believe this, a freaking TIE.

For the love of all things sacred, I could barely tie my shoe- laces (I always went barefoot back then), let alone a bloody TIE, so wagging began in earnest. I scammed a nice, pretty young girl to wag with me, and we began a very torrid childhood love affair.

Her name was Cassie, and she was the prettiest girl I had ever talked to, let alone been allowed to KISS, and on the lips too, and many other things that I shall not repeat here, for fear of embarrassing her. I was king of the heap in my books.

Our days were spent climbing Mount Cootha smoking ciggies, and understanding that the leaves of the plant I touched were in fact the dreaded Gympie nettle and did I itch for days, but the fun we both had was amazing. I lost contact with her after I returned to Darwin, and often wonder where she is today.

So after my brief, yet very happy time in Brisbane, I did return to Darwin, and restarted my schooling at Ludmilla Primary for a couple of years, and then onto Darwin High School, the scene of many of my post-cyclone memories, both good and bad.

I didn't do too well in high school, so halfway through year 10, I left in 1978, and went to work for my stepfather as a brickie's labourer for a year or so, with the choice of

doing an apprenticeship or going my own way in a job of my choice.

I chose to be a trolley boy at Casuarina Shopping Square, which by now had been rebuilt and was on its way to becoming what we now enjoy as a great shopping hub in the northern suburbs.

Silly move, I now think, but back then I didn't have any idea of what I wanted to be, and nor did I care, so I just did as I pleased for a few years, drinking, smoking lots of weed, and getting into lots of trouble. I travelled Australia many times, and to this day continue to do so, finding odd jobs as I go.

I am now residing in Gympie QLD, for now, and like it here very much. I work part time carting hay for a local farmer.

I very much doubt that this will be the end of my journeys, and hold even more doubts that I will ever settle down for any great length of time in any one place.

The sounds of thunder still excite me, and to hear heavy rain on a corrugated iron roof soothes me immensely. I have returned to Darwin many times, but feel my old city has lost its most cherished features.

The old buildings and people are all but gone, (try and find two or more locals not related, from back then, in the same room), and the city has just lost its appeal for me, although I do miss the Barramundi fishing and mud crabbing, and when I revisit, I can often be found at any number of locations in and around town, with rod in hand, flicking lures for my favourite adversary.

Oh, and as for the pushbike I mentioned at the very start of my story, it was waiting for me, with flat tyres, when I returned from Brisbane in 1975.

It seems it was, as I suspected, stashed next door at the neighbours' house, and when I finally grew out of it, and got my motor bike, I gave it to the kids of Bagot.

Picture of bike is not the original, but an exact match.

Written and will always be remembered, Ian Heron.

Photograph by Ramon Williams

CHAPTER 11 – KATHRYN HOLDEN

(Née Kathy Jukes, then Kathy Henderson)

Potts Street, Moil.

All through my years of growing up in Darwin since 1962, you would get "WARNING, WARINING CYCLONE COMING, CYCLONE COMING," so you would say "oh no, not again, just another warning, nothing to worry about!" Ha what a joke, the joke was certainly on us.

At the time my ex, Russell Henderson, was working for Scaturchio and Sons, who were builders (he had done his apprenticeship with them) and I had just got a job with John Lysaght Steel. Well, we were invited to a party at the Scaturchios' place in Winnellie, where Nonna and Papa Scaturchio lived, and we were having such a great time of it, eating Nonna's fantastic Italian food, having lots of drinks and listening every now and then to the radio about

the 'WARNING CYCLONE TRACY', and as usual not taking any notice, but partying on. About 10 p.m., Russell and I said our goodbyes, as we had to get out to the place 17 miles (27 km) away, where Russell's parents were.

Keith and Kath Henderson lived on Wells Creek Rd, just behind what is now Coolalinga Woollies; there was nothing built there back then. We had a few drinks with them and then went to bed, waking up a few hours later with water coming into the bedrooms, as down the hall of the house it had open-face besser blocks, to let the cool breeze in. The four of us sat on the bed just listening to the wind, rain, loud noises, and tin being torn off the roof, and whatever other noises we heard. This went on for what seemed ages and ages, and because we were getting very wet we decided to go down to the end of the house where the laundry and bathroom was to keep dry and warm, so we stumbled all the way down and by this stage all the noise had stopped and it was very airy, it was so very, very quiet, then all of a sudden, bang! The eye had turned and the noise was even worse than before. Well, that had done it - the whole end wall of the house was sucked out where we were, and the inside wall came down on us. How we survived God only knows. So we stumbled back up to the bedrooms, back onto the bed that was now soaked with water, and it was the first time in my life that I have ever heard a man cry. Poor Keith; all he could say was 'how am I going to start all over again at my age', and we just all held onto each other and rode it out.

When morning came we went outside to see the devastation. Trees uprooted, trees with no leaves on them,

tin roofing everywhere. I said to Russell, 'I need to go into town to see Mum and my step-dad (Edna and Bruce Pratt) and my brother (Brian Jukes). So off we went in our Toyota utc, driving on the Stuart Highway, looking over towards Palmerston (which had not then been built) you could see Darwin Harbour, we were in shock. Never, never in all my years had I ever been able to see the harbour from the Highway. All the power poles were as if a giant had stepped on them; they were all bent and twisted down to the ground. We turned right onto McMillans Road to get to Rothdale Road, and this was a task in itself, as there was devastation everywhere, and it was hard to make out what road and suburb was what. Driving on Rothdale Rd was a mammoth task; we had to drive over trees, tin, you name it we drove over it, up one side of the road to the other side.

Mum lived in Potts Street and that was where we needed to go; we drove to where we thought we were near her place, and all I could do was get out of the car and yell out, 'Mum, Bruce, Joe, where are you?' and thank God, Mum yelled out to me, so we walked, and this was hard to do as well, from the corner of Rothdale Road and Boyle Street. Again we were in shock, for although the house either side of Mum's and the one behind were all standing, Mum's house was gone.

Mum and Bruce were evacuated days later, as Bruce was injured. They were lucky, as they got to go on a Jumbo Jet. When they returned they moved into the house behind them, which belonged to the Gleesons, who were on holidays. Russell and I stayed with his parents and helped get things cleaned up. I remember we had to go down the road a bit to a creek to do our washing by hand and get our water, as there was no power, or water. This went on for a few days and Russell asked me, as he and his dad talked, if I would go with his mum down to Melbourne where her parents lived, as she was not coping very well with everything, so I said I really didn't want to but I would. So off to the airport we went, to line up with hundreds of others to get on a plane. We got the luxury flight, a Hercules, and would you know it? We were right up the front on the right-hand side, squashed in like sardines. Because I smoked at that time, I had to go from where I was, crawling over everyone, down to the back of the plane, then all the way back up to the front of the plane on the left-hand side to the flight deck to have a smoke! I soon gave up smoking!

We could not land in Melbourne as it was all fogged, so we were diverted to Adelaide; this trip took us about seven hours. When we landed in Adelaide we were met by the Red Cross who were wonderful, they wrapped us up in warm blankets, fed us and then drove us up to the hills to a Girl Guide hall. The next day they had arranged for Kath and me to be flown by TAA to Melbourne.

I stayed in Melbourne for a couple of months, but then I wanted to get back to Darwin, so it was arranged for me to be flown back. I had lost my job with Lysaghts, and Russell had to go to Roper River for a year to do a big building job with Scaturchio's, and they asked me would I like to go with him and be the camp cook? I jumped at the chance.

This is how Russell and I started our life together, and

paid cash for our five acres on Lowther Road, and bought a new Toyota. Life was good.

I have since had a wonderful son, and moved interstate to New South Wales ten years ago.

Kathryn Holden.

Above: Leaving Darwin. (Diane Hunter)

Photograph by Ramon Williams

CHAPTER 12 – DIANE HUNTER

I was a single mum, and my dad had just got back from Darwin and he paid for us to go up. I was to spend two weeks with each of my sisters, and they had all sort of trips around and about to take us on.

We went with my sister Sharon to the Casuarina shopping centre, and the children each bought presents which we wrapped up.

Sharon cooked spaghetti, and in a moment of madness we had a bit of fun with the un-sauced spaghetti that was left over. I remember it sticking to a wall.

My children were to sleep on a mattress on the lounge room floor, and we listened to the constant cyclone warnings, and probably because I was not from Darwin I took it very seriously and eventually convinced my sister and her husband (now deceased) to come downstairs.

The first half of the cyclone came over and did some damage, so their car was moved away from a wall, and

REGISTRATION CARD

Family Name: BARKER

First Name(s): DIANE
Usually Known as

Date of Birth: 27-2-42.

Sex: Male ☐ Female ☑

Place of Birth: ENGLAND

Nationality: BRITISH

Pre-Disaster Address or Last Known Location: 11 EASTHER CRES NIGHTCLIFFE DARWIN

Occupation or Profession: CLERK

Signature of Registrar: W Lewis   Holder's Signature: DBarker

Place of Registration: Date of Registration:

REGISTRATION CARD

Family Name: BARKER

First Name(s): TIMOTHY
Usually Known as: TIM

Date of Birth: 29-9-61

Sex: Male ☑ Female ☐

Place of Birth: ENGLAND.

Nationality: BRITISH

Pre-Disaster Address or Last Known Location: 11 EASTHER CRES NIGHTCLIFFE DARWIN

Occupation or Profession: SCHOOL BOY

Signature of Registrar: W Lewis   Holder's Signature: DBarker

Place of Registration: Cars Car Park   Date of Registration: 28-12-74

REGISTRATION CARD

Family Name: BARKER

First Name(s): LOC
Usually Known as

Date of Birth: 18-3-64

Sex: Male ☐ Female ☑

Place of Birth: ENGLAND

Nationality: BRITISH.

Pre-Disaster Address or Last Known Location: 11 EASTHER CRES NIGHTCLIFFE DARWIN

Occupation or Profession: Sch. girl.

Signature of Registrar: W Lewis   Holder's Signature: DBarker

Place of Registration: Cars Car Park   Date of Registration: 28-12-74 remained fairly in good condition. We went outside and we could see the sky, but went inside and we were playing a Bill Crosby tape, I think it was Noah's Ark, when I saw the curtains move and thought the window was not closed; that was when it exploded in, The settee was swivelled round at some stage, and the five of us sat out the night, sitting in glass, the air was all sparks and I thought 'this is very evil'. We told each other what we had bought for Christmas, because none of us thought we would survive.

It was six a.m. when we heard someone outside calling for survivors, and we went out. I had got glass in my head and had bled onto my daughter Zoe, and we did not know that she was not injured. Tim had barely been covered by the settee, and had glass cuts on his legs.

We managed to get to the National insurance offices where my other sister's husband was working, and were there for four days till we all, except for the men, got into a plane.

CHAPTER 13 – JILLY LIMB

Jilly Limb (née Delvendiep)

Photo left: View from our bedroom window, taken about 7 a.m. Cnr Ross Smith & Goldsmith Avenues.

I wrote this about twenty years ago when I was doing my memoirs, and these are the excerpts about Tracy I wrote then. I haven't changed anything, so will need to explain, plus personal details have changed. I am now married to Brian Limb, who also went through Tracy with his then wife and three children. He lived near the Casuarina Fire Station.

My husband, Wim Delvendiep, and I had been in Brisbane; Paint N Paper, his employer, asked him to take over the management of one of their shops there. We tried it for a while, but much preferred life in Darwin. This excerpt starts on our drive home to Darwin.

Wim returned to work at Paint N Paper in Smith Street, and was acting manager at the time of Tracy; the manager,

Jim Lyons, was interstate on holidays.

Tamar was my Chocolate Point Siamese cat; my parents had sent him to me in Darwin in 1971.

Doreen Graham and her husband Justin were old and good friends, as was Franz Schoolmeester.

Morgan's company was Simon Transport; that is Morgan, another friend in Toowoomba.

I worked for the Attorney-General's Department, in the law courts, before we went to Brisbane.

Wim and I were members of the Darwin Trailer Boat Club and the NT Game Fishing Club.

It felt good heading home along the Stuart Highway. We had another overnight stop before Katherine, where we stayed, arriving back in Darwin with plenty of time to get ready to surprise a lot of people at the Trailer Boat Club Friday night drinks.

Doreen Graham worked for a real estate company, and had arranged a flat for us at Fannie Bay; we moved in immediately. I had managed to bring enough of our gear to get by until Morgan's company delivered the rest.

I went into the Attorney-General's Department on Monday morning, and was given a position in the Personnel Section as a clerk, which suited me just fine. I started work immediately, which surprised me; I had thought I would have a few free days. I was working in 'Block Three', one of a number of government office buildings along The Esplanade overlooking Darwin Harbour.

We had only been back a few days when Cyclone Selma threatened to strike Darwin. Some people made the necessary arrangements, just in case, by stocking up on tinned goods, batteries, bottled water etc. It wasn't necessary; Selma turned north and Darwin was unaffected.

Christmas Day was fast approaching, and with it plenty of Christmas functions. Doreen and Justin were hosting Christmas lunch for quite a few friends, and we were all contributing food and drinks. Doreen gave me a list of tinned goods she wanted, as well as a salad to make.

On 21 December, the Darwin Weather Bureau issued a tropical cyclone alert regarding a low pressure area that could develop into a cyclone, and later that night it was official: Cyclone Tracy was 700 kms north-east of Darwin. Tracy actually passed north of Darwin on 22 December, and ABC radio said Darwin wasn't under immediate threat.

We, like most Darwin residents, went on with our Christmas cheer and were saying "don't worry about it, Selma went away, so will this." I doubt many did much in the way of preparation.

On Christmas Eve morning I was in the law courts having a few Christmas drinks with the Commonwealth Police and some Territory Police. They had obviously had an early start; when I left they were drop kicking empty Foster's cans down the front foyer and down the stairs to the basement area.

I had some Christmas cheer with co-workers, most of whom I had known for some years, and met Wim at Paint N Paper at lunch time. I phoned Mum and Dad to wish them a Merry Christmas; I wasn't sure if I would be able to phone the next day, due to time constrictions or delays because of the heavy phone traffic. Mum was worried about the Cyclone. "Don't worry about it," I said. "We just had a cyclone alert, and nothing happened". The wind had risen at this stage, and it was raining. We had some more cheer at Paint N Paper, then went next door to have drinks with Greta and Eddie Quong, and the champagne was flowing. The Quongs had numerous businesses in Darwin, including their famous bakery, and were also liquor wholesalers. This business was next to Paint N Paper, and the bakery was just down the street.

The Trailer Boat Club was the next stop, and I switched from champagne to Galliano and orange juice. The club was nearly bursting at the seams, and nobody seemed worried about a cyclone. I was shouted so many drinks I had them stored in the fridges behind the bar, I couldn't keep up; everyone was just having a good time. Later a group of us went back to our flat and I cooked a meal of Chinese soy chicken in our electric frypan. The wind was really getting up by now, and blowing water under our front sliding doors and wetting the carpet about three feet in. The doors were protected by a wide verandah and walls each side, but the water came in like there was no barrier. Doreen, Justin, Franz and other friends now decided it was time to go home and check on their homes and families. We turned the radio o;, it was ten o'clock. Another warning, this time a direct impact by Tracy was inevitable and it was expected to cross the coast in the vicinity of Darwin in the early hours of Christmas Day.

My reaction was to clear the benches and shelves of items and fill whatever containers I could with water and put them in cupboards. I had the electric frypan soaking, so shoved it in a cupboard too. I filled the bath with water and unpacked the transistor radio and some candle holders. At least I had bought new batteries, candles and matches for Selma. Wim and I also tried to put masking tape over the windows, but it wouldn't stick. Wim moved my car so it was as close as possible to our flat, and partly protected overhead by the concrete floor of the upstairs flats. We went to bed.

Wim slept, but I couldn't; it was so noisy outside, the wind was screaming and I was worried; would the concrete floor collapse onto us? I still had the radio on, and heard the announcer say it was 1.40 Shortly afterwards, the air conditioner stopped, I remember Wim waking up and saying, "turn the bloody air conditioner on". Sorry no power. We both got up, naked. I tried to find some clothes by candlelight, but only managed the bottom to a pair of bikinis, a knee-length cotton brunch coat and rubber thongs. I don't remember what Wim put on, possibly his bathers.

Using his cigarette lighter he went into the second bedroom to try and find our torch. We had yet to unpack most of our belongings. I took the candle into the lounge to find Tamar; he had jumped off the bed when we got up. I placed the candle in a holder on the bench which separated the kitchen and lounge areas. Wim, who had found the torch, was by the kitchen door, and Tamar was now rubbing against my legs; there was pounding on the door. I yelled to Wim, "Don't open the door"; I knew if he did it might cause the glass in the floor-to-ceiling front doors to blow in, and I was directly in front of them. "Noooooooo" - Wim didn't hear, or didn't realise, and opened the door, Tamar took off for the rear bedroom and I dived after him, and the front glass doors and windows exploded. Wim and our visitors were protected by the large floor-to-ceiling built-in housing the fridge, and I by the linen cupboard. Long slivers of glass covered the carpet where I had been standing. I don't doubt I would have been speared if Tamar hadn't taken off or I hadn't tried to catch him. A couple and two young children were at the door, soaking wet and hanging on to each other for dear life. They said they lived upstairs and their roof had collapsed. Wim, who was still pretty drunk, just said, "Well what do you want, it's after 2 o'clock? " I said, "Wim, let them in." I think it started to dawn on him then, what was happening outside. We all went into the bathroom at the rear of our flat; the wind was blowing into the front of the building. I lit more candles and emptied the bath, the chap got in with his children and left his wife just standing there. We moved the washing machine out and some chairs in. The wife then said that an elderly Greek lady was upstairs in the end flat. Wim grabbed the torch and left to climb the outside stairs, they faced the side road and towards the harbour, taking the full brunt of the cyclone. I tried to look from the kitchen door, but it was too dark once he was out of sight. Wim said later that the elderly lady was crouching in the small space between the fridge and the wall with a fallen cupboard partly protecting her; the roof was entirely gone. He tried to get her to move but she wouldn't budge; she was probably too frightened. Wim said he just grabbed her arm and told her to "get your fucken arse out of there". That did the trick, she didn't understand English but got the message. He managed to carry her along the rear balcony, down the stairs, across the yard and into our flat. The poor lady sat on the toilet seat with her rosary beads, eyes closed and muttering, I presume praying. I offered a towel but she wouldn't take it. They were all pretty wet by then, anyhow.

Wim had to have a pee; he went to the kitchen door, opened it and he reached the back fence! He came back offering beers: "it will only get hot". I was bursting to use the loo but Mrs Greek lady wasn't moving, no room for any more liquid. Tamar was sitting on my lap and didn't seem the least concerned with the wind howling, the rain and the unbelievable noise of it all. The children were very good, obviously scared, but they offered only the odd whimper. There wasn't much room in the bath for them with their father taking up most of the space. Wim finished his beer and then said the takings from Paint N Paper were in his briefcase inside the boot of my car, and before I could say anything he was gone again. He returned intact, along with the case.

Sometime after 3.30 a.m. it became quiet and still. Wim and I went outside but couldn't see much by torchlight, just my car and others, plus roof beams hanging down from the upper flats. It was quiet for such a long time that we hoped it was over. It was wishful thinking; we were in the eye of the cyclone.

Knowing the wind would change direction once the

eye passed, I said we'd better move to our bedroom. The big guy from upstairs didn't want to leave the bath; he was terrified, I have heard of people being a mumbling mess, and he certainly was that. His wife was trying to talk him out of the bath, but he didn't want to move or listen about any wind change. Wim hoisted the children from the bath, the chap's wife and our Greek lady followed him into our bedroom, I took the last candle and also left; the chap followed a few seconds later, not wanting to stay by himself in the dark. I took the opportunity to return and use the loo - what a relief. I had just left the bathroom and shut the door when the wind returned with a vengeance, and the bathroom window shattered. I was very lucky, again.

Back in the bedroom, the chap was trying to get under our bed. It was laughable; here was this heavyset guy, about 6' 4", trying to squeeze under our low double bed, unforgettable. Wim and I took the mattress off the bed to prop over the large centre window; it could offer some protection if it smashed, and it also held the venetian blind reasonably flat against the glass; the two outer windows were already gone. We put the bed frame on its side for protection and to lean against the mattress, and then we sat on the wet floor and waited for dawn. It wasn't far away. I was the first to look outside and I couldn't believe what I was seeing. My first words were, "It's all gone, there's nothing there."

The children were upset now; they could see the devastation and no Father Christmas, I had some presents wrapped and safe in a wardrobe, but nothing suitable for children. Wim opened his briefcase and tried to give me

my present, but I shook my head, "Later." The children's father just wanted out and left virtually straight away; his wife thanked us and declined an offer of clothes, but took some dry towels and Christmas lollies for the children. They drove off; their car wasn't very damaged and had a clear path out of the driveway. Amazingly, our belongings in the linen closet and bedroom wardrobe were dry; the concrete roof I was afraid of had protected us and most of our belongings. Another stroke of luck for us was that the tea chests holding the majority of our goods were in the second bedroom, the only room to survive intact.

Our landlord, George, lived nearby, and arrived soon after dawn looking for his mother. He was so relieved to find her safe, after seeing the state of his flats. He couldn't thank Wim enough, and told us not to worry about paying any rent until the flats were repaired. We hadn't got to that stage yet; our minds were still in a state of disbelief. Of the six flats in the group, only three were occupied; the other occupants had gone south for Christmas. Of course our phone wasn't working, but it had been worth a try. We were worried that our familes wouldn't know what, if anything, had happened to us.

Wim was concerned about Paint N Paper, and we managed to extricate my car, which only had dings in the bodywork, and no broken windows. I went with him, and we negotiated the debris-covered roads to reach the shop. Looters were already helping themselves; panel beaters, Wim said, he knew from the products that were missing and what had been dropped behind the shop when we interrupted them. They were quick-thinking, free products to repair just about every car in Darwin. Money-hungry bastards, they must have arrived just after dawn! We managed to secure the rear roller door to prevent entry, and unbelievably, two more employees arrived and we could then secure the gaping holes where the front windows had been. The entire roof was also missing from the shop and warehouse. Luckily Wim, as acting manager, had the takings, close to $10,000 was safe.

Next we made our way slowly to Doreen and Justin's home on Trower Road, via the Trailer Boat Club. The building was still standing but it was full of sand, my drinks were still in the fridge which, being so large and solid, only had a few dents in the doors. The front lawn area was sand, debris and fallen palm trees. Boats in the rear parking area had been tossed every which way.

Doreen and Justin were unhurt, but their house was a write-off,

They had spent the night in a wardrobe which, unlike a lot of others we later heard about, stayed attached to the house and didn't fly away with its occupants inside. They came back to our flat, and Wim and Justin managed to salvage enough unbroken windows from the upstairs flats to replace all of ours. We were very fortunate; we now just had wet floor coverings, a wet mattress, damaged curtains and a secure abode. Not many Darwin people were so lucky. Barry, a Paint N Paper employee, arrived with his wife and two children. They had lost their home in Stuart Park, and we had invited them too when Barry arrived at the store earlier.

The next day I was outside our flat when I heard a

phone ringing in the flat next to ours. I was so surprised, as along with ours we had been checking it regularly to see if there was a dial tone, and of course there wasn't. I answered it and it was the sister of the chap who lived there, calling from Adelaide to see how his flat had fared. I told her, and asked her to phone Mum and Dad and let them know we were okay. I then tried using the phone, but nothing, I was just leaving when it rang. It was Mum, she was so relieved. The Adelaide Advertiser had printed a list of the fatalities from Tracy and another of people missing, believed dead. I, Jill Delvendiep was in the latter, and my husband Wim was shown to have been evacuated to Adelaide!

Mum and Dad had been worried sick, and couldn't understand why Wim hadn't contacted them. How could a name like Delvendiep be mistakenly used this way? The only Delvendieps in Australia were Wim's family, his parents, brothers and sisters plus their young children. Mum later showed me the newspaper article, and it is still with her papers. The next day the phone had a dial tone, and we could call out.

That phone was a lifeline; soon most of our friends, and even people we didn't know, asked to use it to contact relatives and friends. There was a steady stream of people making calls all over Australia and the world. Wim was in contact with Paint N Paper in Brisbane, and they said they would send up a generator for us. What a welcome gift that was when it arrived, a 5 KVA, it would run power to both flats.

Later in the afternoon, after speaking to Mum and Dad, we drove out to Nightcliff and surrounds to check on other friends and one, Sharm, had a generator and gave us our first cold drink since Tracy. It was one of the best drinks I have ever had, ice-cold orange juice. Heavenly.

The evacuation of Darwin residents was well underway by now, and food supplies were pouring in from around Australia. We were able to collect food from the Darwin High School, and would call in on the way home from work to select something for dinner. It was amazing that between us we would nearly all come home with the same tinned goods. A friend, Charlie Grasby, managed to get hold of fresh beef, and this I shared with Tamar. Sadly, a lot of pets were destroyed out of necessity, but I managed to keep Tamar fed and out of sight.

We had no running water, so would go to the Stuart Highway, the water pipeline would be opened and we could shower in our bikinis on the main road. We also lined up for cholera vaccinations, this was before the generator arrived, and later that day block ice was available, one block per person. Doreen, Justin, Wim and myself were in the long line for what seemed like forever when Justin and Wim felt ill and faint from their shots and had to leave the queue and sit in the shade. We missed out on two blocks of ice! We told them what wimps they were; we girls didn't feel faint. Not long after, we were able to get water from the fire hydrant next to our flat, and would cart water to the bath to wash our clothes and sheets. What a job, but at least we had water close by.

By the time the generator arrived, only Doreen and Justin were living with us, and two male friends were in the other flat, their wives and families having been evacuated.

10,000 people were evacuated from Darwin in the first two days after Tracy. The generator would usually run out of fuel between 1 a.m. and 2 a.m., and the guys would wait for Wim to come out and pump the fuel from the forty-four gallon drum. They had overhead fans, we had the airconditioner and they knew Wim wouldn't stay asleep long if that turned off, so they would stay in bed, knowing it wouldn't be long before power was restored.

During this time, Wim and I would go to the Trailer Boat Club after work and open up and serve drinks. The cold room was pretty well stocked, so there was a good selection, but of course no beer on tap. We did this for for a couple of weeks, and it amazed me that some so-called friends and members would still get abusive if their drink wasn't available, or we wanted to shut up and go home. Anyone would think we were getting paid. Years later Wim did take over as manager.

I'm now 67, born 28 October 1948 in Adelaide, where I live with husband Brian Limb at Henley Beach. Brian and I married in Darwin on 8 May 1982 at No 97 Restaurant, Mitchell Street after meeting at the Darwin Trailer Boat Club in April 1981. We moved to South Australia in September 1982; his employer Castrol ("Oils ain't Oils") wanted him down here to set up a new business division. We both had mixed feelings about leaving Darwin; Brian's three children were there, and so many friends; the upside was that our parents, my brother and one of Brian's sisters lived here. We don't have children. I'm fortunate to have his children and their families in my life; all still live interstate but it's a great excuse to travel. We've visited Darwin many times since leaving, and it's always great to catch up with friends, though as the years go by many have left, and sadly, too many have passed on.

I took leave from the Education Department when we left Darwin, and managed to get a transfer to the Department of Social Security (Centrelink) before my leave ran out. I stayed until accepting a redundancy in October 1998. Most of my work with Centrelink was investigating Social Security fraud, interesting to say the least, and one time, life-threatening. Brian retired shortly after me. He's 10 years older, and we enjoyed many years holidaying/travelling on the Murray River aboard our houseboat "The Jilly Bean." We bought her in 1997 and moored at Paringa. We sold a few years ago; we still have some regrets, but we made happy memories and great friends.

We love the Paringa/Renmark area and of course the river, and were planning to move there, when I was diagnosed with breast cancer. During the Melbourne Cup festivities at home in November 2000, I received a phone call informing me that my recent mammogram showed a suspicious lump. More tests followed, and the upshot was two operations, chemotherapy and radiotherapy, and I'm now a breast cancer survivor of 15 years. Once recovered from treatment, I became a dragon boat paddler with SA Dragons Abreast, set up for breast cancer survivors. I enjoyed paddling and competing for a few years, and our Golden Retriever, Banjo, who was only 11 weeks old when I was diagnosed, became the mascot for our team. I still have one photo of him in the pink t-shirt, not that he appears too happy about it.

We planned to visit Western Australia in 2002, and the only way to take Banjo with us was to buy a van. I am so glad we did, I loved the life and our travels, and we have been travelling all over Australia since, and always with Banjo until his death last year; he was well travelled, much loved and is still dreadfully missed. We returned home a few weeks ago after two months away in Queensland, New South Wales and Victoria, which included visits to Charters Towers where Brian's youngest son Martin lives with his family, and the Sunshine Coast where his daughter Rachael is now, having moved there from Darwin 22 months ago. His eldest, Stephen, is single and still in Darwin.

Brian is a keen golfer and very involved with his club. I've been researching our family tree for several years and really enjoy it I love the detective work. It resulted in meeting new relatives here and on our travels, contact with others overseas and even discovering that a former next door neighbour and friend of many years was my second cousin, and also a cousin of Brian's. I can't believe all the relatives I've discovered Brian and I have in common, and we joke that if my mother were still alive she'd make us divorce.

We plan to keep travelling, and are fortunate to be in good health. The next big trip we have planned is to WA early next year, where I hope to pick up the trail of some of our less respectable ancestors in Albany and Northam.

Photograph by Ranson Hill

I love living here at Henley; it's also where I spent most of my early years. I try and get to the beach most days, though it's not the same without Banjo. It's funny how people identify you by your dog, he was such an outgoing personality and made it his business to say 'hello' to anyone and everyone, think it was to hear them say 'he's beautiful'. I'm sure he thought that was his name. (No, I'm not biased!) I meet the same people now, and with most, I have to mention Banjo before they twig who I am. I'm guilty of the same.

Brian and I were doing obedience training with him in a nearby oval in 2001 when a woman came running over. We thought maybe we shouldn't have been on the oval, but no - "he's perfect." She wanted him to appear in Channel 7's "The Book Place" as Boomer, from the book "Boomer's Big Day". It was filmed at home and nearby a few weeks later, and we treasure the video.

I wasn't sure how to take this, but during one walk a woman said , "What a beautiful dog, you look just like him".

I guess that in a snapshot, I'm 67, very happy, healthy, have great friends and family plus a wonderful husband (third time lucky) who also happens to share and enjoy most of the things I do, including a sense of humour. A legacy from Tracy is that I find the noise from strong winds unsettling.

I believe in "don't sweat the small stuff"; I first heard it from a former nun conducting a training course at Centrelink, and I guess after breast cancer it made even more sense. I was in bed feeling sick after another round of chemo when a caller to talk-back radio rang in to complain that his paper had landed in a puddle of water that morning… if only.

Left: Jilly Limb (née Delvendiep)

CHAPTER 14 – COSTA KARAOLIAS & FAMILY

Above: Costa with his brother and his dad and mum taken around 2000, just before his mum died.

In November 1974 we moved into our brand new house at 5 Easther Crescent, then considered in the suburb of Nightcliff.

On Christmas Eve, I left our shop, Andrews Food Fair in Westralia Street, early to go home and get dressed to party at Swingers at the Berrimah Hotel (where Harvey Norman now is). In my haste, I forgot the keys to the house and in the end broke the window to get in. I was angry with myself and started coming up with excuses to explain to my parents the next day how it happened. Our house was one month old, we moved into it in November

CAM. 3 ALL 3-3
DATE 24-5-75
LOT SUB.

1974. It is at 5 Easther Cres, right behind KFC in Nightcliff.

By the time I picked up my mates, Kevin Doolan, Steven Beer, Willy Clayton, Alice Snape and another girl and got to Swingers, it was around 9:00 p.m. If my memory serves me right, the power was cut off at around 11 p.m., so everyone left. We were all pretty intoxicated, so we thought we should go to the St Mary's Cathedral for the other guys to pray that the cyclone would not come.

After we left the nightclub, on the way into town, I was arguing with someone over one of the girls who was sitting in front with me and another guy (Kevin I think) and lost control of the car, and we literally did a 360 on the highway just outside the gates to the Berrimah navy base. We missed all the oncoming cars and the ones driving into town as we turned right around. Luck? We then decided to go to the St Mary's Cathedral for the other guys to pray after that incident, and so that the cyclone would not come.

While we were at the church, around midnight, the stained glass on the concrete arch in front of the church broke, and people started to come out and go to their cars, as did my mates. For years I thought I had imagined this, until I read a post on the 40th Anniversary Cyclone Tracy Facebook site of another person recalling the same event!

I dropped off one guy in Stuart Park, and it took us at least half an hour to drive up Bagot Road; this was around 12:30 p.m. The winds and rain were slamming onto the car and kept stalling the car, and in the end I had to drive in first or second gear all the way to Rapid Creek.

I finally dropped off the last two guys, and one of them was so drunk he could not walk, so I left him on the porch of his house along Rapid Creek road. He was fine after the cyclone, as I saw him down south when we were all evacuated.

When I got home, I went into our bedroom and shortly after that, Dad got us all up and said we had to go downstairs, as his room windows had broken and he was not sure what could happen next. We all moved towards the front stairs, but when we opened the door the front verandah was mangled up, so we went to the back stairs which were still okay. We all went into the room downstairs, which had, I think, three women and two of them had young babies, Their husbands were at the Greek club playing cards and could not get back. I guess this really proved that no one believed a cyclone would hit us!!

There was myself, my brother, Mum and Dad, my cousin John Andreou, the three ladies and two babies.

Dad put the two ladies and the babies in the cupboard, and the rest of us stood against the wall away from the window and waited, if that is the word.

The noise was horrifying and you could hear the clanging of things and the movement of heavy materials. When the eye came over, (although I don't believe we knew that there was such a thing as the eye being over Darwin) you noticed the noise really dropping off, we thought it was over, it was quite eerie. We went outside and we could see around a bit, and the house next door was partly there and all the trees and shrubs in our yard had gone.

The winds began to pick up again, so we went back inside and this time the winds and noise were more terrifying. In one massive whoosh the windows blew outwards (luckily for us), and then in another massive whoosh the gyproc ceiling fell on top of us. At that time I remember thinking that the house would fall on us. Mum and the other lady were screaming. But as things were, the gyproc ceiling actually became our massive umbrella. I and my cousin and dad held it up over our heads and it gave us respite from the dripping water.

We stood for a couple of hours holding the ceiling up, and by the time daylight came and the winds stopped, our arms were so tired. We went outside and the place was a mess. More so when the eye was on its way in. When I saw the site in front of us, I remember thinking, shame job, how am I going to explain this to my mates! Later on when I saw what had happened everywhere else in Darwin, I felt a little better, if that can be said.

My uncle and the husbands of the ladies somehow drove to our house from Stuart Parkaround lunchtime. We all got in and went along Bagot Road to Nelson Street in Stuart Park, whilst the others went to some other people's houses.

On the way to my uncle's house, we went past our shop (Andrews Food Fair) and the front windows were all broken and many people were walking out with goods. Once they saw us, many ran off – you would be surprised at some of the people who took stuff and took off! Once inside we noticed that the cigarettes and all the alcohol

37

Darwin Reconstruction Commission
LOT DATA SHEET

LOT IDENTIFICATION

TOWN	LOT NO	ST. NO	STREET	SUBURB
NIGHTCLIFF	6121	5	EASTNER CRES	COCONUT GROVE

ZONING: RR

TITLE STATUS: P

DAMAGE CATEGORY: 3

EXPEDIENT USE CATEGORY: 3

AREA: 3

METROPOLITAN CONTACT

SITE AS AT

cabinets were empty. We thought it was rather funny that not much food was taken.

My uncle's house only had one window broken and a couple of beams of the roof went, so it was in a good state compared to the others around. My parents and cousin stayed there with my uncle and his mate Arthur, and Eva from Eva's Grill Bar in Wog Alley, where the Galleria is now. Eventually everyone was advised to go to mustering points ready for evacuation. We all went to the Stuart Park Primary school for one night, then we were bussed to the airport.

My brother, myself and Steven Beer slept in the car parked in front of the shops, as we could not board them up. We also had shotguns with us, as rumours were rife that people were breaking into shops and houses to get anything going or unguarded. These were dark times for Darwin after the cyclone.

During the week, we cooked and ate food from the shops' fridges, along with other families, the Cleanthouses among them, as they lived in the two houses above the shops. We kids tried all types of food combinations. We knew that it would go off so we tried any recipe we could think of, even fresh cream with tinned oysters, ouch!

At first, we were told via radio that only women and children under 18 would only be evacuated. All males over 18 had to stay and help clean up. Not sure when, but a couple of days later, it was announced that anyone who wanted to leave could do so.

We all agreed to go as we were not sure what would happen to us and to Darwin. We were advised to go to the nearest school, in our case the Stuart Park Primary School, and register our names for evacuation. Whilse we were there, they asked us to actually stay at the school (need to confirm this) until we were evacuated. We spent a couple of days there, and had to share a classroom with a couple of other families.

On New Year's day we were evacuated. Steven Beer who was an older than eighteen years old and could not leave the week before, was recorded as Steven Karaolias so that he could travel with us, as his family had left town another way, I'm not sure how and where. The week leading into New Year's day, the authorities allowed all men who wanted to be evacuated with their families to do so. So Dad decided that he would come to settle us down and return. Steven Beer also came with us, but we forgot to change the recording of his name. My parents decided to go to Sydney, as we had friends there.

We flew out on an Ansett T-Jet and the plane was jam-packed, can't recall for sure but there were four people in the row of seats that normally used to seat three. One of the hostesses asked us about the Tripp family, and we had seen Gus somewhere and told her so.

When we arrived in Adelaide, we were greeted by thousands of people who lined up behind the barricade fencing on the tarmac. It was a funny feeling walking through to go to the terminal. I saw a school friend who had been in Adelaide on holidays when the cyclone hit, and she asked me about someone who luckily I had seen, and I advised her that he was on another flight after ours. It was great feeling to see a known face.

In the terminal, there was a board with missing people and guess what, Steven Beer was listed! We went to the authorities and fixed the matter up, but Steven had to go as they knew where his family were.

From Adelaide, we flew to Melbourne and again, sitting at the airport waiting to get to Sydney was lonely. But lo and behold, when I was walking around, there was this guy reading a newspaper and I had a feeling I knew the body. It was Eddy Motlop, and we embraced and I can tell you this was a great moment.

We then flew on to Sydney, where we were picked up by our friends and taken to their house. On New Year's eve, my brother, myself, the Cleanthous kids, Clem, Leo, and Chris all walked for miles along the Princess Highway, we walked to the Tom Ugly Bridge and back! I guess there was nothing else to do.

The next day, the Cleanthouses went to Melbourne, I think, and we were bussed to Pennant Hills Hostel. There we met up with another Darwin family, the Alexis (father Nick, their mother, sons Andrew and Alex and daughters Meriforo and Chloi), who had driven to Sydney in an old Valiant.

In two weeks in Sydney, we learned the train system and caught the train to the city from Pennant Hills. One time in the city, we came across a cinema which was showing the ABC film, "When will the Birds Return"? or something like that. That day was very moving for us. The cinema was packed and you could hear people gasping at the sights of Darwin and saying things like "Oh, those poor people," and so on. We remained quiet, and sort of proud

that they were talking about us, but we just sat there and said nothing.

Sydney was far too big for me, and when my dad was to return to Darwin and clean out the shop, I applied for a permit as his "interpreter", otherwise they would not let me back.

Dad was going to come back, do some cleaning and sell everything, and we were to move to Sydney.

However, Chris stayed in Sydney to do his apprentership as an electrician, and as an investment we bought a house on the river. Chris actually won one of two apprenticeships that were going, because he was a refugee/survivor from Cyclone Tracy. We thought that the Apprentiship Board who decided that were very good people.

Once we cleaned the shop, we realised that its condition was very good, and within 5 or 6 months it was operating again, so we thought we should stay in Darwin. The navy cleared the rubble of our house at 5 Easther Crescent, then Nightcliff, we cleaned the mess inside the downstairs flat and made it liveable. It had two bedrooms, kitchen, toilet and bathroom.

Mum came back a couple of months later, once the house was all cleared.

Left: The family home after it was rebuilt. (late 70s)

Costa Karaolias.

CHAPTER 15 – GABY LANCASTER.

Corner of Bauhinia and Bougainvillea Streets, Nightcliff.

I found it hard to grip the reality of the night of Cyclone Tracy, on entering the rubble that was left behind and knowing how lucky we were to survive. But yes, it really did happen. I was only fifteen then, and we had just enjoyed our Christmas night (Germans celebrate on Christmas Eve).

Things were getting a bit rough around 9.30 p.m., so we were packed off to bed a little earlier than normal. By 10.30 the rain was pouring in horizontally at a million miles an hour, even through closed and locked louvres.

When the louvres started smashing through, we knew it was time to get up. We got as far as the corridor of our house, an elevated, only to see the end (Mum's room) get totally blown away; then we saw the next one go (that was mine), at which time we could see out into the wild and terrifying night storm.

A rash decision was made by my stepdad, Reg Cusack that we should immediately get downstairs, which meant climbing over a fridge and freezer which were piled up on our stairs. So we – Mum, Dad and us 5 kids - clambered into our tiny, disorganised little storeroom under the house, sitting on top of the lawnmower, car tyres and all kinds of other gear to ride out the storm. It was a terrifying night, watching out through the holes and gaps in the fibro walls to see what was happening outside.

The wind never let up, and as the eye passed over I thought we were goners for sure. The roaring sound of the wind was so deafening, we could only look at each other, as you would never hear what anyone said. It wasn't until about 6 – 6.30 in the morning that we were able to come out of our so-called safe haven.

What we had to witness in the following days still haunts me to this day. We searched our yard looking for what was left of our beloved Christmas presents, any tinned food we could salvage and whatever clothes we could get our hands on, which wasn't much. Our house was flattened up top, except for two walls of the bathroom which were only just there. Everything else was just totally gone. It was just so hard for us young ones to comprehend why or how this had happened.

But I know how lucky we all were to have survived.

The most horrifying image I still have is of a young girl; her parents came wandering down the street, asking if we had seen her. Sadly, we looked up at one stage, and the poor little lass had been tossed like a rag doll into the now-

Above: Bauhinia Street, Nightcliff.

stripped bare tree not far away. (I knew writing this would undo me).

I'll never forget that.

We didn't know her or her parents, but how awful it was.

We had to walk for hours from Nightcliff to the pipeline at the Stuart Highway/Ross Smith Avenue junction to stand and wash (there was no soap) under the opened valve controlled by others, after waiting in an endless queue.

My stepdad was involved in the rebuilding of Darwin, so he and my two elder brothers were allowed to stay, whilst Mum, my two younger brothers and I were finally evacuated at the end of January, returning six months later. I have endured the following cyclones that came via Darwin, but thankfully nothing ever like Cyclone Tracy.

People seem to think it's fun to stock up and have a cyclone party to ride it out – I never want to experience another one ever again. We did survive it, so that is our blessing. I finally left Darwin in February 2003, and cannot live back there again.

Gaby Lancaster with her husband.

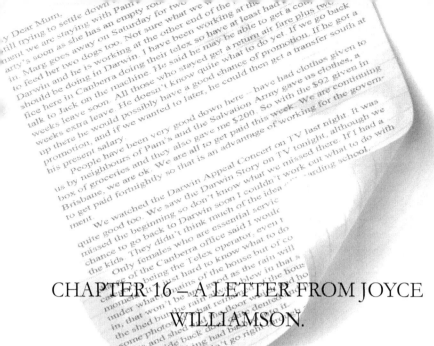

CHAPTER 16 – A LETTER FROM JOYCE WILLIAMSON.

My Dear Mum,

Still trying to settle down but each day seems to get better. At the moment we are staying with Pam and David Cass. May go to Marg Moriarty's soon as she has an empty room under her house that we could stay in. Marg goes away on Saturday for two weeks and she needs someone to feed her two dogs too. Not sure what we will do yet. Jack is still in Darwin and he is working at the other end of the telex machine that I should be doing in Darwin. I have been working at the Department of N.T. Office here in Canberra doing their telex so have at least had a chance to talk to Jack on the machine. He said he may be able to get a couple of weeks leave soon. All those who stayed get a return air fare plus two weeks extra leave. He doesn't know quite what to do yet. If we go back up there he would possibly have a good chance of promotion. If he got a promotion, and if we wanted to later, he could then get a transfer south at his present salary.

People have been very good down here – have had clothes given to us by neighbours of Pam's and the Salvation Army gave us clothes, a box of groceries and they also gave me $200. So with the $92 given in Brisbane, we are ok. We are all to get paid this week. We are continuing to get paid fortnightly so that is an advantage of working for the government.

We watched the Darwin Appeal Concert on TV last night. It was quite good too. We saw the Darwin Story on TV tonight, although we missed the beginning so don't know what we missed there. If I had a chance to go back to Darwin soon I couldn't work out what to do with the kids. They didn't think much of the idea of boarding school.

Only females who are essential services can go back but Mr Plant in charge of the Canberra office said I would just about come under that category, being the Telex operator, even though Jack is doing it at the moment. It's just hard to know what to do for the best. Jack is sleeping under what remains of the house but of course, when the wet season sets in, that won't be any good as the rain will come in. There is floor over the shed but the rain always blew in that side anyway. Les Jacobs took some photos of what remained of the house which was only the cement posts and shed and the floor which had holes in it anyway. The car had the left side back door quite dented and Lesley said there was a hole in it where something had bashed into it.

Luckily it didn't go right through as that was where Lesley was sitting. I think we were very lucky we didn't stay in the bathroom as people were told to do, or we may have had injuries as I think we would have either been hit by something or been blown off the house. We sat in the car from about 2 a.m. till it finished about 6 a.m., and the car just rocked all night and as the window on the back left-hand side had smashed, we had rain and wind blowing on us and were freezing. We couldn't get out of the car and back into the shed as the wind nearly slammed the door on Jack's legs. It would have been ok in the shed as that's where Peter and Sambo (the dog) ended up after he got out of his car. I don't ever want to go through anything even half as bad as that again. Still we were lucky we got away with our lives which is more than some people did.

Not sure what you gave us for Christmas but thanks anyway. The kids found some presents but we weren't sure what was what.

A neighbour of Pam's brought down a present for the kids the day after we arrived. Very nice gesture I thought. Marg bought us some underpants. Pam brought me a nice dressing gown so all in all we ended up with something. Another neighbour sent down a turkey, so we had Christmas dinner on New Year's Day.

Must away to bed for now as I have to be at work at 8:30 tomorrow.

Love from us all, Joyce.

PS. Trying to get an envelope to post the letter. Going to Marg Moriarty's tomorrow night and will send the new address.

CHAPTER 17 – LESLEY DAVIS

Lesley Davis (nee Williamson) was fifteen years old at the time of Tracy.

On the afternoon of December 24, 1974 we knew that this cyclone was on a direct path to Darwin and was so close that there was no way it could veer off now. We usually had warnings during the wet season, but those cyclones came to nothing except heavy monsoonal rains.

I remember my dad coming home in the afternoon saying that Tracy was definitely going to hit us, and we went around doing the usual preparations, such as filling up bottles and putting away all the fold-up chairs from under the house. The sky started to look rather ominous. I have never seen a sky quite like it. It was very heavy, with greenish-grey clouds, and almost looked the colour of my mum's famous pea soup. We knew we were in for a big storm, but I don't think any of us really knew how big.

We went about our usual business of dinner and finishing off present wrapping for Christmas. My brother was at Nightcliff at his girlfriend's place. Throughout the evening we listened to the radio and heard the frequent siren of the cyclone warnings. That siren still gives me chills when I hear it. At about 11:00 p.m., the winds were getting pretty strong and my brother arrived home. He said that his car was getting blown across lanes on Bagot Road, and that he had had to really pull on the steering wheel to keep on the road. Sometime close to 12:00 p.m. the radio stopped transmitting and the power went off. The wind was howling outside and we could feel the walls of the house beginning to shake. I could see my dad was getting pretty worried. We had torches, and he told us all to go and get some shoes on, and we also pulled the mattresses off a couple of beds and put them in the hallway. There were six of us: Mum, Dad and the four kids, so we couldn't really fit in our small bathroom, which we were told was the safest place in the house. We all sat on the mattresses in the hallway with the doors to the bedrooms, bathroom and living room closed. The walls were moving behind our backs now, and the roar outside made it difficult for us to hear each other.

Then Tracy began to unleash her fury. We could hear the shrieking and tearing of metal and thought it was our neighbours' roof coming off, but realised later that it was probably our own. Next we heard the very worrying sound of shattering glass, as all the louvre windows in our living room began exploding. I am thankful that my dad was a very practical ex-navy man, and he decided there and then that we weren't staying in the house. That was a very good call, as I don't like to think of the many people who were sheltering in bathrooms that night.

My dad said that we would get into the car under the house as again, we wouldn't all fit in the solid cement shed, and that could be dangerous if it fell, too. He looked at me and said, "Lesley, you're the bravest, you can go first!" My dad still had his sense of humour, as it was really that I was just the first in his line of vision. He escorted us one by one down the stairs and around the corner into the car. We kept our heads very low and held on to the stair railings. I remember looking up a bit, and although the sky was very dark, during lightning flashes I caught a glimpse of our roof all crumpled up in the yard, and debris flying through the air all around the house. My older brother couldn't fit into the car with us, so he and our black labrador sheltered in his car, which was parked beside the house.

We spent the next four or five hours in the car, not daring to lift our heads from the brace position as the car was buffeted about as though it was on an ocean. Sometime during the night, the back windshield shattered, and we were covered in broken glass. We didn't realise how close we had come to injury until the morning, when we discovered that the balcony had come down over the side of the house and a huge sheet of fibro had dug halfway down the springs in the back of the seat behind us. Something also smashed into the left side of the car and shattered that window. It was freezing with the rain pelting us like stinging sand, and we weren't even sure if our parents were alive, as the roar of the wind was so loud, they couldn't

hear us kids occasionally screaming out their names to see if they were okay.

Sometime during the night I looked up to see our dog with his paws on the windows, peering in at us. My brother was frantically trying to see if we were okay. We couldn't hear him, but Mum and Dad told us they screamed out at him to get back to his car. As he was running back, I saw the whole kitchen virtually spew out over the side of the house. I could see the stove and fridge falling and at the same time, my brother was running. We thought that the contents of the kitchen had fallen on my brother, and my mum told us, she screamed at my dad that she could see his hand underneath the rubble. He wouldn't let her out of the car and she feared, the whole night, that he lay there dying. Thankfully time has a way of being distorted in times of distress, and he had actually reached his car before the kitchen disintegrated. He told us the next morning that he had a feeling he should start up the car and move it forward, and just as he did, the kitchen pulverized the back corner of his car.

At about 5:00 a.m. when the winds were still shrieking, my sister and I both had to pee. We sort of shouted out to each other and decided that we'd just have to let it go. It was actually really nice, as we were absolutely shaking from cold and it momentarily warmed us. There was to be no embarrassment, as the drenching rain soon washed everything away.

We had always heard that there an eye to the storm. We had been sitting in this cramped position for several hours, and our fears were that we were buried in rubble and that if we hadn't had the eye yet, we would have to endure this for another five hours (we were later to find out that the northern suburbs were the worst hit and didn't get the eye at all.) It sounds a little dramatic, but my sister and I started singing the Maureen McGovern song, 'There's got to be a Morning After'. I can't remember if my little brother joined in. Thankfully there was a morning after, and the winds started to die down a bit by about 6:00 a.m. We still weren't sure if this was just going to be the eye, but the sky seemed to have lost its ominous look, although it was still raining. We literally staggered out of the cars and tried to get some life back into our legs.

We, along with all our neighbours, looked around in utter disbelief at the devastation Tracy had wreaked during the night. I think everyone just looked dazed. My brother recounts that he looked at Dad and said, "What are we going to do?" My dad just said, in his usual sarcastically humorous way, "How the f*&%^ should I know?" And then, "I'm sure the navy or army will be here to help us soon enough." He was, however, able to get it together and he and the neighbouring men started going around our street to make sure everyone was okay.

We had no idea what had happened to our cat, as she hadn't come in to the house that night. We heard a pitiful meowing and realized that it was coming from the engine of the car. When we lifted the hood, we found our very bedraggled and frightened cat. We also discovered that a large metal pole had been driven through the side of the car and halfway into the motor, and we were thankful that it hadn't gone through the front door of the car where Mum and Dad were sitting. We later stood on our floorboards and couldn't believe that we could see over eight miles into the city because there was not one tree left with leaves and very few buildings to block the way. It reminded us of photographs of Hiroshima.

The next day or two were surreal, as we all gathered at Wagaman Primary School for meals and a hard bed on the floor. I remember the tears welling up as the army helicopters dropped supplies on the oval, thinking that other people cared. I remember the scratchy army supply blankets. The strangest thing was that we had never been without all the city services, and at night it was so black outside that you couldn't see your hand in front of your face. With all the street and house lights gone and no traffic on the streets, no sounds of TVs or radios, it was eerie.

In that inky blackness we had to go outside with a torch to the deep latrines that the army had dug, and my sister and I held hands and said a prayer as we squatted over the edge. After some of the roads had been cleared by bulldozers, a few families went down to a creek that we used to swim at to take a bath (we just soaped up in the clothes we were wearing). I couldn't believe it was the same place, as the cyclone had changed it so much. It seems the cyclone had killed the birds, or many of them had had the sense to leave town, as there were no bird sounds to be heard, and with so few cars on the road, the days were eerily quiet, too.

We had tied our dog up at the school bubblers along with an assortment of family dogs. We went back to the house often, to check on our cat and to see if we could

salvage anything. We found four bathtubs in our yard, but they wouldn't help much! My dad heard mumblings of the army shooting looters and dogs, as it was feared that dogs would roam in packs. I could understand that reasoning for dogs that were roaming without their owners, but surely that wouldn't apply to all these lovely dogs that had ridden the storm out in their owners' arms? My dad said, "Over my dead body" and took our dog back to our place to tie him up under the floorboards. I remember lying on the floor in a classroom later that day, and under a room divider I saw army boots walk up to a little boy and the little dog on his lap was lifted up. They took all the dogs out and shot them on the oval. I still feel incensed that people who had already been traumatised enough had to mourn another loss.

After about three days, people were being put on lists to be evacuated south. We only had the clothes we were wearing, so we tried to find some clothes in our yard. We found a muddied sheet, and a few muddied items of clothing which we tied up in the sheet. I guess we were thinking that we could wash them when we arrived south, but they were really pretty useless. My dad and older brother stayed, and my mum and the three younger kids were evacuated to any city that the next plane was flying to; we had no choice at that stage. Our plane was flying to Canberra. My mum knew some old navy friends from her days at Harman, so she asked one of those families if we could stay with them.

Our grandmother lived in Brisbane, but Mum didn't think she could cope with us all arriving on her doorstep. My dad stayed on to help for about three months, and my brother drove out of Darwin with our dog. He headed to Wollongong, where his girlfriend's family lived. My dad flew our cat down when we had resettled in Brisbane.

I felt utter helplessness that I couldn't contact any of my friends from school, or my boyfriend. As a fifteen-year-old that was pretty hard, and I spent many a night drinking too much in Canberra. I had been smoking for a while, but like many teenagers in Darwin, had kept this hidden from my parents. At the airport, I threw all caution out the window and said to my mum, "I need a cigarette!" She said, "So do I!" So we bought some from a vending machine and sat and had a puff together. Unfortunately my mum, who had given up twenty years earlier, kept smoking after that day, and I still feel responsible for leading my mum astray.

In those days, there was no such thing as 'post natural disaster' counselling, and I don't think people knew much about loss and grief, however on looking back I know that Cyclone Tracy ripped a lot away from us. I still wonder to this day about people I never saw again, and I know that my siblings and I felt much displaced in the two years after the cyclone, when we had to go to school in Brisbane.

We never lived in the same city as our older brother again, and I still feel sorry that we have very few childhood photographs. On the other hand, going through Tracy has made us very resilient, and I have moved many times since then, and never get attached to houses or material things. My parents lived the rest of their lives in Darwin, and we kids visited many times and still feel that Darwin has a special place in our hearts. Our parents are now at rest in the Services section of the Rapid Creek Cemetery. A good excuse to visit now and then!

Postscript: I married a Canadian in 1991 and lived in Canada until 1995. I then moved back to Brisbane, where I have lived ever since. I spent some lovely weeks in Darwin in 2008 with my mother who lived there all her life. Sadly she passed in 2008, so I haven't been back since, although Darwin is rooted deep in my heart, as both my parents are resting in the Services section of Rapid Creek Cemetery.

I have three beautiful children aged 24, 27 and 30, and

have worked as a primary school teacher for the past 20 years.

Lesley Davis

Below: Lesley with her husband, Charlie.

Photograph by Ramon Williams

CHAPTER 18 – MARG RODERICK

I was working for Repco Auto Parts in the Stuart Park branch (Winnellie being the other), as a delivery driver. My job entailed delivering parts to service stations, garages and various auto outlets around Darwin and the surrounding suburbs.

We'd had cyclone warnings on radio and TV all day, but that wet season we'd had several cyclone warnings already, so we were pretty complacent. It was Christmas Eve, and party mode was overtaking any concerns about a cyclone that might not even affect us.

It was raining and hot and humid, but not really windy. The time was approaching 5 p.m., and I heard the cyclone warning siren being broadcast over the radio. Still not alarmed, we packed up and all headed to our respective families or Christmas Eve parties.

I was caretaking a flat on the second floor of a three storey block of flats for a workmate of mine at Repco, who was on holidays.

On my way home to Nightcliff, I stopped at a number of service stations that were on my delivery route, to wish them all Merry Christmas and to check out their Christmas parties.

Parap Service Station was having a huge Christmas party for staff and friends, so I stayed there for a few hours. We ended up having water fights under their hoses, as if there wasn't enough water around already from the rain and wind that was picking up.

Still unconcerned, I carried on home; the time was around 10 p.m.

I had a quick shower, put on my nightie and went to bed.

I was jolted awake by the sound of an explosion. I sat bolt upright in bed, in time to see the front plate-glass window of the bedroom imploding in at me. The force of the wind picked up the end of my mattress and slung it up against the wall, with me still on it.

Beside the bed was the doorway leading into the living area of the flat, and I went airborne through that door and landed on the floor near the refrigerator, with sheets and pillows landing on top of me and glass from the window landing on top of them; amazingly I did not even receive a scratch from all the glass that was showered down over me.

I crawled over to the fridge and squeezed into a space between it and the kitchen cupboard. I was overwhelmed by the sound around me. The wind was absolutely deafening, comparable to the sound of a train thundering through a tunnel at top speed with all the other sounds coming through, the screeching, tearing noise of metal tearing away from rooftops and houses. I heard glass smashing, trees and branches whipping around in the wind... and I couldn't see a thing in the total blackness.

Then lightning flashed and I could see the venetian blinds in the lounge room window, which was devoid of glass by this time, almost horizontal, blowing and tearing up in the wind. As the blinds were snapped violently in the wind they sounded like gunshots.

Another flash of lightning and I could see all the artefacts and pictures being ripped from the walls and disappearing into the darkness.

Another flash, and to my horror I could see the huge electric power cable that was the main power line to the flats, swinging outside the window. I was absolutely terrified that I was going to be electrocuted. I was sitting in about four inches of water, and rain was drenching me every time it gusted through the flat, which by this time had no windows or doors left standing

I stayed in that position for the next five hours, screaming in fear and watching that powerline every time the lightning flashed. I had no idea that the authorities would have shut down the power station at the first sign of destruction.

I remember wishing I had my cat with me; at least she would have been some comfort. She was at home at my parents place, and I didn't feel concerned for her, because at that stage I had no concept that what was happening to me might have been happening to others as well.

Eventually there was nothing left of the gunshot-sounding venetian blinds but tiny shreds hanging from the top of the window frame.

At about 5 a.m., the greyness of dawn crept in, and the wind had eased off a little. I struggled up from my small space beside the fridge, stiff and sore and in a daze. I looked through the window, and at first I had the strangest sensation that I was enveloped by a thick fog, as I couldn't see the house next door, or the trees or any buildings around me. Then my mind cleared, and the destruction before my eyes was overwhelming. Only then did I realise that it wasn't only happening to me. My next door neighbour's house was almost gone. The cement foundation was there, a few parts of walls, water pipes and troughs. All the tall palm trees that had lined his driveway were flattened to the ground. He was circling his yard in a disbelieving daze, as well.

I looked to the car park and saw that my H.D. Holden sedan had a smashed windscreen and dents across the roof. The cabin cruiser that was parked alongside my car had been picked up by the wind and rolled across my car and landed on the other side. Luckily that was all the damage done to my car. I worked for Repco and knew that they would replace my windscreen at a very special price. There was building material and storm debris piled up around my car, and I knew I couldn't move it on my own.

I was still in my nightie, so I rummaged around in the mess and found a pair of wet jeans and a shirt to put on. Amazingly, our block of flats was mostly still standing; the top floor only had a few walls left upright. On my floor, the second, all the windows, doors, furniture, wall hangings -

almost anything that wasn't fixed was gone.

I had to find my family. My brother, Stan Perron, and his wife Carol and their new baby Yvonne lived about four blocks from me on Nightcliff Road. I made my way through the debris. The streets were almost non-existent, as all around me was like a rubbish tip, consisting of building material, fences, trees, furniture, cars, power lines and power poles, glass, paper, and all of it wet.

I reached Stan's house and couldn't find them. His house was demolished; all that remained upstairs was bare floorboards, and downstairs was his car and bricked-up laundry area. My heart was pounding, I thought they were dead. I turned back to the street. People were starting to panic. Someone had a loudspeaker and was announcing that the cyclone had done an 's' bend over Darwin and that it had turned and was coming back over us. The people in the street were in shock, and at a loss as to where to go for shelter, as most of them had none left standing. I think back and am astounded that someone could be so callous and uncaring, and so ill-informed.

Then radio messages came through that confirmed that Cyclone Tracey had dissipated about 20 kilometres inland. That was a huge relief. I believe the only information we could get at the time was through ABC radio, as our local radio station had suffered severe damage.

We had no electricity and no water, as the water pipes that connected Darwin to its main water supply at Manton Dam had been torn up.

The tropical weather was hot and humid, so our first concern was that any food anyone had would be a mass of maggots in about forty-eight hours, without refrigeration.

I started to walk the six kilometres into town to find my parents. As I walked past Stan's neighbour's low-set brick home, someone called out to me. It was them! They had run next door during the storm when their house had started to break up. Thank God they were safe!

Then I had to find the rest of my family.

My younger brother, Eddy Roderick, meanwhile had set out in his Holden panel van to find us. He drove for about four hours to travel the six kilometres from the inner city to Nightcliff . He mostly had to clear his own road as he went. He drove through back yards, front yards and pathways and footpaths, anywhere that was easiest to clear. He picked me up and then picked up some of his friends, of whom two required hospital attention. We dropped the injured at the Darwin Hospital, which was overcrowded and chaotic, with injured people in corridors, verandahs and outside, still trying to shelter from the rain, which persisted for days after the cyclone had gone.

We continued on in Eddy's panel van to Mum and Dad's (Chris and Roger Roderick) house in Mcminn Street. Thank God they were safe too. Later that day, my other brother, Marshall Perron,, and his wife Cherry, made their way in to us from Stuart Park. They were okay, too.

Dad's house had been very sturdily built in 1937 by Harry Chan, who incidentally was later the Mayor of Darwin. It wasn't damaged except for the fibro walls being punctured along one side by flying roof tiles from the buildings over the road. So we had safe, dry shelter at least.

We stored what water we had in bottles and containers

for drinking only. We also had to put aside some water to flush the toilet. So we created a toilet roster; only after so many uses could we flush it.

Dad was an owner of a trucking company, Darwin Truck Owners, and I had my truck licence. So began the cleanup of Darwin. Dad made all his trucks available, so the first thing we had to do was pick up, dump and bury as many fridges and contents as we could find. As it was Christmas, everyone had fridges full of festive food and lots of seafood, which as I said previously, turned to maggots really quickly in the tropics.

We also hauled water into town in tanks on the trucks, from a disused quarry about twenty kilometres out of town, and delivered it to places where folk were sheltering in schools, hotels ,clubs etc. that were relatively undamaged, until they could be evacuated.

Two things I vividly remember in the days following Tracy were the absence of birds anywhere in Darwin and the fact that there wasn't one tree in a twenty kilometre radius that had a leaf left on it.

Being useful, and not wanting to leave anyway, I stayed and drove a truck and helped in the cleanup where I could. The majority of women and children were evacuated. I stayed until May of the following year before going to Perth with Mum for a two week break. Uncle Stan Perron looked after us in Perth.

The next few months in the aftermath of Cyclone Tracy is another story on its own... dealing with looters, martial law being suggested, vaccinations against diseases, water shortage for bathing, destroying or caring for pets and other animals left behind, cleaning up, and the gruesome finds. The miracle is that only fifty-six people were killed in the massive destruction wrought by Cyclone Tracy.

I had my twenty-first birthday just a month and a half after the cyclone, and celebrated by having a huge party. Dad obtained a generator for power and party lights, and someone supplied a pig, and it was cooked on a spit in the front yard. Most of the women and children had been evacuated from Darwin, so of about a hundred guests that were there to help me celebrate, only around ten of them were women. It was a special time for me, and a much-needed release from the weeks of hard work.

Left: Marg Roderick.

Photograph by Ramon Williams

CHAPTER 19 – MARK SABAN

I was only five when I had the displeasure of meeting Cyclone Tracy. I don't remember everything, but here's what I do remember.

At the time, I clearly had no idea what a cyclone was, let alone what it could actually do. I did, however, understand what Christmas was, and I was so excited about riding my brand new first bike, which I knew I was getting.

I was asleep on Christmas Eve pretty early, I remember the rain and wind on the roof and bedroom louvres.

At around 11 p.m., I woke up and came out to the lounge room. My mother Audrey was there, with my brothers Julian and Nick, and there was one other person but I don't remember her name. Shortly after, we all went to the bathroom to hunker down for the night.

The winds grew, they felt like they would never finish intensifying in strength. I recall my mum had covered me and her with our lounge room cushions. When the first winds had finished, I remember thinking that we were finished. My family knew we weren't.

The eye really did seem to last forever to a five-year-old. The air inside our house felt different, like a pressure feeling, ears popping, that sort of thing. In the distance I could hear explosive noises, and they were coming closer. It was a little like the thirty seconds of warning you have to get undercover when you hear the rain on the roofs getting closer, that we all experienced growing up in Darwin. When the other side of the eye hit, all hell broke loose, in an instant, windows gone, roof gone. The noise outside sounded like the world as we knew it was being dismantled. That ferocious wind felt like it didn't let up for hours.

The morning after was surreal. I remember taking all the soaking cushions off us, I remember sitting in the water that had flooded our home. I remember the cuts on the fronts of my feet where they had been sticking out of the cushions during the night. I stood up and the bathroom floor felt like a pontoon, like it was just floating.

We went to the lounge room and then ventured outside. It was unrecognisable, I still to this day can't describe it any other way.

People were just wandering around lost with what they had gone through and were now witnessing. It was eerily quiet.

My mum stayed in Darwin, as she worked for Australia Post and the mail absolutely had to get through. All of us are so proud of how she handled the situation in the aftermath.

My brother Nick (who was only sixteen, although the evacuee list shows him as nineteen) and I were evacuated a few days later. Mum waved goodbye to us at the airport, not having a clue where we were both being evacuated to. We ended up in Perth with a family friend. We took the scenic East coast route, seemingly through most of the Major cities.

My brother and I returned to Darwin after a few weeks.

Christmas since, to say the least has always been a struggle; not one goes by that I don't think about that night.

We were lucky, others were not and that's tough to take sometimes. P.S. The bike survived without a scratch.

Mark left Darwin and moved to Brisbane in 1987. "Darwin will always be my home in my heart."

In December 2014, Mark returned to Darwin. "This was a very emotional time, but I just feel like I had to go. Thanks to all the wonderful Tracy survivors that I met, you have all made a tough year bearable. Thank you from the bottom of my heart."

Above: Photo (2015) of Mark Saban with his mum.

CHAPTER 20 – BILL McGUINNESS

I was a TAA Maintenance Engineer in Darwin when the cyclone hit Darwin.

On Christmas Eve I went to Midnight Mass at St Paul's Nightcliff; I was singing in the choir. It was quite wet and a little windy as I drove from Stuart Park to Nightcliff. As the Mass progressed the power went out, and water was dripping in through the roof. Father Travers said Mass with the aid of a torch, brushing the water from the Missal before turning the page. At the end of Mass I drove home. The wind was getting stronger and the rain was now horizontal. I noticed several buildings on the way home had lost their roofs, but thought 'just keep going and get home.'

By 1.30 a.m. I had decided to sleep in the hallway of my apartment, as the wind was quite strong and the cyclone warning was out to take cover. I lived in a block of apartments that had ground, first and second floors. I got comfortable and went to sleep. I heard a glass louvre break in the early hours, but went back to sleep. I then woke again and heard my cuckoo clock chime 6 a.m. So I knew what the time was, and that my apartment was still intact.

I got up and discovered the broken louvre in the second bedroom, checked the rest of the first floor and that was the only damage. I was lucky. Downstairs was also untouched.

I went outside to discover that my car had a broken windscreen; the balustrading from another apartment had fallen on to it. And there was quite a lot of water in the car.

I met up with some of the neighbours, and went through the block apartments helping those trapped in wardrobes, and helping people any way that I could.

A family of four moved into my bedroom and spare bedroom. They picked up my phone and were shocked to find it still worked. That came in handy in the next few days.

One of the guys that lived in the apartments was an ABC freelance journalist, so as soon as I cleared my car, we went down to the ABC office and he collected his cameras. We set off driving around the city, and later, the more damaged outer suburbs. We went to the airport and checked out the maintenance hangar where I worked for TAA. The hangar doors had come off, and the four Aeromedical aircraft had been pushed to one side of the hangar but were not badly damaged. In the outer suburbs the devastation was at its worst. Images I will never forget.

Later on Christmas Day I saw the TAA Fokker Friendship flying over, so I went to the airport and met it.

The RAAF Hercules arrived later that day. I was able to take the ABC journalist to the airport, and the film was taken south and screened on the television news on Boxing Day.

For the next few days I spent all my time at the airport, seeing aircraft in and out as the Darwin population was airlifted out of the area.

On one day of the evacuation I found the Qantas and British umbrellas, so those people queueing on the tarmac awaiting aircraft enjoyed the shade of an umbrella during their long wait. Funny - those umbrellas did not ever come back.

Life gradually got back to normal, and I was lucky that I did not lose anything that night, as many others did.

These days I still have trouble coping with high winds.

Life gradually got back to normal, and I was lucky that I did not lose anything that night, as many others did.

These days I still have trouble coping with high winds.

I am sure there are things I do not remember about those early days after the cyclone. The days were busy, sending out the aircraft as they came in.

Bill now lives in Melton, Victoria, with his wife, Sue. They have two daughters. Katherine and Elizabeth.

Photograph by Ramon Williams

CHAPTER 21 - SUE McGUINNESS

Christmas Eve 1974 started pleasantly; I was out with work friends from Burns Philp. Driving home with friends at about 11 p.m., I thought the rain was really very heavy, and the wind was a bit gusty. I was quite pleased I was not driving.

I got home and said goodnight to my mum, who was packing her suitcase in the spare room downstairs. Mum and I were travelling to Singapore the next day.

After the eye passed over, the eye of the cyclone only lasted a short time, maybe fifteen minutes. I cannot really remember, the wind really got very bad. Mum was still downstairs.

Dad came down the hall and said, "get under your bed." He continued into my two sisters' room and got under their beds with them. All I could think about was Mum downstairs and us upstairs, and how she would be worried about us.

The noise of the wind and rain over the next few hours was something I will never forget. The house shook so violently, I thought any moment it would just collapse and kill us all. Dad called out and said, "just stay where you are."

Honestly, I cannot recall how long the next part lasted. I must have dozed off at some time, probably when the cyclone moved on.

I do remember a very loud banging at our back door. I opened it to see our lovely neighbour Arthur So Choy; he was trying to find his wife. He had come home from Darwin Hospital. He was a cook there, and had stayed at the hospital all night; they would not let him leave. When the cyclone weakened he drove home. He came in and sat down in the hallway for a little while. He was very distressed. He left saying he had to find his wife. It was then that I looked outside. The neighbourhood was not what I remembered. Poor Arthur, his house was gone. He did find his wife; she hid in the fridge.

Mum was okay, but so upset. The noise above her room had been so bad that she had thought we were all been killed.

Dad was lucky; the roof and a timber pillar crashed onto his bed. He would not have survived. My bedroom and my sisters' bedroom were the only part of the house not affected. We were one of the lucky families.

The next couple of days are a bit of a haze for me. I remember spending a couple of days with friends in Stuart Park. Can you believe it - they had power and water!

My mother, Audrey Dunn, sisters Patti and Fay were evacuated to Brisbane shortly afterwards. I know it was after the 27th of December, because that is my birthday. No celebration that year. To this day I cannot remember the actual day. I can remember the flight, sitting with someone's child on my lap. Being bussed to a hostel in Brisbane and spending about a week there before heading overseas for a couple of weeks. I had a ticket and it seemed like a good idea at the time.

My mum and sisters returned to Darwin before me. I was pleased to come back later in January, and go back to work with Burns Philp Travel.

My story, compared to some I have read about, is relatively simple. I survived without a scratch, but had terrible nightmares for quite a long time. I still do not deal well with loud noises, or very windy nights, and the cyclone warning signal gives me the creeps.

Sue and Bill now live in Melton, Victoria, where they have lived for 37 years. They have two grown-up daughters. Sue has fond memories of growing up in Darwin; meeting Bill at TAA, and getting married at St Paul's in Nightcliff. They have returned to Darwin many times, and intend returning for another visit soon.

CHAPTER 22 – CHRIS HOPKINS

Above: (front) Amberlee, Merle, Keenan (back) Ted, Chris, and Adrien.

It was Christmas Eve 1974 in the new Darwin suburb of Nakara. We had moved, six weeks ago, into this brand new elevated N.T. government house. The house was of the style built on concrete pillars and of the new cyclone proof design, yes right! As usual in Darwin, the parents had gone to a Christmas Eve party. Us kids had been left at home by ourselves; I think it was the first time we had ever been left at home by ourselves without a babysitter. There was myself, 8 years old, my older brother Adrien, 10 years old, my younger brother Keenan, 5, and our little sister, Amberlee, 2 years old. Having been given strict orders, we were all rugged up in the lounge room watching TV. There had previously been cyclone warnings, but that day it seemed that everyone was either ignoring them or not taking them seriously. After all, we get cyclone warnings all the time and nothing much ever happens, just a lot of rain and maybe some strong wind. Well, that was soon to change. I remember the four of us huddled together on the lounge in front of the TV, listening to the storm outside. We were getting a bit scared; it was not really the storm that was scaring us, but a combination of the storm and the fact that this was the first time we had ever been left at home to our own devices. About 10 p.m. Dad and Mum came home. Dad and Mum tell us they had been gone less than two hours, but to us it seemed ages. I think some people were now starting to take the threat of a cyclone more seriously as the storm outside continued to intensify. But not to worry, Dad and Mum were home now, so everything would be okay. Us kids all went to bed and put the storm out of our minds. After all, it was Christmas tomorrow. If we didn't get to sleep Santa wouldn't deliver our presents.

I was woken up by the storm intensifying. Dad and Mum were already up manning the mops and buckets, as the rain was coming straight through the louvered windows and flooding the upstairs of our elevated house. The mopping didn't last for long, as it soon became evident that they were fighting a losing battle. It started to look like the cyclone was now a real issue. Instructional broadcasts on the radio had recommended that people stay in the smallest room of the house. Other than the toilet, this would be the bathroom, or in our case, the separate shower. So us four kids and Dad and Mum ended up in the shower, which was a small room between the bathroom and the toilet. Not sure how long we stayed there, but it did not seem long till water started to come in between the walls and the ceiling, I remember it being a rust-brown colour for some reason. So much for the smallest room of the house being the strongest! For those not familiar with elevated government houses in Darwin, usually the bathroom area protruded from the rest of the house, which exposed it to the full force of the wind, depending on its direction. With the walls now moving with the wind and the water works getting worse, it seemed prudent to relocate from the bathroom, but to where? That was when Dad and Mum had the idea of putting a single bed over the dog's whelping box.

A week ago our Irish Setter, Bella, had given birth to a litter of ten pups. To contain Bella and her pups, Dad and Mum had built a whelping box, which was basically a wooden box a bit shorter than the length of a single bed, with sides about 30 cm high. A single bed fitted nicely over the whelping box, leaving just enough room between the bed and the sides to crawl in. I think the builders of the new college across the road had given Mum the timber to build the whelping box. In we all went: Bella and her ten pups, us four kids and Mum. Dad was reluctant to get in, as he thought there was not enough room. Not sure what mum said, but I believe there were threats made about what would happen if Dad did not get under the bed with the rest of us. So there we were, two adults, four kids, a dog and ten puppies squeezed under a single bed. We then settled in for the rest of what was to be a very long night in the dark, all of us very cold and wet.

It being Christmas, the obvious choice was to sing Christmas carols. I remember all night we were singing carols and doing whatever else you do under these circumstances. I remember it being very cramped under the bed, especially with our dog and ten puppies, though the puppies were good for keeping us warm. In a normal situation, the last thing you want is for a puppy to pee on you. But when you are in pitch blackness, cold and wet, there is nothing nicer that having a puppy pee on you. It is a nice warm feeling, and we were all wet through anyway. During the night we continually counted the pups to make sure we had them all, either that or it was just something to do to take our minds off everything. Each time we counted ten, until one time we could only find nine. Oh, it looks like we have lost one of the puppies. We continued to count them, each time coming up with only nine. Most of the night was spent awake, listening to the incredibly loud scream of the howling wind outside. It was a very eerie sound, like a big jet engine. Even today, the noise of howling wind still puts a shiver down my spine. I think some sleep was had, but it would have been little, and only short naps. I remember waking up, and you could see some light as the sun started to come up. It seemed relatively quiet compared to what it had been like during the night. The cyclone had finally passed.

We managed to crawl out from under the bed, and what a mess. I remember standing beside the bed in what used to be a bedroom. The house was completely gone, except for the elevated floor that we were standing on. No walls, nothing, just piles of rubble. The outside wall and big window of the bedroom had fallen on top of the bed, protecting the bed, and us underneath it. It appeared we were very lucky when we looked at the destruction around us. It seemed a miracle that we were all able to emerge from underneath the bed without a scratch.

The missing puppy was found in a corner of the box, very wet but alive and well. I guess all the prayers and Christmas Carols did the trick, for us, Bella and the puppies.

When we went downstairs we found the family from next door huddled in our car, which had been parked under the house. They had ended up in our car after their house disintegrated. The floor boards section of their lounge room actually ended up in our lounge room. The neighbours were injured, but nice and dry in our car as the amazing thing was that none of the windows was broken. A good thing for them that Dad had left the car unlocked that night, and that they were able to make their way to it. The next problem was finding the keys for the car. I'm not sure where Dad and Mum had left them the night before, but Mum eventually found the spare one, which had been taped to a strut underneath the car. We all piled into the car for the drive to somewhere, moving timber and iron out of the way so that we could get through. We eventually ended up at Casuarina Shopping center. I think the main reason for going to the shopping center was that us kids were only in our jocks, and all the clothes in the house had been blown away. We also needed to get medical help for our neighbours who were injured. When we arrived at the shops they were still locked up tight. The police showed up and Dad helped them break into the shopping center. We ended up in Coles, where I got a shirt and a pair of jeans two sizes too big for me. There were no belts to be found, so I was to spend the rest of the day holding the jeans up, until a piece of rope was found for a makeshift belt.

At the Casuarina Shopping Center the police asked Dad if he could go to the Wagaman School, as a makeshift shelter was being set up there, and they asked Dad if he could take charge of organizing it as Dad was a Customs Officer and also in the CMF (Citizen Military Force). Each family was assigned approximately a 6' x 6' area in the library, which was to be our home for the next few days. I remember us kids being in heaven, as there were all the soft drinks that we could drink. The only problem was that we couldn't drink them until the milk and juices were drunk. Therefore us kids were busily trying to drink the milk and juice stock so that we could attack the soft drink stock. We made ourselves sick on more than one occasion. I remember one night I was issued with a whole bar of chocolate and proceeded to eat the entire bar myself. Predictably, this made me sick. This meant that I spent the night in the makeshift hospital, which meant a real bed. It was like heaven after having spent the last couple of nights sleeping on the floor.

I remember at one end of the Wagaman oval they were shooting and burying all the stray dogs. They also wanted to put down Bella and her ten pups, but Dad and Mum had other ideas, as it was probably because of Bella and her

Above: Mum and Dad (Ted and Merle) standing under what was left of our house. We spent the night upstairs in our dogs welping box. A large window became jammed between the floor and the stairs, saving us from being swept off the upstairs area by the next house.

...ARWIN

r a Darwin disaster
happy ending!
and EDWARD
d their four children
Cyclone by huddling
elping box of their red
la.

ns were extremely
because, not only was
but so too were her 10
puppies.

cause crumpled around
ut when the time came to
late there was no question of
e Hopkins leaving those pups
behind — let alone their mum.

The children flew to stay with
Melbourne relatives by RAAF
Hercules, and Merle and Edward
set off by car with Bella and the
puppies.

They got as far as Alice
Springs but had to admit defeat
there. Even the wet towels, with
which Merle kept sponging the
puppies, were not warding off the
danger of dehydration by heat.
They sent their car to
Melbourne and got a flight out of
Alice Springs to Adelaide.

Together again — Merle Hopkins, four young Hopkins, Bella and the pups.

Now, at last, the family and
Bella and her puppies are reunited
in Melbourne, and Mrs Hopkins
telephoned Woman's Day to ask
us to spread the news. She says
there are Darwin people all over
Australia who will be waiting to
hear that all went well with Bella.

pups and the whelping box that none of us was injured or squashed. The Police had asked Dad for help to get a caravan out from under a house so that they could set up a command office next to the school, then Dad parked our car with our dogs inside beside the van, and we all took turns to stay with them during the day, and my brother Adrien slept with them in the car every night. Funnily enough, the car never smelt of dog pee. Bella must have been a very good mum as she cleaned up after her pups when they did anything. The police and men searching the houses for survivors would often bring back tins of dog food for Bella.

After about a week living at the Wagaman School, us kids were taken to the airport for evacuation. The idea was for us kids to go to Melbourne to Grandad and Grandma's place, and Dad and Mum would drive down some time later with our dogs, and in the meantime make plans for all of us to return to Darwin as soon as possible. We all waited patiently at the airport to board a RAAF Hercules bound for Melbourne. This was a bit of an adventure in itself, but my memories are of a long, painful trip. Those web mesh seats they have are not very comfortable during a nonstop flight from Darwin to Melbourne, even for an eight-year-old. I remember we were hungry and thirsty during the whole trip, as we were down the back of the plane, and any food or drinks that were passed down from the front never seemed to make it down the back. There was a certain group of greedy people up the front who just didn't seem to care about anyone else.

We eventually arrived at Melbourne airport, where

Dad had arranged for us to be collected by someone from Customs. I remember it was very early in the morning when we drove from the airport to my Grandad and Grandmother's house in Black Rock, and every traffic light was green. I remember the Customs Officer commenting that this was unheard-of. So we made it all the way to Melbourne, and now had the long wait for Dad and Mum to arrive. When they arrived, we moved into a big house in Black Rock, and then Adrien and I were enrolled in the Black Rock State School.

We lived in Melbourne for about two or three months before returning to Darwin. A few days after Dad and Mum arrived, Dad was told he was required back in Darwin by Customs. He did not want to move back without us, but he went back for a while before returning again for the drive back up the Centre with a train ride on the old Ghan in the middle of the trip. While Dad was in Darwin, Mum bought a new Falcon station wagon, lots of other things we needed and a caravan which would be our new home when we returned to Darwin. On the first attempt to return to Darwin we did not get very far. About an hour out of Melbourne the rear of our Caravan was clipped by a semi-trailer, which resulted in the car and caravan jackknifing. We were therefore back in Melbourne, waiting for the car and caravan to be fixed.

When we arrived back in Darwin, we moved the caravan into the back yard of another Customs Officer. After that we moved to the remains of the Catholic convent on Casuarina Drive in Nightcliff. We lived in the caravan and we rebuilt part of the remains of the Convent, so that we eventually had a lounge and kitchen other than what we had in the Caravan. As a kid it was great living at the old convent, as it was on the cliff directly above the rocks area of Nightcliff beach. When not in school, lots of fun could be had by a nine-year-old down at the beach all day. Slip slop slap was not a big concern back then, but I don't think I got sunburned once.

Well, that's it. Cyclone Tracy from the perspective of an eight-year-old, God, that was thirty years ago. At least my memory is still working. Or at least I think these are my memories. Dad and Mum say they are pretty accurate.

Below: The Hopkin's family (and a friend) with Bella and her pups. Eight year old Chris (center front) beside Bella.

CHAPTER 23 – JAN OAKHILL

Christmas Didn't Come To Darwin 1974, But Tracy Did!

I was just a 19-year old-girl, married with an 18-month-old toddler, when I drove from Brisbane to Darwin with my husband and our best friends, another couple, and their 12 month old baby. In the year before our move, the Brisbane floods had hit, and we were sure we wanted a change of scenery, so despite both sets of parents' best advice, we packed what we could of our possessions into our trusty Belmont ute and hightailed it to what we thought would be the adventure of a lifetime in a town renowned for being "a bit rough".

On the journey up, which took about a week, the two men quickly adopted the mode of driving until 2 p.m., then settling in for a night's drinking before getting up before dawn and starting another day's driving to beat the ever-increasing humidity and heat. Air-conditioned vehicles were a thing of the future! Needless to say, we girls were fed up with this before we even got halfway there, and were very pleased to pull into the Bloodwood Caravan Park at what was called "The 13 and a half mile", on the outskirts of the town of Darwin. All this was happening just two weeks before Christmas, and we soon found the laid-back lifestyle and easy camaraderie of the other park residents very appealing, and looked forward to spending a very happy Christmas with our newfound friends.

Parties after work were a regular feature, so the pre-Christmas party planned at our best friend's caravan site was going to be a big event, attended by most of the people who lived on our side of the park. There had been talk of a cyclone off the coast, but because we had sat tight in Brisbane two weeks before we moved up to Darwin, watching another cyclone pass by, we were all fairly blasé about the possibility of this one affecting us, and never really gave it much thought until around 11 p.m. that night. This was because the music we were loudly playing at our party was becoming increasingly hard to hear over the rising noise of the wind outside the caravan annexe. We all thought this was really bloody annoying, and when the walls of the annexe started flapping loudly as well, this was just the last straw, and we all huffed off to our respective vans to fall into a boozy sleep.

I was feeling a bit apprehensive by this stage, because the wind had picked up quite a lot, and was rocking the tiny fifteen-foot caravan we were living in. The fact that it had no wheels and was simply perched on top of some besser blocks also worried me, so I quickly tied a line of flimsy nylon rope around the outside of the aluminium annexe we had and attached it to the van, "just to be sure". By 1.15 a.m. the wind was howling like a banshee, and my now fully awake and sober husband was watching through the caravan windows at the aluminium annexe walls sucking in and out like a set of bellows with each gust. The hatch overhead in the middle of the caravan ceiling started to lift and slam down too, with the air pressure changing inside, so we tied the heaviest object we had on hand, my Grandmother's antique sewing machine inside its carry case, to the handle of the hatch with the only rope we had, my electric frypan cord! This weight, combined with the two of us hanging onto it for dear life, was all that stopped the hatch from being torn off, and possibly the whole caravan roof from being lifted too. How long we stood like this I can't remember, but what remains vivid in my mind was the thought that maybe I should get changed out of my sexy little black negligée into something more suitable for surviving a cyclone! As I rummaged through the clothes strewn on the table, I marvelled at how my daughter could possibly sleep through such an appalling noise, as the wind was now so ferocious that it sounded like something quite unnatural screaming.

The battery-powered radio had long since gone silent, so we had no way of knowing what was happening anywhere else. I was getting really tired, and said to my husband that I just had to let go of the power cord and that he would have to hang on without my help. Well, it was about then that the eye of the storm started to pass overhead, and the sudden silence was nearly as deafening as the storm had been! It was really very eerie, and we cautiously went outside, and to our utter amazement, the sky was just full of stars, and clear! I am so glad it was at night so we couldn't see the dreadful wall of the storm as it approached us again! Everyone nearby in the park was also outside, and we called out to our friends to see if they were alright, and asked them if they had any damage. Over the road, some fellow who was only a temporary visitor was running up and down the road yelling things like, "Well I am ok and the storm hasn't done my van any damage!" To which we all replied "Just wait for the other half! It's coming! Get back inside while you can!" The silly man ignored us, and holed up and drove out. I never knew what became of him to this day.

I can honestly say now that I know what it feels like to be so scared that your bowels turn to water, after I heard the sound of the wind coming back from the other direction. It was a spine-chilling sound, exactly like a jet engine winding up, or a train coming through a tunnel at a million miles an hour. I will never forget it.

Here we go again, I thought, as the annexe walls started their mad whapping in and out, in and out, and it was almost a relief when the first wall peeled away, quickly followed by the roof. Amazing what a sterling job the little flimsy nylon rope had done holding it all together this long! We cracked open some windows on the opposite side of the van to the wind, and just prayed for deliverance, even though neither of us was particularly religious. I remember thinking, "If God spares us, I will never ever doubt His existence again."

Little by little, as the hours passed, the wind started to

die down until we realised that we were going to survive this thing, and we could relax our exhausted grip on the roof hatch. As dawn broke, we peered out through the filthy windows to a scene of utter devastation. We used to live beside a forest of gum trees, but all there was left now was a stark image of completely denuded stumps. Not a single solitary leaf on anything, and as my girlfriend and I wandered through this awful wilderness, we noted that there weren't even any ants or flies, or bird life! And the silence was what completely took our breath away. It was so quiet you could hear people murmuring to each other inside their caravans way over the other side of the park! To say we were all in shock was the understatement of the year. Normally brash young blokes were just wandering around in their underpants, staring at the smashed vans and vehicles strewn around the place. We must have had the gods smiling down on us that night, because over the road where our friend's vehicle was parked, a huge gum tree had fallen between their van and the car, and neither was damaged in any way. Our car was not where it usually would have been parked, but a large tree was now taking up that space!

I don't know why, but we all thought we were the only ones to have been affected by this storm, and the thought was to drive to town to see if we could get any help.

Off we drove, up the now unfamiliar road to the Stuart Highway and the way into Darwin, as we were in the rural area and some distance from the township. The first, and possibly only, words to escape our lips for some time were repeated over and over again as we turned onto the main road, and looked over the landscape to see a tangled mess of cables.

"Holy Shit!" The huge radio masts of some installation, maybe Radio Australia, lay in absolute ruins, as if some giant had just knitted then all together and flung them on the ground. We all thought this was unbelievable, but hastened to get to town and to find help for ourselves. I say the road was now unfamiliar, because having arrived only two weeks before, it had taken us all this time to memorise landmarks, which had now vanished. We drove as far as we physically could, given that the roads were choked with debris of all kinds, and then started to pick our way ever so slowly along the way until we got to the outer suburb of Casuarina and the huge shopping centre, which now looked like a derelict place. I can still see an image of the night before, when we were there doing some last-minute shopping. I was walking behind a man who had a small child perched upon his shoulders, and as they walked along they were singing Christmas carols. I wondered where they were now, and whether they were okay.

The things that stick in your mind.

Time has blurred some memories of what we did in the days afterwards, but some remain vivid. Things like the sick feeling in the pit of my stomach because I couldn't ring my parents to tell them we were all okay. Things like how much I feared having to get an injection against the diseases the authorities said were coming. I had a pathological fear of needles, then. A bit funny when you consider what I had just survived! I never did get that injection.

My girlfriend and I and our two little girls were evacuated two days later back to Brisbane, on one of the many Qantas flights. Six bods squashed into three seats was not the most fun ride, especially since my nearest seated neighbour confessed that he had "just been released from the loony ward," and my daughter seemed to be doing her best to be a rowdy, restless little bugger and this was most annoying to the man next to me! The reception we got from the Salvos at the refugee centre in Brisbane will forever remain as one of the highlights of the whole saga. There was nothing those people couldn't do for us! The two babies were whisked away and bathed and clothed in clean dresses, my daughter remained asleep through the whole process after eventually falling asleep from sheer exhaustion five minutes from touchdown! Our parents were a very welcome sight, and they whisked us home at what I think was around one or two in the morning. One thing which bothered me a lot in the next few weeks was being recognised as a cyclone victim. I soon stopped telling people where I had come from, as I got really very tired of repeating the same tales over and over for the curious and the interested.

A month later, we were back in Darwin and living at the same caravan park, courtesy of the owner, Jack, whose surname escapes me now. He was so tenacious in his endeavours to get us back to our husbands quickly, as we really hadn't needed to be evacuated in the first place. Bloodwood Caravan Park was completely self-contained with its own power generator, water and sewerage, and Jack knew this, and lobbied the powers that be relentlessly until they said we could come back.

Darwin was always going to be an adventure; we just didn't have the first clue how much of an adventure!

Photograph by Ramon Williams

CHAPTER 24 – KEV RUWOLDT

Having spent two years in Alice Springs from 1956 to 1958, I was under the impression that the Northern Territory was the greatest place in Australia. September 1958 saw me joining the RAN as a Radio Operator for a period of twelve years. Three of those years I volunteered for service at HMAS Melville Naval Wireless Station "Coonawarra": 1961, 1965 and 1968/69. That spelt the end of the Alice for me, I was going to live in Darwin on completion of my 12 years.

Upon my discharge from the RAN I joined the Department of Civil Aviation (DCA) in Adelaide, on the understanding that I would work in Darwin on completion of a six weeks' training course in Sydney. I arrived in Darwin in December 1970, and was married in the United Church in Smith Street 13th April 1971. In 1973 I was offered a choice of two houses in the northern suburbs by the NTA Staff Section. The first offer was a previously tenanted house in the suburb of Jimgili, and my other choice was a brand new house in the suburb of Wanguri. The new house won, as my intention was to purchase this home and stay in Darwin, never to return south. The NTA and I agreed on the purchase of this house in October 1974. My biggest mistake then was to insure the house and contents through AMP. They fought me tooth and nail for seven months over settlement after Tracy. Here is my story...

Cyclone Tracy.

Tuesday 24th: The recent airing of Cyclone Tracy, forty years ago, on the ABC reminded me of the events of a night never to be forgotten. In those days I worked as a Communications Officer for the Department of Civil Aviation at the Darwin Airport. My rostered shift was to finish at 8 p.m., but the supervisor let me go at 6.30 p.m. I drove home to my residence at 10 Weedon St, Wanguri, Parking under the house, I got out of the car. My neighbours called out for me to come over and have a couple and stay for tea. My wife and our two children, aged 20 months and 8 months, were in Adelaide, having a break from the muggy wet season weather and visiting our rellies.

I grabbed a few VBs out of the fridge and hopped over the fence into Dot and Len Brown's, to their family gathering of Alma the grandmother, son Leon and his family, and their daughter Barbara and husband, who were visiting from Melbourne with twin babies under 12 months old. The night passed fairly quickly, everyone happy as the wind slowly started to get stronger as the clocked counted towards midnight. As I had a 6 a.m. start on Christmas Day, I returned home around 11.45 p.m. to sober up and get some sleep in my son's room, in his new bed. At the time I thought the wind was about 80 kph, similar to Cyclone Selma, which had passed Darwin two weeks earlier.

Wednesday 25th: I was woken very sharply around 1.30 – 2 a.m., when something struck the house, and I realised that things were very serious, the house felt like it wanted to take off. The bed was saturated, there were two inches of water throughout the house and the roof was missing. Staggering out of bed I pulled on a pair of stubbies, slipped on an old footy jumper, thrust my feet into my ever-trusty thongs and, with my portable radio, headed for the living area. With each flash of lightning I looked out through missing louvres; the vision of debris flying through the air was staggering. The power and the noise of the wind were bloody terrifying. I reached the living room; it was in the process of breaking up, and I noticed the kitchen was already gone. Struggling to open the aluminium door, I eventually made it out to the front porch and looked over at my neighbour's house, and I was shocked at what I saw.

Their whole living area, walls and furniture had blown away, down to the floorboards. They were sheltering in the little passage between the toilet and bathroom with a battery-powered light. I raced down our stairs and was heading for the fence when suddenly I was hit in the head by something. Whatever it was it could not have been very big, or I would have ended up with a split personality. It did hurt, leaving a gash in my forehead. Picking myself up, I continued over the fence and up the back stairs.

Once again I struggled to open the door against the wind, and upon opening the door I yelled out 'Get out, you're gone.' They were shocked at the blood pouring out of my wound and spread all over my face from the wind. Grabbing one of the babies I said, 'Quick, down to the laundry, everyone, and shelter in the store area.' Struggling against the wind with the baby, I eventually made it, and as the others arrived I handed it to its parents and went back up to grab Alma, Dot's mother, who at this stage had lost the plot and was screaming.

Dragging her down the stairs and hanging onto the rail at the same time was hard going, as Alma had no idea of where she was. Eventually we made it, and I shoved her into the store and told her to sit in the corner and shut up. Leon and I stood in the doorway watching the sky as each flash of lightning revealed more and more of the houses in our area slowly being torn apart.

We had no respite; the eye of the cyclone never passed over our area, we were on the outer limits of the Darwin urban sprawl. At daylight a figure staggered out of the wind and rain. It turned out to be Andy, our neighbour from behind, asking for help as the house next door to him had people trapped upstairs in the bathroom area, and they couldn't get out due to the debris on top of them. Leon and I first had to clear the stairs to reach them, and gradually we lifted the debris off them and threw it to the ground below.

There were eight people, adults and children, in the rubble. One lady had a broken collarbone with a baby zipped up in her jacket. We carried them downstairs, one at a time as they were unable to stand, leaving them in the laundry area. Once they were all safe Leon and I returned to his parents. It was during this time that I stepped on a couple of nails with my right foot; thongs do not help!

Glancing at my residence I noticed my XA Falcon Wagon had been blown out from under the house, and the sun visor was hanging by one screw down the right-hand mudguard. The left side had been wind-and-rain-blasted back to bare metal. The windscreen was so badly pitted that it was difficult to see when driving into the sun; eventually I had to replace it. Surprisingly, I had no other damage. My poor old EH Holden fishing ute was slammed into one of the house's concrete pillars, the left-hand side door badly dented.

A sheet of roofing iron from somewhere was wrapped underneath and around the right-hand side of the vehicle. My Ally dinghy, which usually hung under the house above my ute, had disappeared; I never found it, God knows where it finished up, most likely in the Leanyer swamp, where most of Casuarina ended up being dumped. Our above-ground swimming pool was torn in half and one half wrapped around the back neighbour's Datsun 180B, under his house.

Looking at the Browns' neighbours on the other side, we were shocked to see the young couple hanging onto the toilet bowl and holding a plastic clothes basket for protection, lying on the deck of what had once been a house. We cleared the debris off the stairs and climbed up, to discover the wife was devoid of upper clothes and nine months pregnant. She informed us that her clothes had blown off during the night and that she was due to have her baby that day.

I cannot remember their names now, and I never found out if the baby was delivered safely. Looking at the toilet bowl I couldn't believe just how lucky they had been. We helped her down the stairs and they joined us under the Browns' place, where a blanket mysteriously appeared to cover the poor woman. We waited for the rain and wind to die down, looking around at the devastation that had resulted from Tracy. Slowly people began emerging from the rubble, and the dazed looks on their faces told a story of its own.

I could see my bar still standing in what had once been our lounge area, with my three foot fish tank still intact on the top. How that never got smashed is beyond me. Staggering through the mess I went upstairs, and upon opening the bar cupboard found a bottle of whiskey, eleven packets of flagship tobacco and six packets of cigarette papers. I saw our cheque book lying in the mess on the lounge floor and picked it up, thinking it might come in handy, then glancing out what had once been a window, I saw nothing but complete devastation. I threw the cheque book back on the floor, thinking, 'I am not going to be able to use it anyway.' I returned to the Browns, where the whiskey was demolished quickly. The tobacco was dry; the ciggy papers were slightly damp but could be peeled off and held up to dry, and then we discovered no one had a match. This was torture after what we had just been through. Around 10 a.m. a copper appeared in an old Toyota FJ40, and told us to evacuate to the Wagaman

School, as the cyclone was coming back. This was disturbing news and sent a shudder through everyone. Loading the pregnant lady into his vehicle and letting us use his cigarette lighter, he drove off into the debris-laden street. Thus chain-smoking had now became the order of the day.

Slowly trudging through the debris-laden streets, we headed to the Wagaman School. I can recall an HG or HT Holden station wagon parked in the school driveway with 5 wheels in the back. I thought it was rather odd at the time, but later on realised that somewhere someone's car was probably sitting on blocks. Suddenly my milkman appeared in front of me and I asked him, 'Where's my two cartons of VB?' I used to get two cartons delivered every week, and pay him in advance when I paid the milk bill. I don't know where he got them from, I didn't ask, the price was bloody fair at the time. His reply was, 'I had 32 cartons upstairs last night, if you want any, help yourself, they are all around the yard.' A day or two later, thinking back about the wagon with the five wheels, it was probably my first sight of looting. The word was now out that the police were on the lookout for looters, and they would be shot if caught.

My stay at the Wagaman School was not pleasant; it was probably the same for all the other people who were forced to sleep on wet carpet. The toilets in the building were nailed shut because of health risks. There was no water for flushing, and a large hole was gouged out by D8 dozers in the middle of the playing field for people to use in lieu. This, of course, upset the ladies, but it was not a time to worry about modesty. The Army handed out sheets of industrial plastic to lie on, but when the edges of the plastic were depressed, the water seeped from the carpet, wetting your clothes. The authorities had issued an instruction that there were to be no animals allowed. Some people disobeyed this instruction and were verbally abused, eventually leaving with their pets. I slept that night on my back under some roofing iron on a school form seat in an outside area, praying the wind wouldn't blow and would just let the rain fall straight down. Thus ended Christmas Day, it was so different!

Thursday 26th: I cannot remember what I had for brekkie, but I ended up trudging back to my house to see what I could salvage. The fridge had blown over with the door open, spilling the contents over the floor, broken eggs mixed with VB cans - yuck. The pantry door was missing and all our tinned food gone, sucked out by the wind. The upper cupboard doors were open, their contents strewn over the floor and around the yard. The stove had fallen over and jammed against the lower cupboard doors. At least I had some cooking utensils left; the four drawers of knives, forks, spoons etc. were still intact. In the lounge area, our 11 cubic foot Ingus freezer, which was chockablock, had the lid blown open. In those days we bought frozen bulk food from the Farmer Jones store in Perth, freighted to Darwin by State Ships. Our last order prior to Christmas had been 150 kilos of meat, veggies, sweets and other goodies. As my family were away, I had not used any of it.

The linen press, prior to Christmas, contained linen, glassware sets and unopened wedding presents. The upper doors were blown open, the pillows, blankets and bed

covers sucked out. Of the lower linen press doors, one was torn off and the other open, the contents sucked out except for one shelf with about eighteen assorted crystal glasses. I could not believe it. Rubbish, or rather some of the contents, was spread over the ceiling rafters, the floor and around the yard in the mud. I cannot remember seeing the cheque book again. Looking at the bathroom next, I saw that the bath was full of rubbish and dirty water. The Cyclone Warning people used to crap on about filling your bath with drinking water, what a load of bullshit. I considered that area of the house completely unsafe, despite what the authorities advised about sheltering in your bath area. The children's beds were covered in gyprock from the ceiling, doors were either blown off or open, and most of the contents gone. Our bedroom was pretty much the same except that the bed was fully covered in gyprock. I had some clothes, but my wife had virtually nothing; hers had been sucked out.

Grabbing some garbags from the bottom kitchen drawer, I began salvaging anything I considered worth saving. I loaded eight sodden garbags into the back of the Falcon. Next I went through the store under the house, and found my old camping stretcher and some camping gear. Salvaging anything that would come in handy, I loaded it all into the car. Worried about looters knocking off my vehicles, I decided to drive the Falcon to the Wagaman School. My poor old EH ute, I thought it would be safe wrapped around the pier. Returning to the school, I picked up Leon and drove to my milkman's house, rescuing some cans of VB from going rusty. This was to be my first ever, and only, hot beer-drinking episode. Back at the school, Dot and family had moved our stuff, e.g. tinned food, eating utensils and plates, also our bits and pieces of bedding, into the pre-school, so I stayed there that night in my comfy stretcher. The roof was virtually still intact.

Friday 27th: The streets were still being cleared of debris, so I had not bothered going to work. The ABC were broadcasting names of people to be taken to the airport for evacuation. The pre-school was becoming an evacuation centre. People started arriving to register wives and children for evacuation, and the building rapidly filled up. Dot hung onto her space and managed to feed us with food brought from our houses. A Paul's milk truck turned up and I couldn't believe the actions of some of the women, swearing, pushing and shoving to get hold of some milk before the truck had come to a standstill. The bloody truck was full and there was plenty for everyone. This was one example of how people can rapidly change when normality disappears.

As the roads were still being cleared of debris, the story got around that the Police were commandeering vehicles, handing you a piece of paper and taking off with your vehicle. I was not keen on this idea, so did not venture away from the school, but just helped out here and there wherever help was needed. That was to be my last night at the pre-school; it had become too crowded. Tomorrow I would have to find myself some new digs.

Saturday 28th: The school had a mobile generator and mobile freezer moved in during the night. This was my first hot breakfast since the blow: one dessertspoon of scrambled eggs, a slice of bread with butter, a packet of Winfield and matches plus a cold can of VB. I thought life was great, but after consuming that cold can, it became quite clear to me that I could never look at or drink another hot beer. Leon grabbed me to help get a woman out of a nearby house who had been there since the cyclone started. Hopping into the back of a ute, we went to her street and carried this poor woman out on a plank of wood. She had been speared in the stomach by a piece of wood, and had been forced to lie there until her cries for help were heard. We took her into the RAAF Base hospital, as she wished to be taken to Alice Springs. Driving into the RAAF Base, the sight of a DC3 sitting in the middle of the road, blown there from the aircraft hard stand area was unreal. The hospital reluctantly admitted the poor old dear, and we returned to Wagaman.

Upon my return I said goodbye to Dot, Len and family, telling them I was going out to the airport to report in and find out what was happening. After a teary goodbye and promises to catch up again soon, I headed off. Driving into the airport off the Stuart Highway, I crossed over the railway line heading for the Operations Building, and was stopped by an armed Commonwealth copper demanding to know where I was going, and where was my ID. I told him I was heading to work, and that my ID was like the movie, 'Gone with the Effin Wind'. He told me to make sure I didn't go anywhere else and to proceed (this was due to those lowlife scum dressing up as women and trying to jump on the evacuation planes). By now the Southern coppers were getting a bad name around the place; they did not offer much civility to Tracy victims, unlike our own NT boys. I disliked the fact that any suitable motel accommodation went to them while the people of Darwin, who had suffered a horrible catastrophe, were left to shelter under ruined buildings as best they could. In my opinion it was unfair!

I walked into the Annexe and was greeted by Gerry Wareham, who told me to sign the book to register that I was still around, then he told me what had happened to date. To the best of his knowledge all staff were okay, but there had been a few serious injuries to some staff and families. Katherine had taken over our airspace. Some staff had relocated themselves to Katherine; one bloke turned up in Tennant Creek before the wind stopped blowing, others had headed south. There was nothing I could do, as there was no power to the building, which had to be reroofed first. All of the teleprinter equipment had been water damaged and was already showing signs of rust. During this period Barry Hayward, another old navy mate, turned up. He had just evacuated his wife and children on a plane south to Sydney. We decided that if we could find a suitable dry area, we would camp at work.

Heading back out to the northern suburbs, I called in to see Jim Eagles in Wagaman, another close navy mate. Jim and his neighbour were out the front talking to a couple of NT coppers who had just finished shooting their dogs. Both Jim and Lew had evacuated their families south earlier that morning. They were discussing arrangements to drive south to Brisbane and Sydney. Barry and I then headed to his place in Nakara, grabbing whatever we could. I checked my cousin Don's place in Goodman St, Nakara, at the same time. I was shocked; no house, no floor - just the RSJ beams sitting on piers, the floor had landed on his neighbour's house behind. Were Don and his family alive? I had no idea. We returned to the operations building, but the Radio Techs quashed any idea of camping there, so we made the decision to head to Adelaide ourselves.

After registering with the appropriate authorities in the city and receiving the necessary paperwork, we filled up with petrol, then headed down the Stuart Highway. Whilst driving down the highway through Parap, we noticed that people had turned on water outlets of the Manton Dam-Darwin pipeline and were showering. The only restriction was that your privates had to be covered. At the 17 mile mark, we turned into Kowandi Defence station to catch up with Brian and Marylyn Nichols and family, more navy. They had suffered little damage - a couple of broken louvres and some trees down. After ensuring we had something to eat, Marylyn asked me to give them written permission to enter my abode to salvage whatever they could. I gave Brian the keys and asked him to to rescue my EH ute. I said goodbye around 11 p.m., then Barry and I headed off, stopping somewhere later on the side of the highway for a kip on the front seat.

Sunday 29th: We drove through the dawn to find the highway was blocked at Pine Creek, with a policeman directing us into their small township. The idea was to make sure everyone had a good feed before heading off to Katherine. Some local station people slaughtered beef to ensure there were no empty bellies leaving Pine Creek.

While I was eating a steak, Sergeant Graham Bowning came up and said hello; I had known him since he joined the police, and he had been stationed in Alice Springs when I lived there. Graham noticed a 7 ton truck pulling in covered with a tarpaulin; he got up and walked over to the truck, and pulling back the tarp we saw beds, washing machines, kids' toys, fridges and whatever. Graham arrested the driver and took him over to police station. When he came back he informed me the bloke would be charged with looting. We bid him goodbye and headed off to Katherine, not knowing when we would catch up again.

Pulling into a Katherine servo, we filled up, grabbed some ice and some eats and headed off. No money was needed, thanks to the paperwork we carried. A couple of hours later I pulled over for a toilet break, Barry pulling up behind also, when lo and behold, out of the bush staggered two blokes with an esky. They wanted a ride to Tennant Creek. As they were both smashed, we decided it should not be a problem and agreed to take them. When we pulled into Dunmara for petrol, food and toilet relief my passenger insisted on buying me a carton of VB cans for the ride. When he came back with the carton he also had an expensive leather-bound stubby holder for me. Thanking him for his kind gesture, we hit the road again. We arrived in Tennant Creek about 4.15 p.m. All evacuees were told to line up in a lane behind the main street for petrol. This was pumped out of 44 gallon drums. My passenger was happy, thanked me for the ride and headed off with his mate. They were jackeroos and had been paid off from some station.

When we both finished filling up, receiving the all

clear from the local authorities we headed out to the airport. Brian Scherr, another ex- Darwin boy, was on duty, and Jimmy Ward the OIC, they made us a cuppa and once we were comfortable, they asked about our experiences. Brian invited us to his place for dinner. They allowed us to have a hot shower and set up our beds in the equipment room, and showed us where we could make a cuppa in the morning prior to an early departure. The dinner at Brian's was greatly appreciated with a couple of cold VBs, then we left to return to the airport for a good night's sleep.

Monday 30th: Getting underway at 5 a.m., we had an uneventful trip to the Alice, arriving around 11.30 a.m. We reported in to the Alice High School, as instructed by the roadblock people, and were informed our cars had to be inspected before we could drive the dirt road to Port Augusta. Leaving the cars in the hands of the mechanics, we started to walk to the main drag, only to be passed by a vehicle which made a sudden u-turn, the driver screaming out, 'Kevin'. It was, to my surprise, Veronica, a girl I'd known in the navy many years ago, and she had been our house-sitter in Darwin, fifteen months ago. She leapt out of her car and grabbed me, saying, 'I was worried about you and your family'. I explained that I was on my own, and Anne and the kids were in Adelaide. Ronnie had returned to the Alice before we accepted the new house in Wanguri, and she was unaware of our new residence. She was staying at her brother's, who was a truckie, and was away at the time. Once again we repeated our story and our adventure down the Stuart Highway. Ronnie provided lunch, which was greatly appreciated.

I had no money on me, so I was told to head to the CES office and register for a handout. I filled in the paperwork and received $62 to last me for the journey to Adelaide. Back at the school where the cars had passed inspection, we were given the all clear to hit the road. We filled up at a local garage, and the owner was upset when we informed him that we did not have to pay, being Tracy evacuees. He still refused, so I told him to contact the people looking after Tracy evacuees. After much argument he was instructed to let us go, and that he would be paid by the Tracy Fund. We stopped at the Gap on the way out for a couple of hamburgers. There were only seven miles of bitumen left now, and then we were on the gravel road. The drive to Kulgera in the dark was no problem, and we arrived around 11 p.m. The pub was pretty busy and the Police were in attendance. We filled up for the last time on free petrol, bid goodbye to the NT and headed for the South Australia border.

Tuesday 31st: Sometime in the early morning we pulled over at Marla Bore and camped in the vehicles. Dawn broke with a windmill happily pumping water close by, and a clear sky for the day. Somewhere near Welbourne Hill we came across a Salvation Army post, set up to help evacuees with tea, coffee, new tyres and puncture repairs. Good old Salvos. I never expected to see that, but they were greatly appreciated. Just out of Coober Pedy I got a flat, changed tyres and on arrival had it repaired. While that was being done we went to the pub and had a counter lunch. No one was interested in us; we were completely ignored. I paid for my puncture repair, filled up and headed out of town. This was where the $62 came in handy. At Mt Eba Station a sign was posted indicating that Tracy victims had clearance through the Woomera Rocket Range. This was a great saving in both mileage and time, plus the road was in great condition.

We arrived at Woomera around 4 p.m., and the roadblock people directed us to one of their Sports Clubs, where volunteer people looked after us. They had tables with clothes spread out, you could grab anything you might need, and toilet gear, and there was a choice of a hot meal with sweets and lots of beer. The committee would not take any money from us, so what could one do but appreciate all their good work and tuck in. There were a lot of Darwin people there, including two blokes we worked with, Phil Harris and Bob Rogers. Around 8 p.m. we were on the road once again bound for Port Augusta, and just after 11 p.m., there was no more dirt road. A Police road block checked our arrival, taking some details from us, then we were escorted to the Willsden School to rest up. The volunteers wanted to billet us out for the night with local people, but we refused, and slept in their hall, under the tables loaded with clothing.

1975 Wednesday 1st: After brekkie, Barry and I headed off for Port Pirie where we separated. He continued on to Adelaide and I headed to Kadina, where my parents lived. On arrival at the house I discovered that Anne had just been informed by the local constabulary that I was alive, but they did not know of my present whereabouts. I had asked three or four people evacuated out of Darwin by air to send Anne a telegram telling her 'House gone, all gone but am okay.' She never heard from anyone, and when she rang DCA in Adelaide enquiring as to my safety, the standard answer was 'to the best of our knowledge all staff in Darwin are okay.' Anne and Mum pulled the 8 garbags out of the car, spreading the contents on the grass to start drying out, and then Mum started the process of washing the lot.

By this time I was in deep trouble; those nails in my right foot had sent a red flash up my leg into the groin area, and I was having trouble getting around. I had tried to get a Tetanus injection at all the major places on the way south, but had been told 'We have run out.' Anne located a local doctor, who quickly assessed my condition and gave me an injection, and told Anne to take me home and put me to bed, 'Give him these pills and if he throws up don't worry about it, make him rest and continue taking the tablets and fluids.' At the time I was shocked to learn that if I had not received attention then, I was in great danger of having my right leg amputated. I never did get any stitches in my forehead either, and had a white scar for a long while. After a few days' rest, I told my parents I was feeling a lot better and intended to go Adelaide and go back to work.

Monday 6th: On arrival in Adelaide, I visited the Royal Adelaide Hospital to check out my leg, and was given the all clear. My father-in-law had arranged for us to stay with his lady friend while we began the task of seeing what would happen next. First up was the CES to get some money, only to be told that as Anne and the children had not gone through Cyclone Tracy they were not entitled to anything. I had had my fortnightly allowance paid in Alice

Springs, which was to last me for two weeks. Next up was the Commonwealth Bank for some cash from our Darwin account. As I had no ID, the female enquiry officer was giving me a hard time when a man stopped and looked at me and said 'Kevin'. looking at him I said, 'G'day, Harry.' We had grown up in Port Augusta together as kids, and his brother John Kernahan had been in my class. Harry asked what my problem was, and I explained to him about having no money and wanting some out of my Darwin account. Harry told the teller 'Give him what he wants,' and her face said it all: it's not what you know, it's who you know. The next step was to go to the teller for the cash, lo and behold Robert Mullen said to me, 'Hi Kev,' another Port Augusta bloke whose younger brother Ray had gone to school with me, and we had also worked together in the PMG on leaving school. A brief conversation with Bob, then I accepted some cash. The next stop was to the AMP office to lodge both contents and house claims. The contents would be paid out in five weeks, but the house was another matter. It had to be assessed by an assessment officer, which was fair enough.

I visited the DCA offices in Grenfell Street about working back in Adelaide for the time being. First up the pay officer wanted to see me. Sitting in his office, I was asked a lot of questions about what had happened in Darwin, and why didn't I go out to the Alice Springs Airport as the manager was holding $10,000 to assist anyone driving south. I told him that I had been unaware of any help being available in the Alice, and had used the CES. He was not impressed on hearing how I had been treated. He asked did I need any more money, and I told him not at the moment, but I might in the future. I needed to find a place to rent for now, until our future could be planned out. My car had been taken to the smash repairs for a paint job; luckily my father-in-law lent me a motor vehicle.

Looking at the real estate each morning in the Advertiser resulted in placing an application for a two bedroom flat in Unley. There were a lot of applicants, but the phone rang around 8 p.m. and I was informed that we had been lucky and could rent the two bedroom unit. DCA paid the $600 bond and the first month's rent, which was of tremendous help. Once my contents money was paid I would be able to clear this debt. Life started to take on some sort of normality except that we did not own anything, and work was a problem, with too many people working in a small area. I caught up with my old school mate Ray Mullen and his family; his brother Bob had told him where we were staying. It was good to talk about our schooldays growing up in Port Augusta.

Monday 13th: Starting work at Adelaide Airport, I was asked if I was interested in going back to Darwin, as they needed staff urgently to get the Comm Unit running again. My answer was yes, and I was then taken by car to the Department of Labour and issued a pass for my return to Darwin. Anne was unhappy, but understood my desire to get back as soon as, to try and sort out our problems and to enable them eventually to return. My mate Ron Beaumont and his wife Pat came around to see Anne and me that night. We had joined the navy together in Alice Springs on

29 September 1958. On one leave period in Adelaide I had introduced him to my cousin Pat, and they ended up getting married. Ron worked on the ABC site for Radio Australia on the Cox Peninsular upon his discharge, purchasing their NTA house in Alawa. They returned to live in Adelaide as we were moving into Wecdon St. Anne was to pick up the Falcon when it was repainted, and use it for herself and the kids.

Tuesday14th : Before I boarded the aircraft, Don Hodder from Darwin asked me if I would go around to his house in Rothdale Road, Moil, and see if his car was still under his house. I boarded the DCA aircraft at 8 a.m. for my return, with 10 other fellow Darwinites, plus a lot of freight strapped down where seats had been removed. The flight in the F27 took over eight hours, with a brief stopover in the Alice to refuel. Lunch loaded, we were on our way again. We experienced a rough ride through an electrical storm between Katherine and Adelaide River, finally arriving over Darwin in clear weather. The pilot flew around Darwin and Casuarina before landing, to show us the path of Tracy's destruction, an impressive sight from the air. After landing at the terminal I was met by Brian with whom I had arranged to stay.

First up I went over to the Ops Building to see my boss Eric Bergholtz, who was most happy to have me back. He had enough people to commence 24 hour coverage, passing traffic to and from Sydney via Telex. Happy with my roster, leaving the Airport I asked Brian if we could head out to Rothdale Road so I could check on Don's Holden wagon. Lo and behold it was still under his house; the right hand window was wound down but the interior was dry. I hopped into it and turned the ignition switch on, and surprisingly the car started straight away. I told Brian I now had a set of wheels and would follow him back to his place. I sent a telex message to Don Hodder, telling him I had wheels. Marylyn and the kids were happy to see me. They had been up to our place a few times and had salvaged the freezer, lot of bits and pieces and our Wedding Certificate, although all the amendments I had written on the back were gone. The ink washed away. I never did find my cheque book. My EH was not under the house on their first visit; some mongrel apparently had a greater need, a bit upsetting at the time. The freezer had a full bottle of Airwick in it trying to erase the smell. Brian and Marylyn were happy for me to stay with them while I returned to work.

Back at work there were two messages for me from close navy mates, one from Tony Miles in Brisbane, another from Tony Sullivan in Derby, offering help and money. When not at work I visited home, poking around the ruins, looking under the rubbish, throwing more rubbish out on the verge. It was a very lonely place, no one around, a bit spooky at times. A couple of times I was challenged by security people checking to see if I was a looter. Once I proved who I was, they left, wishing me all the best. At the end of January I eventually got the Army in, and they cleared my block for me, at the same time saving anything of value. My garden was looking the worse for wear, so I began cutting the grass, pulling weeds, trimming the shrubs and trying to straighten trees. The hanging baskets under the house needed some tender loving care. I had called into the AMP office and was waiting for an assessor to assess the damage.

DCA rented the North Australian Haulage Quarters over the other side of the Stuart Highway from the Ops Building, and I was allocated a room sharing with another worker. Gerry Wareham was made manager of the Hostel and did a great job; they gave him the keys to one of the Falcon Wagons outside the Ops Building. The vehicle wouldn't start, and when we lifted the bonnet we discovered that the complete motor had been knocked off. I thanked Marylyn and Brian for letting me stay with them. Occasionally I would visit the Marrara Pub for lunch, and again for tea. They were open for two hours each session, no drinks until you ordered a meal. Drinks and smokes were on the house; I guess old Gough was covering the bill at this stage. Eventually this had to come to an end, when Woolworths opened in the City. DCA started to charge me full board, so I found things were getting tough financially. I was still paying for Anne and the kids in Adelaide, and having to pay for myself as well was not good. My boss Eric offered me a Departmental house in Rapid Creek. After checking it out, I thought it could be cleaned and made habitable; the Navy had temporarily reroofed the dwelling. Dutchie Phillips and his wife were living there in a caravan in the back yard, and they were transferring to Ceduna in South Australia. I agreed to take it.

I came across my old mate Jim, who had just returned from Sydney; he worked at the Met Bureau. He told me he was camped in a dormitory at the Rapid Creek School, and it was not very good. I made him an offer that if he helped me clean my DCA house he could move in; this he promptly agreed to. It took eight days of hard work getting rid of the mould everywhere, scrubbing floors, walls, ceilings and cupboards. When it was clean I went back to Weedon Street, pulled all the gyprock off the bed and there was the basket of clothes I had taken off the clothesline before going to work on the 24th. They had been protected from the wet as well as the bed; it truly was unbelievable. The bedspread, sheets, pillows, mattress and base were all totally dry. Good old gyprock came in handy after all. I carted the lot over to 1025 Norcock Place in Rapid Creek, informing Jim that I had a bed. He managed to get a bed from his place. After moving in, we decided to go to the Raid Creek School once a day for a hot meal, $1 for breakfast and $2 for dinner or tea; this worked out well. We had an esky containing butter, vegemite, bread, milk and our diet food of VBs. Our only light at night was a little kerosene lamp hanging from a fan. We visited the ice works every day for a bag of ice on the way home from work, or Jim would do it.

The southern states' Lions and Apex Clubs, just to name a couple, donated portable generators for people without power, flown to Darwin by the RAAF on the Hercules transport aircraft. I put my name on the list and waited patiently to be allocated a generator. I checked periodically, but there were never any available, and I was always told to try again later. People who had generators were expected to return them when their power was restored. This did not happen in many cases, with excuses of 'it was on the verandah when I went to work, someone must have taken it,' or 'it was under the house and when I came home it was missing.' Funny the number of fishing camps that had generators in the dry season.

Each time the F27 came up from Adelaide, food, fruit and beer would be dropped off for the staff, donated by fellow workers at the Adelaide airport. The brew room fridge was always well stocked. I was able to have a hot shower at the start of my shifts. The Supervisor had a phone on his desk, which we could use to ring our families in the southern states, keeping in mind to keep the calls reasonably short, not to abuse this privilege. We were even allowed to have a TV in the office and keep an eye on the test cricket.

Volunteering to help others on my days off kept me occupied. Workers turned up one day and fully rescreened the house and replaced missing louvres, which had a habit of falling to the ground when opened. The window frames were slightly out of whack. Quite often I would visit empty houses, grab a few spare louvres and stow them under the house in the store. Our Wanguri place was starting to look good garden-wise now that I looked after it, cutting the grass every week and watering when necessary.

Finally an assessor from the Insurance Pool turned up at Weedon Street. This bloke was from Sydney, and had no idea of Darwin's reliance on building materials brought in from southern states, higher freight costs, etc. First up he offered me $16,000; the stove and clothes line had been fixtures, and were not included in his figures. I pointed this out to him, thinking that this bloke was supposed to be a professional. I refused his offer, as the place was insured for $24,600 and I wanted the full insured value. A fellow neighbour from my Smith Street Government flat days told me that I should consider getting an engineer's report. I followed his advice and requested an engineer's report. A short time later I received a letter from AMP stating the engineer's assessment was $17,600. I still refused to sign the release.

Sometime in March I heard a truck pull up in Norcock Place, and upon investigating found a crew from Wollongong starting work on the power lines. I asked one bloke, 'How long will it be, mate?', his reply was about a week. I offered them a VB with the excuse 'It's hot out here, do you blokes want a coldie?' They were only too happy to have a short break and a cold refreshment. A week later when the power was ready to be reconnected, I was the first one in the street to be connected. The old VB trick, it worked again, better than money. Now I had power, it was time to arrange for Anne and the kids to return to Darwin.

Not long after the Greek Liner Patris berthed, my boss informed that I was wanted at the NTA Staff Section. At the end of my shift I went to their office in Mitchell Street and asked, 'Did you want to see me?' They asked if I was living in the house when the cyclone struck, and I said no, that the Department had placed me in it. The clerk then said 'you're a squatter, you will have to get out and live on the Patris." I knew that Ray McHendry, the boss of the NTA, had issued an instruction about squatters, but considered that my Department knew what they were doing. Telling the clerk to jam the Patris up her backside, I stormed back to the airport and told Eric I wanted a transfer to Adelaide; there was no way I was living on a ship with two very young children. My wife and children were due back to Darwin at this stage. Eric said to me, 'Slow down, you're not the only one, there are six of you in the same predicament, two air traffic controllers, two flight service officers and 2 Comm officers. As luck would have it, the First Assistant Secretary of DCA from Canberra was in Darwin, and when he heard about our situation he demanded a meeting with McHendry.

The Secretary told McHendry that he could not operate Darwin Airport without sufficient staff, and that if we were evicted the airport would be shut down. McHendry told him he could not do that. The Secretary told him that he could, and there would be no more R and R flights in or out of Darwin. McHendry immediately saw the problem he would have with angry Darwin residents if the R and R flights were cancelled, and backed off, giving permission for the six of us to remain in our allocated houses. A short time later I was given permission in writing to stay, and immediately arranged to have a few photocopies made, just in case.

Good old TAA arrived from Adelaide on a Saturday at the end of March, bringing my family back. As I was considered staff they allowed me to walk out to the plane and help Anne and the two little ones back to the terminal. Anne told me that she had put the car on the train in Adelaide and it should be there in about a week. The railways would notify me when I could expect the car. On the day the car arrived, I drove down to the wharf area, where shunting was taking place. My car was going backwards and forwards while I waited. The diesel engine pulled up where I was standing and a voice from the cab said, 'What the bloody hell are you doing, Ruwie?' Looking up I saw Bob Green, another navy bloke I had served with seven years ago on HMAS Derwent. I told Bob that I was waiting for my car; 'which one,' Bob said, 'the brown Falcon,' I replied. On Bob's speaking to the shunter, the train was split and my car delivered to the unloading area. I thanked Bob and told him I'd catch him later on. I checked the car over, signed the paperwork and was given the keys. It was great to have my own wheels back.

When I arrived back at Rapid Creek, Don Hodder turned up and wanted his car back; he had a pass to stay for five days to salvage anything from his house. Talk about great timing. As there were no keys, I told him 'it's all yours' and thanked him the for loan, it had come in very handy. He told me if I wanted anything from his house that I could use, I was welcome to take it. Calling in on the way to Berry Springs for the day, I went into the house and had a look around. His Christmas tree was still intact with his children's presents still wrapped under it. All he wanted was a cap given to him by his grandfather at some pommy football final when he was a kid. Telling him I would take the fridge, we headed to Berry. On our return there was nothing left on his block. He had the army clear the place, ropes around the piers, pulled it down, scooped the lot into trucks and dumped at Leanyer. There went his offer of the fridge. Unbelievable, I could not understand him; the house could have been fixed for someone to live in.

Life never became normal again; there was always someone contacting me to sign them in to spend five days salvaging anything of value, plus 'can I stay at your house'. Anne was not happy with the constant visitors, but I made it clear that if they stayed they looked after themselves. As each one departed south, they kindly left me a fridge or a washing machine, sometimes both, saying, 'here, Kev, you may as well have it rather than throw it out.' It did not take long for my place to start resembling Steptoe & Son out of the ABC comedy. Sometimes at work I'd hear someone say they wanted a washing machine or a fridge. My new venture now was 'I can get you one for a carton of VB!' Barry Hayward was one of the early ones, and when he was leaving I bought his Datsun half-ton ute; Anne and I both now had our own wheels.

Now I had a new problem; both the kids liked playing downstairs, but there was a problem with louvres falling from above, and small debris on the ground still. I'd removed the front fence from Weedon St and it was still in our store, also the 60 concrete slabs and some 16x8 patio cement slabs I'd used around the yard. I gradually moved the lot to Rapid Creek in the little ute; it took a few trips. My cousin Don called around and gave me a swing for the kids that our grandfather had made in the blind school in Perth. I hung that up under the house. He was now working with NTA based in Brisbane. We now had to put up with three lots of bullshit: Canberra, Brisbane and Darwin. The three of them left a lot to be desired as far as communications went. Don was in the Draftsman Office, so I didn't pick on him. After fencing in the back area under the house, I laid the concrete and patio slabs to have a decent entertaining area. On one of my trips to Leanyer I knocked off a bath, brought it home and set it up for the kids to play in. Every night I would pull the plug and water the plants; I had installed some piping to allow me use the waste water on my veggie patch.

AMP sent me a letter saying they had a surveyor survey the house, and came up with a new offer of $19,000. I knocked it back again: back to square one. The surveyor rang me at work one day, asking me why I would not sign the release. I told him I considered the damage to my house was such that to rebuild would cost the full insured amount. He replied, 'Okay, I will go back and have another look.' I asked him when, and told him I would meet him there. The surveyor was friendly enough, and we walked around together. I pointed out things like the fact the breezeway brick wall in the laundry would fall with a slight push. The concrete piers under the house had moved. Another breezeway brick wall at the end of the house was not cemented to the piers; it was just sitting there waiting for a strong breeze to knock it over. In the end he said 'Ring my office tomorrow at 11 a.m. and I will have a favourable reply.' I rang his office on the dot, and he said 'I have reconsidered, and we are giving you the full amount plus the six months' motel rent.' This was in lieu of the twelve months stated in the contract if the house had to be rebuilt. We accepted his offer.

As I was starting to get a bit jaded by now from helping people in their houses, removing fridges and freezers full of mould, it was starting to get to me; the smell was no longer tolerable. I decided one of the R and R flights being offered would be just the ticket. I requested and was given a flight to Perth, return, for the four of us. We stayed with Anne's adopted parents in Mosman Park for a week. During our visit, Nell babysat the kids while Anne and I looked at homes. We found one in Maddington that we liked, and we decided a transfer to Perth would be ideal. On our return to Darwin we made an appointment at the Commonwealth Bank for a housing loan. Because I did not have a credit rating, I was knocked back. Unbelievable, we had $25,000 in the bank at the time. We decided to change banks, but the ANZ advised us not to, just find a better manager. We would need to bank with them for six months before they would give us a loan. I thanked him for the advice; it made sense.

A trip around to Weedon Street shortly after really hurt me. Some bastard had been around and knew about my exotic plants under the front stairs. I couldn't believe it; the whole lot had been dug out and taken, leaving holes where they once stood. This rotten act brought me to my knees, I shed some tears and was down on everyone in Darwin who had rebuilt their home and wanted an instant garden. I drove around checking out restored gardens, especially those people that knew I was a keen gardener.

I never found out where my lovely plants finished up. Now I had no choice but to apply for a builder's pole and rent the block out. Once the pole was installed, a young couple with small children replied to my advert. He was in the building trade, so I gave him permission to demolish the remains of the upstairs area, using any materials to build in underneath. They remained on the block until I sold it back to the Reconstruction Commission.

Not long afterwards, Jim asked if Angus, a workmate, could board with us, as he was having accommodation problems. After a short discussion with Anne it was agreed that Angus could stay as long as he contributed to our living costs. He was no problem, very quiet, tidy in his habits and fitted in well. Jim and Angus shared a room, as the children had the other room. Ralph Franklin, who was in Port Hedland, requested a five day stay to check his house and see if he could rebuild it in Moil. I agreed to his request, as Ralph was not only a talker but he was a doer as well; he had given me a lot of help in the past. Ralph thought the house repair would be okay, and returned to Hedland to arrange his transfer back to Darwin.

Sometime shortly after this I applied for a Regulation 98 airfare for an R and R flight to have another break from Darwin. I told our next door neighbour Nancy that I was thinking of heading south for bit of R and R; she worked at a Travel Agency and advised me to get a warrant to go to Singapore.

This was quite a common practice for Darwin people in those days. When I received the warrant, I would give it to her and she would arrange our trip for us. I followed Nancy's instructions, handing the warrant over to her on receipt. Nancy arranged for the four of us to fly to Derby for five days to stay with Tony and Shirley Sullivan, and thank them for their offer of money after Tracy. Then onto Perth for 4 weeks with a hire car, staying with relatives and visiting Anne's girlfriend Trish and her husband Colin for a week in Bunbury. Then we flew to Adelaide for a week, staying at the Taft Motel in Glenelg, then returned to Darwin. I don't know how she wangled it, but I did not ask any questions. As we had Jim and Angus living with us, they looked after the house.

Nell looked after the kids again while Anne and I started house-hunting again, eventually finding a four bedroom house in Beckenham. I asked the agent if he knew of a friendly Commonwealth Bank manager. He said he had one at Cannington, and made an appointment for us. The manager was very approachable, and approved our loan straight away, under the proviso that we had to live in it, and not buy it or an investment. We assured him that transferring to Perth was not a problem for me. I felt like going back to the Darwin Branch and telling the loans officer there what I thought of him and his credit rating, but Anne said 'let it go'.

No sooner did we get out of the car upon our return, than Ralph pulled up with a caravan and his family, to stay. I had only signed for his return, and did not expect Denise and his two girls. Anyway, they set the caravan up in the back yard. Denise was of Mauritian descent, and started to get on Anne's nerves after a while, cooking her meals in the kitchen leaving strange odours, and always jumping in early. Anne was frustrated at this, because our two children would have to wait until Denise was finished. Her girls teased Peta with spooks and stuff, which gave her nightmares. I was told by Anne to help Ralph work on his house as much as possible: 'the sooner it's repaired, the sooner they are out of here.' It took six weeks in total.

There was a pile of rubbish in the yard which I kept adding to, and tried to burn without success. A D8 Dozer team were working in the area, so I asked them if they could remove it for me and I would give them a couple of six-packs. They agreed, and within half an hour I had a clean yard. Then my neighbour Ron, who was the manager, arranged a tipper with a five ton load of good soil to be delivered. I forgot to add that the D8 driver noticed something flashing in the heap; stopping, he got down and picked the object up. It was a glass jar full of round 50 cent pieces. He was kind enough to open the jar and give Anne half a dozen of them, and he took the rest. Someone must have been a keen collector. At least they didn't finish up in the melting pot, like a lot of 50 cent coins did.

Watching the TV one night, I heard a knock on the door around 8 p.m. Getting up out of my chair and turning the porch light on, I opened the door to see a little clerk with a clipboard and a big NT copper behind him. I asked him what was his problem and he replied, 'you were not in this house when Cyclone Tracy hit, therefore you are a squatter and have to vacate the premises'. I told this upstart to stay where he was, went back inside and grabbed a copy of the approval from McHendry, went back outside and handed it to him. He replied 'I know nothing about this,' I replied, 'that's your effin problem,' turned the light off and shut the door, leaving them in the dark. Christ, was anyone going to leave us alone!

Jim, my old mate, was not much better; he never told the Met Bureau he was boarding with me. They were under the impression that 1025 Norcock Place was a Met Bureau house. One Sunday morning I had a visit from another little clerk, who asked me, 'does Jim Eagles live here?' I told him yes and he came out with 'we need this house for a Meteorologist and you will have to vacate the premises.' Unbelievable, another dickhead who hadn't checked with Jim first. Anyhow, after telling him that it was a DCA house, I gave him short shrift with two words, the second one being the word 'off'.

We still had the occasional visitor, but passes for entry were no longer required. My Steptoe collection under the house was still growing. I purchased an Ally dinghy and outboard on a special deal in Cavanaugh Street. Now old Ralph came in handy to weld a frame on the ute to carry the dinghy on. Once that was completed, I chucked an old tyre in the back to rest the outboard motor on, and had room for some crab pots, now I was ready to tackle Buffalo Creek. It was nice to catch a few mangrove crabs again. I chased barramundi in the river below Manton Dam wall, but I did not have any luck there.

Ronnie, my friend from Alice Springs, arrived from Indonesia looking for a bed. I told her it was not a problem, and she stayed for a bit more than a week. Unfortunately she had picked up some kind of flu-like virus overseas, and she spent the whole week in bed while Anne nursed her. Once she was better I showed her around what was left of the Darwin that she had once known so well. Ronnie had been a WRAN at Coonawarra in 1965 and was shocked to see her old quarters; the top floor was totally destroyed. I drove her around through the various suburbs so she could assess for herself just how bad Tracy had been.

My transfer to Perth was underway, with a departure date at the end of November. Suddenly Malcolm and Gough had a little spat in Canberra and cancelled supply; money was stopped to all government departments. The day of our uplift no one turned up, Anne decided to ring the Airport clerk to find out what was happening, the packers had not turned up.

His reply was that there was no money for transfers and they had cancelled ours that morning. Anne was shocked, and rang me at work to relay the bad news. Deeply shocked, I visited Bruno St Lucia, the airport clerk, and asked him what the score was. Poor old Bruno, he was copping it from all the staff affected by this decision. I mentioned our problem to Ron, our next door neighbour, and he said 'if you want, I can get you a container on an empty truck returning to Perth.' I asked him could he let me know how much the damage would be. He told me a day later that it could be done for $600. He would arrange for one of his trucks to bring the container around and allow me to pack it over a weekend.

Now the big question was 'what do we do'. Bruno advised me that I had a Reg 98 available, so Anne and the kids could fly to Perth, and when my transfer was approved I could join them. The house in Beckenham was empty, decisions, decisions, decisions. Finally Anne was happy to go to Perth with the kids, and I would stay with Brian and Marylyn again. Now we had to work out what went to Perth, what got disposed of and what went to Leanyer.

I managed to get rid of another washing machine and fridge, and someone from work bought the slabs and patio slabs. At this rate I thought I would need another container just for VB cartons, but it was certainly better than having cash lying around. I advertised the ute, boat and outboard in the NT News as a complete deal. A young RAAF gentleman turned up and only wanted the ute; I knocked him back, telling him I would not separate them. He ended up taking the complete deal; unfortunately he paid me in cash, not VBs. Over the next couple of weeks, we started to pack items for Perth in cardboard cartons. Jim had been accepted by DCA, and was required to do a course in Melbourne, transferring to Perth on completion. Angus had decided it was time to be reunited with his family down south.

Now it was getting close to the middle of November. The packing was completed, the container had been loaded over the weekend, taken back to NAH Haulage on Monday morning, and loaded on a truck for Perth departing that night. Anne and the kids left on Ansett that night. We had cleaned the house, but the Housing Inspector had not shown up at the set time. I had moved all the stuff under the house to Stuart Auctions on the highway in Stuart. They would send me a cheque once all the items were disposed of. After loading all my gear into the car, I turned the power off, locked up and departed for the 17 mile.

I drove into the city and parked by the NTA Staff offices shortly afterwards, to return the house keys. The clerk asked 'What are these keys for?' I replied, 'They are for 1025 Norcock Place,' and told her I was vacating the premises. 'Has it been inspected?' she asked nastily. I said 'no'. Then she became really nasty and 'You have to have the house inspected before you leave.' I told her 'I don't give a stuff, your Inspector never turned up at the appointed time, I'm off to Perth.' Then she had the audacity to come out with, 'It has to be in the same condition it was when you moved in.' I said, 'Give me the bloody keys back, it will take at least eight buckets of mud to make it look anywhere near what it was when I moved in.' Then I stormed out the door, and never heard again from the NTA.

The following day I realised I had left my .22 rifle, two burner gas stove and a couple of other items in the linen press. Returning to Norcock Place, I knocked on Ron's door and asked to borrow a screw driver. He laughed when I told him why. Breaking in through the louvres was easy. I grabbed my gear, locking the door and replacing the louvres upon exiting. I gave Ron back his screwdriver, had a VB, and bid him and his wife goodbye. They had been good neighbours. Life was quiet now, I just had to do my shifts at the airport and sit on my bum at the 17 mile, occasionally stopping at Casey's at Berrimah for a liquid refreshment or two.

There was no sign of Mal or Gough giving in, so we just had to wait. At last an election, they had gotten rid of Gough thank Christ, the man who invented the 'Gimme mentality'. Each time I knocked on Bruno's door he'd say 'not yet, Kev'. One day Bruno said to me, 'Kev, you have three and a half months' leave up your sleeve, two Reg 98's, take one and go to Perth for Christmas with your family, and if your transfer is not approved I will send you a return ticket at the end of your leave'. Great, now I had to work out which way was I going to go. I rang my father up and asked him did he want to meet me in Alice Springs and accompany me to Kadina by road. He was only too happy to accompany me.

I rang Anne and told her to hop on the Indian Pacific and we would have Christmas in Adelaide and then drive back over the Nullabor. Next I applied for a Reg 98 by road via Port Augusta, which Adelaide approved. I set the date, gave Dad the date to meet me in Alice, and lo and behold, what does that bloke in the sky do. Dropped bloody nine inches on the railway and road south of the Alice, washing both out. I told Bruno right, cancel the trip by road, put the car on State Ships to Fremantle and I will fly to Perth. Dad was extremely upset over this, but it was beyond my control. I rang Anne and told her to cancel the train, as I was stuck in Darwin.

I was able to get on an Ansett Special departing Darwin at 2.15 a.m. I delivered the car to State Ships, went back to work to bid everyone goodbye, and with some other close friends, mustered at Brian's for farewell drinks. About 1 a.m. Brian drove me out to the airport, after I said good bye to Marylyn and their children. The flight from Perth still hadn't arrived, so it was a case of try and stay awake. Once the flight landed it did not take long to turn around and load, then depart for Broome. I remember seeing lightning flashes at one stage, but nothing else. Departing Broome, I had a VB and slept again until arriving in Perth. I caught a cab to our new house, catching Anne and the children still in bed. They were very surprised at seeing me, as I hadn't told them I was coming. I should have stayed in Darwin; now I had a brand new house, no garden and a heap of work in front of me.

Bruno sent me a telegram in the New Year telling me my transfer had been approved. My commencement date at Perth Airport was 9th April. Life was very different in Perth; they hated anyone from the eastern states and tolerated anyone from up north. I must confess I found them different also, even although I had been born at Merredin, 260 kilometres east of Perth. Thus ended a year of more downs than ups; I was not sorry to see it pass although I did miss the Darwin lifestyle.

I visited Darwin in 1979, staying with my cousin, Don, at Wulagi for a week. As we drove around the city, the evidence of Tracy was still very visible. I returned again in 1989, staying at Howard Springs, and Darwin was now really a different City. Another visit in 2000, again staying in Howard Springs. I was very surprised at a dual highway just out of Noonamah, with a set of Traffic Lights at the Humpty Doo Intersection. I had another six weeks at Howard Springs in 2002, but Darwin was now nothing like the old Darwin that I loved. I have no desire to return any more; I just keep my memories of what was once a great life. I hope to do the Ghan trip upon my next visit to the Top End.

Kev Ruwoldt.

Photograph by Ramon Williams

CHAPTER 25 - CHRISSY SCHUBERT

"On Christmas Eve of 74 a warning sounded out, on all the broadcast stations a great storm was near." Forty years ago the beautiful town of Darwin was blown away by a devastating wind.

My mum & dad still live in the home that was ours on Christmas Eve of 1974. Our family survived without too many dramas, but I remember coming out onto our street on Christmas Day and there was debris everywhere and people just looking around with horror on their faces. I was twelve years old and I remember every detail as if it was yesterday. Cyclone Tracy stripped many thousands of children of their innocence. The rebuild of Darwin showed how resilient and strong the residents were. I call Darwin my home, and I love it and miss it every day I am not there.

So the plan for Christmas Day 40 years ago was a fun-filled lunch with our good friends Gwen & Boyd Scully and their kiddies Marise, Sheree & Jodii. Mum and

Gwennie spent the day before preparing the food for our feast. What then eventuated changed the lives of many.

After spending the night awake and praying in our shower room (1.5m x 1.5m) the six of us walked out into the street at Borella Circuit, thanked God we were all safe and sound, caught up with our neighbours and friends the Turners, and again thanked God they were all okay. So our next concern was for the Scully family. Gwen mentioned that they were wondering how we were after they spent the night huddled under their dining room table, and then we walked down the street to their home just around the corner in Jingili. Our families had Christmas lunch together, using a gas stove to heat up the wonderful curry that Gwen had made. We made of it the best we could with all the emotion and sadness. Then commenced the cleanup and evacuation of 35,000 people. We are all still here, thanking the man

upstairs for looking out for us. Thinking of Michael Turner at the moment, love to the Turners.

Chrissy Schubert (left) I now live in Mandurah WA, but my 4 siblings & their families live in

Darwin and my mum and dad still live in our home that went through Cyclone Tracy, 60 Borella Circuit in Jingili.

Photograph by Ramon Williams

CHAPTER 26 – VICKI SHEAN

Christmas at 7 Symes Street Nakara.

For many years I have tried to put pen to paper and write our story. Now, through the wonders of Facebook and the Cyclone Tracy Survivors forum, I have found the peace of mind finally to do it.

I once went to Fannie Bay Goal to view the Cyclone Tracy display with a psychologist, and found that I could not go through, so she told me not to worry, it would happen one day when I was ready.

My husband, Jim Shean, and I moved to Darwin in September 1971, and in January 1973 we moved into our new NTA house, in the new district of Casuarina in the suburb of Nakara. Our house was in Symes Street, behind the Post Office.

In September 1973, our son Daniel was born.

A few weeks before Christmas 1974, we prepared for a cyclone whose name escapes me, but like so many other cyclone warnings over our short time in Darwin, this one turned away at the last minute.

Then on 24th December 1974, Christmas Eve, we were preparing to go to the airport to pick up my parents who were coming to share Christmas with us. We were concerned, because for a couple of days beforehand, we had also been preparing for a cyclone that had been named Cyclone Tracy. At one stage we were advised that the plane had been diverted to Katherine, to wait until the weather was clear. Next we were advised that the cyclone had turned away and was heading back out to sea, and that the plane would be landing as per schedule. When we were on our way to the airport, it came over the radio that Cyclone Tracy had changed course yet again, and was heading for Darwin.

We picked up my parents from the airport and headed home, with no idea of what was ahead of us. We suggested that my parents not unpack their bags, but put them under their beds, and we locked all our valuables into an overhead cupboard.

We went ahead and cooked Christmas dinner for that night, just in case there would be no power the next day.

By 7:00 p.m., we had cleaned up and were taping the windows, then we were mopping up the water off the floors. About 9:00 p.m. there was this mighty crash, and so Jim forced open the back door, only to see a part of the roof from Casuarina Shopping Centre heading our way, so he forced the door shut, as it was about to hit our house.

We decided to get some sleep, and my dear Dad, being ever so faithful, decided to listen to the Midnight Mass from St Mary's Church, and suddenly the radio went off the air. We no longer had contact.

We had filled the bath and all the sinks, both upstairs and in the laundry downstairs, and we knew that we had the pool filled too. We had done all the things that we had been told to do, but no one had told us what was to happen next.

Suddenly the windows started to crack and split apart, and we could hear the deafening winds as the roof started to tear apart. We were huddled together in the bathroom and suddenly the walls started to rip off. Jim called to us to gather at the back door.

We grabbed our baby boy and followed Jim out the back door, where the roofing iron had formed some protection for us by means of a tunnel. But we could only get halfway down the stairs, and then had to jump the rest of the way to the ground. As we made our way to the storage room under the house I will never forget the vision of devastation through the lightning flashes. Jim had already taken the budgies and our dog downstairs, and some towels to keep us dry.

We stood with our backs against the block wall to prevent it from falling in on us. Funny, but it wavered in and out behind us. The roof had gone, and we saw our bath disappear as the floor boards were being ripped off board by board from over the top of us. I will never forget that sound. As the rain pelted down on us we could taste the Dieldrin that had been used on the floor boards to prevent white ants from eating it. Oh and because I was four months pregnant, I needed to pee a lot, and my Dad gave me a bucket, but after a while it blew away and I peed where I stood, as we all did.

Outside there was a deafening roar as the winds ripped and tore the world apart, it just never stopped, but at one stage, despite the winds, the sky cleared and we could see stars in the distance. We were told that in our area there was no eye, hence the damage. Then we thought the wall was coming down on us as a block dropped on my foot, but because we were standing in water up to our knees (there was a high tide which had been caused by the cyclonic winds) it broke the fall, so I was not injured.

As the winds became even stronger we embraced each other, and prayed until daylight. What we saw then was unimaginable. Nothing, no one could have prepared anyone in Darwin for what they saw that morning as they rose with the light of day and ventured out from the rubble. Our birds had gone, but our dog stuck close by us at all times. From out of nowhere came a knock on the store-room door, and there stood two firemen – this was about 7:00 a.m. They helped us outside, where we saw our neighbours, Jeff, Julienne, Andrew, Craig and Lara Brown, being helped out of the rubble that lay on top of them upstairs at their home. Together we were all taken to the Casuarina Fire Station, where we grouped with other families from Nakara.

Most people were taken to either the Nakara Primary School or the University. By the end of the day there were only our next door neighbours, my Dad and Mum, Jim, me and Daniel, along with some of the firemen, camped at the fire station.

My father and Jim went back to our house, where they managed to get all the meat out of the upturned freezer (it had a whole side of beef in it) and take it in a wheelbarrow to the university so they could cook it up for the displaced people who camped there that night. Then they happened to retrieve some belongings and fit into the store room so that we could get it on our return. Of course, being pregnant, I had my suitcase all packed ready for hospital, as you do, but imagine my surprise when Jim turned up with it for me, but when I opened it, apart from my clothes for hospital and some babies' clothes, the rest of the contents were cans of beer. Men! But the beers were a welcome relief.

Of course they say that Santa never made it into Darwin that fateful day, but he did, in more ways than one. We were alive and together, and that is more important than presents. Despite that, my neighbour Julienne went out and found a present from our yard that was for Daniel; it was a Tupperware ball. My husband also brought me a present he had found still sitting under the tree (yes, the tree, an amazing sight; a very soggy-looking six foot Christmas tree still sitting on the only floorboards remaining over our heads); it was a Bible still wrapped and slightly damp on the cover. The power of prayer and the Bible protected us that night. I still have that Bible today.

We were well looked after by the firemen, who would crawl in at night totally exhausted and extremely distressed at the carnage they had to deal with. They told us of one family with five children they had found dead, huddled together in the wreckage of their home, and other, similar stories. All the bodies were taken to the Post Office at

Casuarina. I often wonder how those brave men have evolved today. They had helped us dig latrines outside, and made makeshift showers from the gutters, with privacy. The rain was our only means of showers and toilet and drinking water.

My neighbour and I went into the Casuarina Police Station to register our families. While there, we discussed where we were and what we had, and before we knew it we were escorted over to the shopping centre and taken into Coles, where we were given a suitcase each and trolleys, and told to get what we could. We filled them with necessities for the children, and some changes of clothes for all of us. One policeman came up to me and gave me a radio and some batteries. We kept that radio for almost forty years, and only just dumped it last year.

At one stage we heard a gunshot as a police officer had shot at the ground at a group of what they called scavengers. In my mind I thought to myself, "but aren't they doing what we are doing? Surviving."

They helped us back to our retreat, and as we passed the police station, they gave me extra cloth nappies, baby bottles and powdered milk for Daniel. I often wonder if, even though he was just fifteen months old, this experience is why he is now a superintendant with the NT Police today.

By day three, the roads had been graded enough to get our car out and prepare to drive it to Adelaide. I had tried to get a flight by registering at the university, but was told I was a low priority, even though I was four months pregnant and had a fifteen-month-old.

Dogs were being put down by the police, who would drive along the roads and shoot any roaming dog. This was for the safety of the people. We took our poor dog to the police station, where they were euthanizing animals. We left him and returned back to the fire station, where we found our dog had raced us home. My dear father then returned him to the police and held him until he went to sleep. This distressed Dad immensely.

The police directed us into Darwin where we could get fuel vouchers, so the men got the cars and made them roadworthy. Our car had not a window in it, and so we had to cover each window including the front windscreen with plastic and black tape. The fuel tank had also been punctured by a piece of wood that had lodged through the wheel hub into the boot. We packed the cars and headed into Darwin where my neighbour and I went in to get the fuel vouchers and the men went in to register our departure by road.

I was confronted by a well-dressed woman, in high heels, make up and coiffed hair, with jewellery hanging off her. She had been brought up by the Government from down South somewhere. Her rudeness was confronting, because she was putting us all down, and so this got right up my nose, because like everyone else in the room, I was dressed in what I had been standing in for several days, and with matted hair, no makeup and no shoes, so I lashed out at her and screamed for her boss, who came out and, along with half the room, had to calm me down. We then got our vouchers and headed off.

Anyway on that day we departed from Darwin along the Stuart Highway, with hundreds of others. Our hearts were heavy and tears were many, but we had to go and leave the devastation behind us. Our first stop was Pine Creek, where we got fuel at rather inflated prices, and a bed for the night. At Adelaide River we were given a change of clothes, cake and coffee. On to Katherine the next day, where we were greeted by the CWA women, who went out of their way with coffee and food for everyone. I don't remember where we stopped after that until we arrived in Alice Springs, where we went to the showgrounds. The next day Jim, my Dad and Jeff drove on their way to Adelaide. Julienne, my mum and the kids and I were taken to the airport where we went on a flight to Adelaide.

In Adelaide we lined up with everyone else and registered with the Red Cross, and were given a green Refugee Card, which I still have today

Darwin really gets into your blood, and eventually we returned in June 1986, after living in Adelaide and then Papua New Guinea. We built a new home – elevated – and stayed at Howard Springs from 1987 to 2013, when we retired to Cairns.

Darwin has grown and changed from 1974, and continues to blossom. There will never be a Darwin like pre-Cyclone Tracy, but Tracy made Darwin a much stronger city, and like the Phoenix she has risen from the debris.

I congratulate the people of Darwin for making Darwin into what she is today.

After Tracy we moved to Adelaide, where we built a

beautiful home in Happy Valley and had our second Son Matthew, with whom I had been pregnant during Tracy. Both Daniel and Matthew went to school for a short time, before we moved to PNG. By this time we had, had our third son, David. We spent four wonderful, adventurous years in Lae, PNG. A time never to be forgotten. We returned to Adelaide in June 1986 and within two months we returned to Darwin to take up where we finished in January 1975.

We built our home in Howard River Park and our boys were raised here. As it was a rural area, they were free to be themselves in their out of school time.

Daniel moved to Adelaide and lived with his grandparents, where he joined the SA Police Department, and then in 2005 he, along with his wife Tammy and two children, Isaac and Tahlia, moved back to Darwin where he transferred to the NT Police Department. Daniel now has another beautiful little girl, Bella, and he and his family live in Bellamack, and Daniel has worked his way up the ranks to become a Superintendant who is often in an acting position as Commander.

Matthew is married to Lisa, and they have two beautiful children, Ellie and Jaxon, and they live in MacKay. Matthew works in the mines and is good at his job, a true provider and a wonderful husband and father.

David and his wife Sam have four adorable children, Lincoln, Sienna, Zachary and Ivy, and they are now living in Redlynch Valley near us. David is the North Queensland Area Manager for NBN Co.

I am a breast cancer survivor, and Jim and I are living

in our own little paradise in Redlynch Valley, Cairns. We have lived a wonderful full life and are thankful in one respect for the experience of Cyclone Tracy because, despite the devastation that Tracy dished up to us, we have learnt that life goes on and that no one gives you anything, you must stand on your own two feet and earn your living and reap the rewards. There is no such thing as luck, life is what you make of it.   Below: Jim and Vicki Shean.

Photograph by Ramon Williams.

Photograph by Ramon Williams

CHAPTER 27 – JOYCE SPRUNT

My name is Joyce Sprunt, I'm a Cyclone Tracey survivor and this is my story:

The year was 1974; my husband, Malcolm Gordon Sprunt (affectionately known as Mal), and I were living in our home town of Perth in Western Australia, when Malcolm, who worked for the Australian Government, was offered a promotion. The promotion required us to be relocated to either Port Moresby in Papua New Guinea or to Darwin, in the top end of Australia. We finally settled on the top end. So, midway through 1974, we moved to Darwin, where Malcolm filled a position on the government's Promotions Appeals Board. As part of our package we were accommodated in government-allocated housing, our new address 3955 Allwright Street Wangeri, directly opposite the primary school. The house was of the typical Darwin architecture of the time. The house itself was fibro with a tin roof, elevated on concrete stilts with a laundry and second toilet centrally located on the ground floor. Access to the house was via external staircases to both the front and rear doors.

With much excitement we looked forward to this opportunity, the new adventure. We quickly made friends with some of our new neighbours, Judy and Terry Wooster and their two very young children Michelle and Phillip, along with Glad and Eric Turner and George and Maxine Waters. It wasn't long before I also had a new job, a position behind the bar serving patrons at the Marrara Hotel. Before long we also purchased a brand new vehicle, a Volkswagen Kombi Van, with the intention of road trips, fishing and camping in and around the environs of Darwin.

The end of the year was fast approaching, and we were busy making preparations for our Christmas holiday, a fishing trip. A brand new blunt punt dinghy was on order, we'd taken delivery and the Kombi Van was all but packed. With Christmas Eve upon us, Malcolm attended an after-work party and I was working my shift at the hotel. Much earlier than expected, Mal arrived to collect me from my duties. I sensed a degree of urgency; he was keen to head home and make sure everything was securely battened down for the bad weather ahead. I was insistent I stay until the end of my shift. Once home, we both endeavoured to tie down and store belongings in and around our home, in readiness for the predicted inclement weather.

It was late; Mal was tired and went to bed. I felt uneasy, so sat up and listened as the rain and wind whipped at the louvre windows; the weather was closing in. It was the sound, the sound of things going 'bump' in the darkness, that made me wake Mal from his slumber; it was time to seek refuge. Having been in bed asleep, Mal was scantily clad; in haste on went a pair of shorts and a suit coat into which he slipped his cigarettes, matches and a torch. With one hand he grabbed a bottle of scotch and the other a bottle of brandy, declaring that it could be a long night. As he opened the front door to exit, the wind ripped it from Mal's poor grasp, and the bottle of scotch was lost to the wind. With some effort we managed to close the front door and secure our home from the elements. Turning to descend the steps to the ground floor, we found the path blocked; a refrigerator on its side was wedged into the staircase.

The brandy was now sacrificed; the only thing to do was to climb over it, hanging on for dear life. Finally refuge, both of us ensconced in the laundry under a plastic outdoor table, so scared but somewhat safe. The sounds of destruction carried on long into the night, sounds of twisting metal, darkness closing in as time ticked by and no sleep. Interestingly, we thought it was just our home ripping apart, which was funny as we'd climbed over a refrigerator to descend the stairs to the laundry. As daylight was breaking there was quietness, a certain stillness; we decided to emerge from under the plastic table and venture out into the morning light.

Nothing could've prepared us for what we were about to witness. Destruction as far as the eyes could see, not a single house intact, a neighbour walking down the middle of the street dazed and confused. A stray dog wandered over for a pat and some reassurance. We never found her owner. A lovely placid dog, who became a close companion for many years, we named her Lady.

Over the next few days, neighbours and strangers banded together to create makeshift shelters. Loose sheets of tin were used to roof standing structures where homes had once perched. Surprisingly, we still had an operational toilet, although there was no water, so some effort was made to make the area a private place for people to use. Counting the losses, our home and our belongings were gone, the Kombi Van that was a few months old had extensive damage to every panel and the brand new dinghy was never seen again. However the bottle of scotch was found in the grass; it was shared among friends and neighbours, and sipped with great vigour. I imagined the brandy to be with the dinghy!

Over the ensuing days we shared our stories of survival, and here is one I'd like to share. Most of us had been judging the severity of the cyclone by the intensity of the noise that was occurring, as the power outages had robbed us of lights, and without lights to see by there was no telling what the level of destruction already was. In the blackness of the night, the noise too loud to bear, my neighbours placed their two very small young children into the safety of a bedroom wardrobe. How could they possibly have anticipated that their home and everything in it would blow away? They found the wardrobe at the bottom of their yard; it had landed on a mattress with the children still inside, a little bruised and shaken, but alive.

It wasn't long before emergency accommodation caravans were being delivered to house the homeless. We received the second caravan that came to Darwin. This we provided to the Lockhart family, relatives of Mal's, who had lost their entire family home. So while the Lockharts and their young boys sheltered on one side of our block in the caravan, I slept with Mal on a mattress we had found, under a corner of what remained of our home. The school directly across the road became a designated drop zone for supplies like food, cool drinks and water. Days started to run into weeks, and progress was slow.

As time dragged on it was becoming obvious that I needed some medical attention. At Mal's insistence I was a passenger on the last Hercules plane to Perth, part of an evacuation plan for the displaced people of Darwin. I sat next to two lovely young married girls. They seemed rather anxious and were clutching their shoulder bags with real intent. I enquired if they were all right. I must have looked trustworthy as each of them gave me a peek into their shoulder bag - a dog in one and a cat in the other. They had drugged their pets for the journey. With my promise not to tell anyone, we all had a secret.

I spent several weeks in Perth with my daughter and my grandchildren, and eventually Mal joined me. When the time came to return to Darwin we had to apply for a permit to do so.

Malcolm and I made Darwin our home for fourteen years. We did all the fishing and camping trips we had planned to do. Darwin certainly delivered adventure in more ways than I could have ever imagined. I'll be 90 years old this year, and my sight is fading, but the memories of that fateful night, the memories of Cyclone Tracy, are permanently etched in my mind.

Joyce Sprunt.

Photograph by Ramon Williams

CHAPTER 28 – LEESA PLESTER

My name is Leesa Plester, and I'm Joyce Sprunt's granddaughter. This is my memory of Cyclone Tracy.

I was seven years old when Cyclone Tracy flattened Darwin in 1974. My Nanna Joy and my Poppa Mal had only just moved to Darwin for my grandfather's work.

My grandmother Joyce, who's turning 90 at her next birthday, is a survivor of Cyclone Tracy. And although I was only seven years old at the time I'll never forget that Christmas Day of 1974. My mother was frantic for news of her parents. I remember, like it was yesterday, going out to the Perth Domestic Airport and standing at the cyclone fence waiting for my Nan to disembark from the belly of that air force aeroplane.

Her many stories of that night and the following months in Darwin have moved me, sometimes to tears. When I visited her for Christmas 2014 she gave my almost

13-year-old daughter a cardigan. This was a handmade crocheted cardigan crafted by a samaritan, a cyclone Tracey survivor. She made one for all the women in her street, it was the only thing my Grandmother owned at the time. My grandmother has lived in several locations since Cyclone Tracy; it's clear that the cardigan, which no longer fits and is no longer fashionable, has been kept safe for the journey. Such a precious gift to my daughter, representative of a terrible moment in time, but also of the community Aussie spirit that pulls us through.

Leesa Plester.

Photograph by Ramon Williams

Photograph by Ramon Williams

CHAPTER 29 – WAYNE STUBBS

In December 1974 I can remember my last two days of school in the library on the first floor. You could see the sea over Nightcliff. There was a huge waterspout, which we had never seen before, and you could see the change in the weather as clouds from the wet season were rolling in as usual. There was a lot of fuss about the waterspout, but never was there any mention of a cyclone.

About four days before Christmas the weather became still, and the indigenous people were saying, "A big wind is coming." They knew, as they were leaving Darwin, and it was almost like they disappeared, so whether you believed them or not, they were spot on. The birds had all gone; as to where they had gone, they were nowhere to be seen. And you could bet they went for a reason.

On Christmas Eve all the boys and girls were excited that Santa was coming tonight, and there was joy and people planning their Christmas parties. I was home with my sister as usual tormenting me, doing the usual brother-sister silly fights about nothing. So I turned on the TV and I saw that there was a cyclone warning and it could hit within 24 hours. I was only nine years old, and I tried to ring Mum and Dad with no luck, so being the boy of the house I decided to take charge and pack away any loose items like chairs and anything else around the yard so they would not be missiles. In the schools in Darwin you learn about cyclones and how to prepare for one.

My mother and dad arrived home, and were very happy with all the things that I had done. They sat my sister and me down and told us that a cyclone was going to hit that night, and they called it Tracy. By about 8 p.m. the wind was howling and the rain was horizontal and starting to get really scary. We listened to the radio for updates, and the cyclone was getting closer to the coast of Darwin. I went to bed and could not sleep, as the noise was getting so loud you could not hear yourself think. At about 1:30 a.m. the house was shaking, so we decided to go into my room, and after about ten minutes the brick wall was shaking and it looked like it was going to fall in, so we ran out of there and into the middle room. As soon as we ran out of the room and closed the door the wall collapsed, so we huddled on the floor.

It all went quiet, and we knew at this point the eye of the cyclone was above us, and everything was dead still. You could hear the people next door crying, and knew that nobody was safe, and what was next, that was the big question. This lasted for about an hour, and then Mother Nature unleashed all her fury. This cyclone had rain, hail, fireballs, devastating winds king tides and lightning, which nobody could have prepared for. You just had your family.

Merry Christmas, said Mum and Dad. Then, sounding like a freight train with a deafening noise roaring towards us, the house out the back of us exploded apart and a piece of roof, a twenty foot sheet of iron, went through our house like a spear from one end to the other. At that point Dad and my sister headed under the bed, and I looked up and saw the roof take off into the night. I looked at my dad under the bed, thinking I should join them when Dad reached out and grabbed Mum by the hair and dragged her under the bed, as Mum could not move. I then tried to dig myself a position at the end of the bed; there were books to pull out first so I could get in. We also had four small dogs and a cat under the same single bed, so there was not much room. The bed was shaking and we were lying in six inches of freezing cold water. We thought we were going to drown, but could not move.

About three hours later we heard someone outside calling out for help, but could not get out to see who it was. At 6:30 a.m. the cyclone had passed, so we crawled out from under the bed, pushing bricks and gyproc away so we could get out. To our amazement, from our back verandah we could see Nightcliff Beach. There were a few walls left up, and all we could see was total devastation.

People were wandering around in a daze, in a city that had been wiped out. People were saying it would never be built again. I looked around the house, through the broken walls, over shattered glass, and remembered it was Christmas Day and wondered if Santa made it to Darwin. I looked for our Christmas tree, but it had blown away with all our presents, so I looked at Mum and said, at least we did not die. All we had was the wet clothes we were wearing. Dad had a footy jumper that was dry in a cupboard, so I put that on. As we were looking around in disbelief all our neighbours dug themselves out. The person who had called out to Dad during the night was there. He had taken cover in the neighbours' car, and told us that his wife had been killed by a piece of iron. So, what do we do now? We had little food, only water from the bathtub, and no power. We had to dig for clothes to dry out, as we had lost almost everything we owned.

I went down to the shop just down the road, and the owner was there. Outside the shop was a cockatoo with not a feather on his body, swearing like a champion. The cockatoo in the cage had blown four kilometres away and was lucky to be alive, so no wonder he was cranky, but he had found his owner. The shop owner said to me, "take anything you want," so being a young boy being told that, I thought all the lollies in there would be mine, but I thought about it and instead of being greedy I decided to take a box of deodorant for mum cause she needs to smell good, and I wanted my dogs to eat so I took dog food for them and did not forget my cat, her name was Mary and she received food also. The shop owner and I remained friends, as he remembers what a good boy I was doing the right thing that day.

This cyclone, Tracy, did not have mercy on anything. Even all the leaves were ripped off the trees. It was a category 5, and to this day there is no proof of how fast the wind speed was. The weather barometer at the wharf had been wiped out, and the new one at the airport was also blown away. You can compare other cyclones with data or photos and you will see how bad it really was.

As the news said, CYCLONE TRACY WAS A BITCH!

We were evacuated on a Qantas 707, just my sister and myself, to family in Sydney, along with other children. If you want to know what it is like to be in a cyclone, go the museum in Darwin and see the cyclone display. Go into the room, sit on the floor and listen to it twice and close your eyes. I hope this gives you an insight to what it was like.

Left: Wayne Stubbs.

THE SYDNEY HOS

Photograph by Ramon Williams

Photograph by Neil Williams

CHAPTER 30 – SAMANTHA TROTT

Samantha Trott (née Mackie).

My parents arrived with their family, three children including myself, between the ages of thirteen and nine, in February of 1974. The prospect of bringing their young family to a vibrant and fast-growing town was great, and Dad was a meat and stock inspector working under the Federal government, so when he was asked if he would like a transfer in early 1973, both he and Mum were very eager. They lived in Sandalwood Crescent, Nightcliff, till they were allocated a brand new Elevated Housing commission home in the new suburb of Tiwi in early October.

They settled into life in this wonderful city immediately, with the friendly people and relaxed lifestyle. Work was available, and colleagues, schoolchildren and neighbours were welcoming and warm.

The weather was a new challenge to us all, as we had

lived our lives till then in a sleepy country town called Nourlunga in South Australia.

On Christmas Eve I had visited the only cinema in the city and watched a movie called "the Dove", then caught the buses home; the final bus went only as far as Casuarina shopping centre, and I then had to walk home the rest of the way to Annaburroo Crescent. I arrived to find mum frantically preparing for yet another cyclone threat, packing things away into cupboards and the shed, and filling the bath and as many containers as she could find with water, and I helped her reluctantly, because this had happened many times before; I knew the routine. My brothers and father returned home later that afternoon after a day of fun on the motorbikes, and joined in to help also.

As the evening progressed, so did the strength and ferocity of the cyclone.

Our house fell apart around us.

First the louvres on the opposite side of the wind direction would not stay open, and we all understood that we had to keep them open, otherwise the house would just explode with us in it. I remember trying to hold the louvres open, and not having the strength to; the louvres slammed shut so hard that they smashed into a thousand pieces, I then watched with amazement the glass being sucked out of the house. This is when I became a little frightened (that I had to hold on for dear life to something so that I didn't get sucked out of the house too).

We were in one of the end rooms of the house till we began to see what seemed light moonlight, but was actually constant lightning across the sky, through a crack that was forming where the ceiling met the wall in the room, and ran out to the corridor because we knew that everything would be sucked out when the wall came off. We got out in time to see the beds being blown away into oblivion, along with everything else in that room and the other room next to it, and that was both my brothers' and my rooms gone.

Next we went into Mum's and Dad's room (where we very rarely were allowed) and huddled under the bed and in the corner of the room. At one point while there I remember feeling a sense of the house being lifted, then watched the roof go off in the wind, at the same time feeling the whole floor bump back down again with an almighty bang, it nearly deafened me. A wardrobe then fell onto the bed which Mum and my younger brother were under, Mum was stuck, and we had to drag her out after trying in vain to empty the wardrobe, throwing out books and clothing to lighten its weight.

We all then went to the bathroom, because we had heard that this was the strongest room in the house because of all the pipes in the walls, but when the door was opened there was too much flying glass and so we then went into the corridor where we stayed till morning.

Throughout the night we as a family became closer, both physically and emotionally, reassuring each other through the evening that we were still okay, by just answering each other when one of us asked in the black, wet, howling, windy night, "Mum, are you okay?" "Dad, are you okay?" "Yes," came the reply each time. These answers were as warm as the woollen blankets that we had found and huddled under for the night.

Photograph by Ramon Williams

The feeling of being stunned by the bare landscape the next morning is something I have never experienced since, knowing that we had lost almost all our personal possessions was meaningless to us all. We had made it through the night and we were all still alive, and still had each other!

We're alive! But was anyone else?

Looking out of what remained of our house, the landscape looked a lot like the pictures you see of the old World War II zones in Europe. The bush area that was nearby to where we live (which is now called Tracy village) was all bare tree trunks sticking up out of the ground, not a single leaf left on them. Clothing and mattresses were up in the branches, looking almost like a makeshift Christmas tree. I remember making some sort of comment about the similarities to Mum and having her get cranky with me over it. I later found out that Mum had noticed that what I was pointing to was her debutante dress strung high up in the tree about 150 metres away, and she had seen it earlier but not said anything to anyone, more than likely because she understood there were more important things to be concerned about, like where were we all going to sleep, and how were we all going to eat.

We began to see other people moving around in the yards of other houses nearby, so we weren't alone, people were waving at us across the six-block distance between us. Tiwi was a brand new suburb then, and houses were being constructed in clusters of six or so together. Of the other houses in our little cluster, two residents had gone south for Christmas, and these houses had literally exploded, because of being entirely locked up, and the pressure difference between inside and outside the house during the storm, there were only floor boards where elevated houses used to be, and the belongings that were inside were everywhere. Feeling that I really had to do something to help these people who weren't home to pick up their stuff, I began identifying the things that I knew belonged to them and us and other neighbours and retuning it to what was left of their house. Forgetting that I didn't have footwear and was still in my PJ's, I guess it was just something to do, because I just didn't know what I should do, having never found myself in a situation like this before in my life. Well this lasted for all of about half an hour before I put my foot deep down into some mud and cut it on something, and it was a pretty good cut too. That stopped that bit of fun, so I then had to sit and hold on to that foot. I guess that was when it really struck me, we were literally stranded in this sea of rubble, stuff everywhere, with people walking around in it just looking around themselves, then stopping for a minute or two, then taking a few more steps and stopping again, not saying anything, just looking at the ground or at the distance, in the silence, the eerie silence.

Dad had been trying to get the car (a pale blue 1966 Ford Falcon) started, and after a little time turning it over, "Ole Agatha", as I used to call her, had started up. It would have been the best sound I heard that morning, and it broke the silence. Dad wasn't too sure how far we were going to get, but he said we had to try and get to a shelter of some sort, just in case Tracy turned around and came back. And some of the neighbours wanted us to let the authorities know that they weren't able to get out because their cars weren't starting. So we slowly made our way up the street, stopping occasionally and getting out to move stuff that was on the road, and going up on the footpath at times because stuff couldn't be moved. I remember making comments about all the power poles that looked like they had all just melted, because they were all bent down and lying on the ground blocking people's driveways, and how every now and then there was a house that looked like it hadn't been touched, surrounded by a sea of stuff. It took Dad quite a long time to make it to Casuarina, where I noticed there were police cars parked amongst the rubble in the car park, and men walking around with rifles Later I found out that there had been a lot of looters trying to take food from the shops, and the police were arranging for the food to go to the local shelters that were at the high schools. Dad decided to go to see some friends in Jingili that had just had a new baby, Libby & Peter Brown, and my friend Alice Parschen lived nearby to them, so I was happy with that; I would be able to say hello to her too.

Dad turned off Trower road and onto Rothdale road, then all of a sudden the car stopped moving with a sudden jerk, with the motor still running. Dad got out to have a look. He found that some electrical cable had got tangled around the rear axle of the car, but with some help from some really friendly people who lived nearby, it got quickly untangled, and we were on our way again. When we made it to our friends in Jingili, we noticed that no one was home at any of the houses that we knew, and their houses looked pretty bad. I remember being really sad, and crying because I didn't know what had happened to Alice. I don't remember much then, till we got to Nightcliff High School, this was where we all ended up going, probably because that was the only shelter we knew of that we were familiar with, because my brother Jock had been at this school.

The family stayed at the shelter for four days before being evacuated. In that time, we were reunited with many friends that we had made in the previous year while living in Sandalwood Crescent. I remember hearing gunshots every now and then when dogs were being killed, and seeing a backhoe being bogged in the high school oval, when it was on its way to dig a pit for perishables that needed to be buried, and for a pit toilet. The nearest Salvos' second hand clothing depot had dropped off clothing, but there was no underwear, which was all I really wanted apart from something warm. I found a jumper, bright purple with a yellow and red stripe across the chest, and I put that on straight away over my purple and white checkered PJs. I was happy then, all warmed up with the most beautiful jumper that I had found. The family slept in one of the classrooms, on the floor with about four other families, and helped offer blankets and cook meals for the people organising the shelters.

Our family were advised that we were all able to get on a bus to go to the airport after being at the shelter for four days. Dad had decided to drive the car down to Adelaide, so he would be going in a couple of days. The ride in the bus was really quiet, people riding with us were just looking out the windows not saying anything at all, some were crying quietly. I was really sad because I didn't know if any of my friends were still alive, and I didn't know if I would ever see them again or be coming back to Darwin. I didn't know what I wanted to do, but I was happy that we were going to our family in South Australia again. The plane trip was different, there were seven people sitting in the seats that normally could only take three people, seat belts were put on at the longest length around two or three people at a time, the Ansett hostesses, still dressed in their orange uniforms with little orange pillbox hats, were giving out cartons of orange juice and chips. I talked a lot with other kids on the plane about how we hid from the storm, till we arrived in Adelaide.

Adelaide was cold and wet and it was about 8:00 at night when we arrived. We were given blankets by Red Cross volunteers who were at the bottom of the stairs as we got off the plane, then asked to sit in a waiting area that had been set aside with rope around it for Darwin evacuees. Mum had a talk with Normie Rowe, who was visiting and just talking to people, and we were given toasted sandwiches to eat and hot Milo to drink. There was a huge crowd of people just standing around the ropes, just looking at us evacuees, and I remember feeling really awkward about being stared at by strangers. Then in the crowd I spotted Grandma Cooke (Dad's mum) and then, understanding that we were going to go, went around saying goodbye to all the other kids that I had made friends with on the plane trip, saying 'I'll see you back in Darwin'. Then I hopped in the car with Grandma and Uncle Vern, then the last thing I remember was seeing the display building with the first airplane flown to Australia by Sir Charles Kingsford-Smith, which was at the gates of the Adelaide Airport in those days.

Six Days Later

I was on the bus from Kadina to Berry, where my Aunty Steph and Uncle Graham lived, and I was really looking forward to being with my favorite aunt again. Steph got to the bus stop about two minutes after I got off the bus, and kept apologising to me for being late, but I didn't care. I was safe now with Steph.

There is still a six day gap in my life where, forty years later, I still don't remember a thing.

Relatives have told me that I went to the family farm in Agery in the York peninsula and stayed.

I have no recollection of this, and family say that I was not myself, normally being into everything on the farm, I just slept, or just sat and stared at nothing. When I was asked what I wanted to do, the only thing I would say was, "I want to stay with Steph". So that's where I went.

This was the best thing that could have happened. I spent about a week with her, I have memories of spending the day climbing up and down the 100 or so steps out the back of her home which backed onto the river Murray, and sitting in the huge Mulberry tree (as big as a mature African Mahogany tree) just eating mulberries, and then making mulberry jam, apricot jam, and tomato relish, and spending time with her and her sons, who were just babies at the time. These are memories that I have and will treasure.

I had surfaced from the haze!

The family had been given permission to return to Darwin in two months, but school was about to start again. Samantha Trott.

Samantha Trott returned to Darwin Mid 1975 and has continued to live there since her return. She now lives at Dundee Forrest, 120 km south west of Darwin.

Having previously been a company director, and chef, Samantha has retired and is now a poultry and game keeper. Below: Samantha Trott.

CHAPTER 31 – TRACEY COLLINS

I wrote this at age 15, for a school project in the year following the cyclone. At the time of the cyclone I was almost fifteen, and my brothers Craig and Martin were thirteen and eleven respectively.

It was Christmas Eve and we were all excited, as we would be leaving for a trip by car to Queensland early in the morning. As we were leaving early on Christmas Day, we had decided to open our Christmas presents that night. About seven o'clock we had had tea and cleared up, so we sat in the lounge and began to open our gifts.

We kept the radio going quietly as there was a

cyclone somewhere near Darwin, and precautions and the latest news on its whereabouts were being broadcast often. This was not the first cyclone warning this season; there had been several others which had all passed Darwin and hadn't affected us. We didn't take much notice of the repeated news and warnings until the excitement of unwrapping our presents had died down. We turned up the wireless to listen to the next report, thinking that the cyclone would have begun to turn away by now, but instead it was still heading towards Darwin and building up strength. At this stage we weren't terribly worried. I think we were still expecting it to turn away any minute, but we still followed the broadcast precautions, and took all our ornaments and pictures down and put them in cupboards. Our Christmas presents were all put away safely, too. We had only put our Christmas tree up that morning; it was all white, and brilliant coloured satin balls hung on it, it was so pretty that we decided not to take it down.

The rain had been falling steadily since about lunchtime; it was now ten o'clock and still pouring, and the wind was becoming uncomfortably strong. The trees were bending double with every gust.

Ever since we had been in Darwin we had decided on sitting in the car under the house if ever a cyclone hit, and at about ten thirty that's exactly what we did. My two brothers, who'd already gone to bed, got up and dressed again. We took our pillows and a few blankets, some biscuits and a container of water. At the time we had a Holden station wagon, and dad put the back seat down so we could get some sleep. He had the front seat and Mum, my two brothers and I made ourselves comfortable as best we could in the back. We had to keep the windows up, and it soon became pretty hot and stuffy.

By about midnight, we realized we were experiencing the force of a cyclone. Reports continued over the wireless. The car was fairly soundproof, but if we wound down the windows a fraction the sound was incredible, a deafening roar and the continual sound of smashing glass. Every now and then we dared to half sit up and look out the windows. We couldn't see much until a flash of sheet lightning would light up the whole sky and we could make out objects flying and crashing about, but really it was beyond our imagination exactly what was happening.

At about a quarter past two everything quietened down and was still, and we noticed the wireless had gone dead. If it hadn't been for all the broadcast warnings we would have thought it was all over, but we knew that this was only the eye passing. Dad quickly ran around and had a look at the yard; when he came back he told us that our shed from down the back yard had completely gone and our clothes line was a twisted mass of wire and metal. The fly wire had ripped off and was draped over the stairs. Mum was rather concerned about the electricity wires hanging down from the house, but fortunately the electricity had been turned off earlier.

About ten minutes after it had stopped, the wind returned with equal force, only this time everything had been loosened by the first half, and was now free to be carried and thrown about by the terrifying force of Cyclone Tracy. The car rocked and heaved continually, and was struck by sheets of flying corrugated iron and other air-borne objects which we thought would crash through the car windows any minute, but by pure luck the windows remained unbroken. The horrible roaring and crashing sound continued on through the morning. It began to die down as it became light. Soon it was safe to sit up and look about us, and we were gradually working out what the different mangled objects strewn about the yard were. The most upsetting discovery was our piano, which lay smashed and waterlogged on the remains of our lounge room wall in the driveway. The piano had belonged to Mum's parents, and was a really beautiful piece of furniture.

About seven o'clock it was daylight and the cyclone had passed. Everything was grey and silent. It seemed as though the whole town was dead. We climbed out of the car and looked about us. None of us broke down and cried or went hysterical at the sight; I don't think we quite believed what we saw.

Not a leaf was left on the trees, and every bit of ground available was covered with twisted, broken objects and enough scrap metal to last a company for a hundred years! Our orange lounge room curtains were found ripped, wet and mud stained amongst the rubble in the middle of the road. Our first reaction was to clean up, senseless though it was. Walking around the yard picking out belongings, I came across our beautiful white Christmas tree, now bent and shapeless lying in the mud and rubble.

Coloured satin balls faded by the rain could be found scattered about the yard. I suddenly remembered it was Christmas morning, although we were sure not in a

Christmassy mood.

When we dared to go upstairs and discover what damage lay there, the sight was equally shocking. About an inch of muddy water covered the floor throughout the house, and as the floors were just wooden boards it wasn't long before they began to buckle and swell. The ceiling and walls were starting to sag under the weight of the water trapped in the roof, so we poked a few holes in the ceiling to allow the water to drain away. We looked in the lounge room first. Nothing remained dry, the record player was upside down on the floor but we couldn't find our TV; it was found later in the yard with only a leg missing. The kitchen was a quagmire of mud and glass, and our new kitchen curtains had blown out of the window and got hooked up on the roof. Part of the bathroom wall had smashed in, and the linen cupboard doors were ripped off. As we walked through the house we were seeing but not believing, it was too much to take in all at once.

My bedroom was a wreck, my bed was coated in smashed glass, all my posters were lying wet and ripped on the floor and all my clothes were wet through. The sun remained behind a colourless sky and not a breeze stirred, so we couldn't dry anything. When we realized it was hopeless trying to clean up we decided to go and see how our friends were. We drove to our friends who had just carpeted and redecorated their home.

I think the sight of them and their house was more upsetting than what had happened to our house; everything they had done was just ruined. After talking to them for a while they said they'd cooked a Christmas turkey the night before, and would we like to share it with them; as we hadn't cooked anything and there was no electricity, we accepted. They came back to our house and we got things together to have a Christmas dinner. Mum and Dad's room was the driest, so we set everything up in there. We put up a card table and a couple of TV trays and covered them with some Christmas placemats. Mum used a small gas ring to make some gravy, peas and potatoes. When it was all ready we forgot the devastation around us and enjoyed a simple but delicious Christmas dinner.

In the afternoon the sun came out and we began to feel tired from our sleepless night, and so each of us found a dry spot and attempted to get some sleep. Mum and Dad found their room quite dry enough to sleep in, and one of my brothers fell asleep on the couch in the lounge while the other, never too tired to play, went next door to try out his new roller skates. I settled down on an airbed in my brother's room. After about ten minutes I noticed water dripping from the ceiling, and from then on it seemed to get louder and louder. Deciding it was hopeless trying to get any sleep, I went and sat on the stairs and thought. A slow hour passed and I was still thinking, what was going to happen, would Darwin ever be the same again? Would they rebuild it? What were we as a family going to do about the situation? Then I thought about the hundreds who had lost everything, including members of families.

I was very grateful that our family were all safe and unhurt. All of a sudden my thoughts were interrupted; one of our neighbours had come over to see if we were all okay. He said his family were staying at one of the primary schools, and he suggested we did too, as we would be able to find out what was going on and could receive food, etc. When Mum and Dad woke up I told them what I'd been told, and we got some bedding and food and set off to Ludmilla Primary School. The co-operation amongst the people was fantastic; everyone helped each other in any way they could. Towards the evening the Army came with bundles of blankets, Hurricane lanterns and fresh drinking water.

Dad had heard that there was a creek that people were bathing and cooling off in, so he suggested we go and have a swim before it got dark. It was such a relief to cool off after a hot depressing day. We had managed to dry some clothes, and returned to the school refreshed and ready to have some tea. After tea Mum and I went down to the office where people were coming to register that they were safe, and to say where they wanted to be evacuated to. Mum took over from the person there, as he had been taking names for several hours. It was very depressing to see the people that came in to register. Many could barely walk because of injuries, some were followed by dazed children and others couldn't talk properly through tears of grief and shock.

At about eleven o'clock the office was closed up and everyone settled for the night. Several people took turns sitting up and listening to the wireless for the latest information. At about four in the morning we were woken by shouting and banging on the windows. I wondered what the heck it was, and got up to find out. It was a group of policemen come to tell us that evacuation had started, and all those wanting to be evacuated should be prepared to leave any time now. Mum and Dad wouldn't leave, as they had to clear the house, sort our belongings, etc., but they wanted us to leave as soon as possible, as there was a great risk of a disease outbreak. My two brothers and I had a suitcase between us packed with some clean, dry clothes. We had some breakfast and went to join the crowd of mothers and children waiting to be taken to the airport. Hours and hours passed, and several truckloads of women and children were taken off to the airport for evacuation.

By lunchtime we had still not left, and were exhausted by the heat and frustration. We were just about ready to give up hope when another truck pulled up. It was the last one for the day, they said, so Dad got us on that one. We said a quick goodbye to our parents and told them we would head for Adelaide and meet them there.

The sight of the crowd at the airport was frightening, nearly all the people were women and children all in a state of shock and many injured. We climbed out of the truck and joined the crowd waiting to leave. There were over a thousand people, and every time a plane landed, hundreds of south Australian police had to keep pushing the crowd back. After about three planes had landed and taken several hundred people, it was beginning to get unbearably hot standing out on the tarmac just waiting. It was about 35 degrees Celsius, our faces were sunburnt and my head was throbbing Would we ever get out of this depressing mess?

We got talking to this girl, she was about 20 and was visiting from America, and we were still talking to her when dad came down to the airport to see if we'd left.

When he found us still there he was worried that we wouldn't get away before dark, so Rose (the girl we were talking to) said that she would stay with us till we got to Adelaide, as she was in no hurry to get anywhere. This allowed Dad to relax, and he said he and Mum would drive down with all our gear and probably see us in about two weeks. He then said goodbye and left.

We managed to get on the next plane that landed; it was a RAAF Hercules and was going to Sydney, where we would catch another plane to Adelaide. It was no luxury jet, but who was worried, at last we were going somewhere. After about two hours of flying we landed at Mt Isa for refuelling. We all got off the plane and went into the terminal where we were given food and hot drinks; it was really great, volunteers had made hot dishes for us and brought out clothes for us to change into if we needed. Craig and Martin, my two brothers, and I had a good feed and some hot coffee. We then found a jumper each, as we were only wearing light shorts and T-shirts and found it was getting a bit cold. An hour later - about 10 p.m. - we boarded the plane again and continued on our way to Sydney.

As we were passing over Queensland, one of the plane propellers broke down, and a message was sent round that we would be landing in Charleville, a small town in Queensland. We had to spend the night in Charleville. Half of us were taken to a small hotel, and the rest were billeted amongst the people of the town. At the hotel we were given something to eat and a hot drink; we were then taken to our rooms and those that wanted to could have a shower, which

I did. After a hot shower I got into some clean clothes and sank into a soft bed, and I was asleep before my head hit the pillow.

In the morning we were served a nourishing breakfast of cereal, fried eggs, bacon, tomatoes and toast. News came that the plane wouldn't be fixed until about two in the afternoon. Meanwhile the town had rallied and gathered clothes and comics for us, and the hotel had opened their pool table so the kids could play without having to pay. That kept Craig and Martin busy for the morning. Lunchtime came, and we had salad rolls and iced cordial.

While in Charleville I took the opportunity to ring our grandparents in Adelaide to tell them we were all okay and that we were on our way down.

At two o'clock we were taken to the airport, and waited half an hour before boarding the plane again. After we had been flying for a couple of hours it got quite cold, and we were glad of the jumpers we had.

We landed in Sydney about six o'clock, and were taken to a big open shed where there were hundreds of other evacuees. The Sydney airport was huge, and there were thousands of people and Police and Ambulance cars were everywhere. They took our names and details, and we told them we wanted to go to Adelaide, but they said we would probably have to stay there overnight. I felt a bit scared then, and my youngest brother started crying. By this time I was ready to cry, I'd had enough, I didn't want to spend another night in a strange place. I wished my parents were there then, to take over and work out what we were going to do next, but they weren't, and I was determined we were going to get to Adelaide that night. I started asking some of the people in charge if we could get on a plane to Adelaide that night, but I was just told they were all full. I kept on asking around until one man I asked found out for us that there were just enough vacancies left for us on a TAA jet that was leaving for Adelaide at about nine o'clock.

It was the best news I'd heard for three days! We were taken to a terminal where we were given a ticket each and a label we had to pin on us, bearing our names and the word ADELAIDE.

I was really happy now, and Craig and Martin were restless with excitement. At last we were on our way to what would be home for quite a while!

The year in Adelaide following Cyclone Tracy was traumatic, with us all missing our old homes, lifestyle and friends, and feeling culture shock!

City life and people in Adelaide were so different from laid-back, warm, tropical Darwin!

Nothing was really discussed, though, and we just got on with it.

Dad had been transferred to Quarantine in Adelaide, a very different Quarantine job from the one he had at Darwin airport and wharf! The Education department had transferred Mum to a teacher's aide position in Adelaide, also a very different work environment from that of her job at Parap Primary School in Darwin!

I was lucky enough to go back to Darwin and stay with a friend, in the September school holidays. When I returned to Adelaide and spoke excitedly to the family about how Darwin was all cleaned up and liveable, it set the wheels in motion, and we returned to Darwin to live in time for Christmas in 1975!

Mum and Dad were transferred again in their jobs.

We were given a Government house again, with Dad's job, but this time out at Anula, in a new, "cyclone proof" design!

Mum was given a Teacher's Aide job at Wanguri, closer to where we lived now than Parap Primary. My brother Craig and I went back to Darwin High, and Martin, the youngest, went back to Parap Primary in time for grade 7 with Mr Stiller. All seemed right with the world again for a time, but the cracks soon appeared, and it became obvious that Mum and Dad were not happy. Darwin, for them, was no longer the same.

While they were grateful for the relatively smooth transition back to life in the Territory, the solid concrete house out in the northern suburbs was like a different planet compared to our established tropical gardens and high-set house in Parap, down the road from Fannie Bay rocks, where dad and the boys would fish at every opportunity.

By December 1978, Mum and Dad announced that Dad had got a transfer to Mackay, Queensland, and that they and the boys were leaving.

I was 18 and had a good job at the ANZ bank, and decided to stay in Darwin, moving in with friends.

The following year I met my husband, Stewart, who was from New Zealand, and had moved to Darwin to work in the uranium mines of Jabiru and Narbalek. Within a few years Stewart and I married and moved to Mackay in Queensland.

We settled well in Mackay. Craig and Martin became professional reef fishermen, Dad continued to work in Quarantine for a time before becoming an oyster picker, and mum was a teacher's aide for many years before becoming a telephonist with Telstra.

Sadly, Dad passed away in 2006 with a heart attack. He was 66.

Stewart and I had three children, a girl and two boys. Our daughter and son-in-law have recently blessed us with a granddaughter.

Life is good, and we feel reasonably confident when cyclones are hovering close these days, because in 1988, when we moved here permanently, we built a solid masonry block home and made our ensuite bathroom a cyclone shelter by putting in a concrete ceiling, effectively making it like a concrete box! I definitely had some influence in that decision! Tracey Turner (nee Collins).

Below, a recent photo with Tracey and her husband, Stewart, with their children.

CHAPTER 32 – TIM WEST

Above: Cunjevoi Crescent Nightcliff

Still Here - Just! A lifetime spent in the Top End is full of near-death experiences ('NDEs'), but the one that holds the most vivid and emotional memories is that night in '74 that stole my childhood innocence and changed my world view forever!

I awoke about midnight, the last of the household to be jolted awake. I remember putting my feet down onto the floorboards and thinking I had stepped into a pool. The several inches of cold water immediately heightened my senses, and I was instantly wide awake, and acutely aware that the situation was not good. I opened my bedroom door to the hallway on our elevated house, to a scene of organised chaos as my parents were barking orders to my elder siblings to get everyone into the bathroom. Mum and Dad and the elder siblings had been through a bad cyclone in Port Vila (Vanuatu) in the fifties, so they knew what to

302

expect, but they had no idea of what was about to unfold. I remember huddling under the bathroom wash basin with my sisters, with Mum periodically popping her head in the door to check on us.

We had all grown up with pretty severe wet season storms, but this was different. The sound was unique; the constant base roar was like being in close proximity to heavy machinery at full revs, interspersed with the shrill screams of an enraged banshee. But what was really alarming was the relentless crashing, banging and smashing that was all around us. To put it in local terms, to say we were 'gunnaring' ourselves was an understatement!

Mum stuck her head in the door and snapped, "C'mon, we're going." Where, was my immediate thought, but you never questioned Mother, she was a teacher! We immediately assembled at the edge of the hallway and looked left to see our father and elder brother with their backs against the bulging plate glass sliding doors of the living room. Mum screamed at them to get the hell out of there as we made our way down the hallway to my bedroom. As we made it to my doorway I turned to see my dad and brother coming down the hallway with the house exploding and disappearing behind them. I ran and jumped on my bed as the family assembled and caught their breath. We had only been in my bedroom a few minutes when everyone started staring above my head, with faces of sheer horror. I turned and looked up to see the top corner of the room cracking, and then the ceiling lifting and dropping like a set of gaping jaws. I was first to the door, "I ain't staying here!"

Dad barked the order, "Right! We are going downstairs, now! Hold onto each other and don't let go." Again I thought, how? That end of the house is gone and probably the stairs too! I realised we weren't going down the staircase as we hurriedly moved through our parents' bedroom to the fire escape. It took Dad and Steve all their might to push open the fire escape door and then hold it open, as we all huddled together on that little landing. Thinking back, we probably owe our lives to the huge Tamarind tree in our front yard, which shielded that end of the house from the seaward side. A remnant of the old Nightcliff market gardens, no doubt.

Dad immediately slid down the ladder, and my younger sister Vanda was lowered down to him. They disappeared into the darkness along the besser block wall that ran along underneath the end of the house. Out of the darkness I heard my name called, and I was lowered down by my brother with a vice-like grip on my wrists. I felt my dad grab my ankles, and then heard the piercing scream of my little sister. Dad immediately released my ankles and was gone. Sheer terror arrived for the first time! Where was Vanda, where was Dad? The next thing I knew I was airborne on a gust of wind, flying like Superman, with my brother frantically holding onto me. As I fell back down against the steel ladder of the fire escape I felt Dad's hands grab my ankles again. Vanda was okay; she had just panicked being left alone, away from the rest of us, as any seven-year-old would.

We all finally made it down from the disintegrating house and slid along the protective concrete wall and under the house, to our final safe haven. Dad, being a carpenter's son, loved his timber, and had recently completed a solid Jarrah storage area for his downstairs bar. It was back against the block wall, had a vinyl curtain along the front of it, and was tall enough for an adult to sit under. It had all the Christmas beverages stored under there and most of the family had bomb-racks or cartons of beer to sit on; me, I got the crate of Quench bottles. I was on the end closest to the wind, and was the least clothed as well. I only had a pair of jocks on, and like many that night, I experienced the coldest night of my life, and I've stood on the summit of Zugspitz! But ay! I was still alive! Just!

Once Dad had us safely under the bench, he ventured out to see if the storage shed and workshop down the other end of the house could offer us any better shelter. He was probably just scouting out the possibilities and constantly assessing more options; his RAAF training, no doubt. As he was lucky to weigh 55 kg wringing wet, as he got to the end of the breezeway brickwork he was swept out from under the house, to everyone's horror! More sheer terror! Luckily the Hills Hoist caught him, and he crawled his way back under the house, to our relief.

As Mum and Dad were cyclone survivors, Mum started discussing tidal surge, much to Dad's disdain. This had caused the greatest loss of life in the Port Vila cyclone, so Mum was rather concerned, because we could taste the salt water in the horizontal rain that permeated everything that night. I remember this scaring me to the core, because I knew we would have a hard time surviving the raging floodwater; even as a 9-year-old I understood how powerful water was, from swimming in Freshwater (Rapid Creek) in the wet season, and bodysurfing the dumpers at Nightcliff Beach. Mum kept raising it, too; "I can still taste salt water, Ray!" She needed an answer to the question of what we would do. It was obviously worrying Dad until he thought it through. As always, his comeback was calculated, precise and factual. "It's a bloody low tide, woman; stop worrying, it ain't going to happen".

I remember sitting on those mongrel bottles, shivering and falling into a trance-like state from the incessant howling of the wind and the flashing of lightning. Amazingly, there was no thunder; it was drowned out by the relentless roar, no doubt. I became captivated as to what I would see in the next flash of lightning from my protected little hidey-hole. Furniture, fridges, and endless sheets of corrugated iron were it, until the eye was upon us. The silence was surreal and the yelling started from around the neighbourhood. 'Is everyone okay,' was the common shout, with Dad shouting back, "it's only the eye, stay put, it's coming back!" We heard a vehicle, and that same enquiry from Paddy Peckover, the local fireman. I will never forget Dad's dry Aussie reply. "Yeah, we're alright, but you bloody won't be if you don't get back under cover!"

Those short ten minutes of relief were glorious. Then that bitch Tracy started again, from the other direction. With what seemed like even more fury and determination. I was now seeing what seemed like great chunks of houses flying through the air, in the intermittent lightning flashes. It all seemed like it was never going to end until everything was gone. I started to think about my mates as I sat there in sheer terror, shivering my bony little arse off! Were they all right, did they get under cover like us? This preoccupation with seeing them again kept me occupied until the first rays of dawn appeared, and the raging hell of that mega-storm started to abate.

Dad and Steve climbed out of our shelter and ventured out to the front yard, Dad saying "everyone stay put!" As if; I followed them out a few minutes later to a scene that is indelibly embedded in my psyche. I looked out towards the sea and there was nothing left! Just piles of rubble and bits of house everywhere! The trees! Where were the trees? Not a leaf in sight, just skeletons of what had been lush tropical vegetation twelve hours before. My mates! Where were my mates Joey, Danny and Pauly? I found out later that they had all bolted down the track earlier in the night, as most of the local mob did.

I turned and looked up towards the top of Cunjevoi Crescent. To my disbelief the Bones' and McIntoshes' houses were still standing, but everything else was flattened for as far as the eye could see. My next thought was the pets, and as we ventured out into the back yard a little 'yap-yap' came from the floorboards above. We turned around to see our six week old Corgi pup and cat peering out from under the collapsed bed in the parents' bedroom. Mum had shoved them under the bed as we went down the fire escape, and they had miraculously survived the onslaught. A single positive in a mountain of negatives! But ay! We were still alive! Just!

The neighbourhood slowly started to assemble in the Bones' lounge room. They kept all of the kids inside as the men scouted the wreckage to account for everyone. I vividly remember peering out the window, watching the men removing the body of the young naval officer from the house next to McIntosh's. They placed him in the back of an EH ute and brought his hysterical wife and young baby over to the Bones' house. The women hurriedly got her and her very blue baby warm. I remember Dad later commenting on how brave that man had been, as he died shielding his wife and baby in the bathtub.

There were many heroic stories like this that came out of Tracy, and every Christmas since I stop and pay respects to those that didn't make it, to the many lives cut short and the many families affected by the loss of a loved one. The words "Lest We Forget" resonate just as loudly for me regarding Tracy as they do for those great men that made the ultimate sacrifice for this country.

It will be at our peril if we do forget!

Tim West.

Photograph by Ramon Williams

CHAPTER 33 – ELEANOR GRAVES

At first this was just another cyclone warning. We'd had one a short time before. Cyclone Selma. My father had been required to accompany the Speaker of the Legislative Assembly to Canberra for meetings, and my mother stayed up most of the night playing cards with a friend, until news came through that Cyclone Selma was no longer a threat, and so school and normality resumed.

Not so for Tracy. School holidays had started and Christmas preparations had been completed. My father, a last-minute shopper, had left work just before closing time and bought presents for my mother and me from one of the electrical goods stores in Smith Street. They remained in the boot of his car. My mother and I had stored our gifts in the spare room. We had, this time, also put some spare clothes, some food, and a small bag of my trinkets in our unfinished brick tool shed underneath the house.

We lived in Fannie Bay, in a typical government

elevated house. Our house was what was commonly known as an "L-shape", and my parents had renovated it a few years beforehand by simply extending the lounge room and running a wide verandah along the new extension, with double doors forming an entrance to the main living area.

Our Christmas Eve was a little tense; we had TV, but it was the battery-operated radio that kept us up to date with what was happening with the cyclone. I went to bed, but when the power went out at about 10.30, I woke up, probably noticing the lack of movement of the ceiling fan. (A common complaint of Darwin people when they holiday in homes down south is that there is no air movement from fans!)

My parents had moved our dining table to the area which formed the right angle of the "L" of the house. This had greater structural integrity to it, having cupboards which backed onto the bathroom, with a small corridor which lead to the toilet. We then, along with our neighbour's dog Mandy, whom we were minding over the Christmas period, positioned ourselves under the table on an old eiderdown and cushions, with the radio and gaslight and a flagon of sherry.

Just as a toothache builds in intensity, so too did the winds, rain and noise. On one of my frequent trips to the toilet, I reported that the water had been sucked out, causing the toilet to whistle due to the low pressure.

During the first half of the cyclone, we sat under the table, listening to the howling wind, and with each gust of wind, the house shook, more violently than any earth tremor I had ever experienced. The leaves from the trees

were being sieved through the fly wire and louvres and were propelled across rooms to land on the opposite walls, releasing their sap to run down to the floor. I don't know at this point whether we still had a roof, but the rain found its way in, and we sat with our backs to the cupboard wall and had a stream of water cascading down behind us.

The wind slowly abated and the eye of the cyclone was upon us. Nature had provided relief from the sound and shuddering, as painkillers provide their relief. We walked out onto the balcony and saw that the huge tree that sheltered the house and our verandah had been blown over, as had many other trees on the neighbouring properties.

It didn't seem long before the wind returned: small zephyrs at first, which increased in intensity. The painkiller's effect was gone, and the gusting wind caused the house to shudder more violently than previously. I have no idea how long it was before we began to hear the sound of breaking fibro and glass. It was a sound we recognised, as a few weeks earlier we had been woken to this same sound as one of our neighbours had thrown a beer jug through the end of the house, breaking one of the fibro sheets. This sound was accompanied with the screeching sound of the rigging of masts at the sailing club a block away, and the clanging of halyards against their masts. At some point one of our neighbours' cars seemed to short out, and the intermittent car horn became another sound in this chaotic symphony.

Having the gas light next to us, it was difficult to see beyond the table. At one point, my father moved beyond the table, much to the consternation of the dog, to see what

was happening in the kitchen, only to witness a piece of timber smash through a sliding door, ricochet around the top of the stove and land at his feet. He made no more forays into the kitchen, but as the noise of destruction got closer to us, my parents decided we should move to the living area, away from the area that seemed to be taking the brunt of the damage. We began moving, dragging the table with us. We were halfway there when a huge gust of wind forced open the double glass doors that led onto the verandah. My father pushed the doors back, closed and locked them. We now had the table in place and just as he joined us there, the walls of the house were pushed over like a pack of cards, the wall which housed the double doors blew in toward us, and the wall against which we had taken shelter blew out, over the edge of the floorboards. I have no memory of the next few seconds, but I was later told that I too began to be dragged toward the edge of the floorboards. My parents grabbed me, and the next thing I knew we were heading back again with the table above us to our original place, where we stayed for the rest of the night. Having your house taken apart, recklessly destroyed around you, totally beyond your control is a really difficult thing to accept. There was absolutely nothing you could do to stop it.

We waited out the rest of the cyclone under the table. Light and shadow played tricks on the eye and mind. Looking out beyond the table, I saw what I thought were reflections of lightning on the passageway wall. I imagined it was the roof lifting with each gust of wind. As dawn broke, so did reality. There was no passageway wall. The

effect of a remnant of jagged wall being moved by the wind was enough to cause the shimmering effect against the lightening, empty sky.

Dawn and realisation came together. Slowly the wind abated and no longer shook the house; the rain was a slight drizzle and we began to move tentatively around.

Two bedrooms had been destroyed, leaving only floorboards. The third, closest to us, remained, with torn fly wire. There was no roof on any of the remaining house. The toilet and bathroom remained intact, as did the kitchen, despite holes punched through the door and walls. The sideboard in the living room had remained standing, and our small plastic Christmas tree had been wedged underneath it, with some baubles still intact. Clothing from my bedroom, including a ballroom dancing dress given to me by my dancing partner's mother, ended up in the tree in the yard of the house behind us, and the mattress from my parents' room was under the trunk of the large tree that had sheltered our balcony. Our 15 foot aluminium boat had been pushed out from underneath the house and flipped over, although the battery had landed right way up. The cumquat tree was left standing, albeit stripped of many of its leaves, with a few cumquats remaining like baubles, and adorned with stockings like tinsel. In the midst of all this I found a small silver locket, in which a photo of my father's parents was still intact. The caravan from the house next door had pushed over our poinciana tree, and swollen tampons littered the ground as well.

Because it was Christmas, many of our neighbours had left Darwin and we were, at that stage, looking after four houses around us. The house next door to us had just been sold to the government, and all that remained of that were the pillars. The house behind us, the same design as our own, had similar damage, and the house diagonally at the back, on the corner of Giles and Lampe Streets, which had been recently renovated, was severely damaged. The owners never returned to live there.

Not knowing how fragile the remaining structure was, we moved kitchen utensils and cooking pots from the house to the store room underneath. We then wrapped blankets around ourselves as protection from the drizzling rain and began to walk around the neighbourhood checking on others and marveling at the damage that had been caused. Probably in a state of shock, my father was remarking about the state of one house, to which my mother replied, "Don't laugh, take a look at your own house". With relief we found everyone we knew to be in residence was okay, and we returned home to begin burying food that we were not going to be able to cook and eat.

The days after the cyclone are blurred. We cleared the way in order to take one of our cars out, and found out there were various registration points, one next to the Parap Service station at the Quees' old house, and another at the Darwin High School. I remember going with my father to the Legislative Council to check on the damage to the buildings there. There was extensive damage, we had to pick our way around the back of the Chamber to the members' lounge where a lot of the ceilings had fallen in. Dick Ward was there with a friend, also checking on the damage. I think my father, who was Acting Clerk at the time, ensured things were as secure as possible, and we proceeded to call on his acting Deputy, Ray Chin, at his home in Litchfield Street in the city.

For the next two nights I think we slept in our cars, my mother and I in the back of the Holden Station wagon and my father in the small Toyota Corona. Both cars were remarkably undamaged, having been protected by the hedge of Aralias, common screening plants for the under stories of houses at that time.

Injections to protect against tetanus, and possibly other diseases, were being given at some of the gathering points, and telephones at the main exchange in Smith Street and at the post office were connected. We were able to contact my uncle in Melbourne, and daily people queued to let relatives know they had survived.

On the second or third day, the 27th or 28th of December, we were at Darwin High School when Gough Whitlam and his entourage swarmed in. He was obviously affected by the high humidity, if not the gravity of the situation.

My parents decided I should be evacuated. The authorities were pretty insistent that women and children should go, and I had developed an infection on my leg which was treated, but it was necessary to leave. I joined the queue at Darwin High School, my parents saying goodbye to me, only to return hours later to find me in much the same place as before. In the meantime, friends of theirs were trying to get their daughter, Moira, evacuated to Melbourne, which was where I was going, so I agreed to look after her on the journey. We, along with all the other evacuees, were given luggage tags to wear on our wrists giving our destinations.

We got on the bus to go to the airport in the early evening, and my parents turned up just in time to see us go. They were relieved, and phoned Melbourne to let my uncle know we were on our way. Little did they realise the queue of busses at the airport and the situation there. The airport, an old airforce hangar, had rubbish bins strategically placed to catch the drips from the holes in the roof, however the storm that ensued that night rendered futile any efforts to keep the place dry. We sloshed around in ankle-deep water, and any seats that were available were used to store our precious few belongings to keep them dry! I went to use the toilet only to be hailed by one of my friends there and told that I had gone to the men's! Did it really matter in these circumstances? I didn't really care! During the night, someone on a loud hailer announced that a plane had come in and that those people headed for Melbourne were to board a bus to go out to the plane. We boarded a bus, but by the time we got there, the plane was full. The plane was an air force carrier, and despite everything, I was quietly relieved we didn't have to go on that plane.

Just as dawn broke the next morning, a Jumbo jet arrived. Again we were herded onto a bus and out to the plane. This time there was room. I think this was the record-breaking flight for the greatest number of people ever carried. There were one and a half people per seat. I was struck by the juxtaposition of air hostesses who at the time wore a jungle print uniform and were beautifully made up, handing out carefully cut sandwich "points" to the evacuees in our skimpy tropical clothes, sparse footwear and generally disheveled appearance. Moira and I shared three seats with an older woman and her three-year-old son who was also going to Melbourne. I noted many of my school friends also made it onto this flight as well. I don't recall speaking much, or swapping tales about what happened. There must have been some conversation, but I think it was mainly about where we were going and whom we had left behind.

The flight landed at the International Airport in Sydney. The usual customs checks were set up with social security people, and after filling out some forms we were given some money. I later found out I had been given "mother and child" allowance for myself and Moira. There were some news reporters and cameramen waiting outside as we boarded a bus to go to the domestic terminal. The woman with the three-year-old and I stuck together, and we boarded the flight to Melbourne. The flight was occupied mainly by businessmen reading their newspapers, and once again I was struck by the difference in our clothing. Suits contrasted with skimpy little tropical dresses and sandals. Briefcases with Qantas airline bags carrying our worldly possessions! My travelling companion must have taken care of my charge on that flight, as I fell into a deep sleep. I had not slept for two days. We arrived at Melbourne Airport, and I was struck by the sight of the mountains of clothes and the kind volunteers who implored us to make a selection from the piles of clothes. I smile now at my choice of a mushroom-coloured, stripy crimplene pantsuit and some turtle-neck t-shirts. I think Moira may have chosen a toy or two. My uncle met us. He had slept the night at the airport, and was no doubt relieved to see us and pleased his wait was over. We journeyed home, and I suppose the tension and tiredness caused me to remark on his driving, the tram tracks providing a less than smooth ride home! Teenagers!

My uncle's home in Deepdene was behind and above some shops. Usually I slept on the outside, on what would originally, I think, have been a balcony. This time, however, I explained I could not sleep there as I felt I was falling off the edge. I didn't understand this sensation until six weeks later when my parents were able to visit on R&R leave, and explained to my uncle and aunt the event during the cyclone when I was almost dragged over the side of the house. To this day I have no memory of those few seconds. At that time there was no such thing as post traumatic stress counselling, and I feel I was probably a victim of PTS. I stayed up most of the night and slept most of the day, not eating and getting the shakes when I suspect my glucose levels were too low. This slowly started to sort itself out, and at the end of January my father's cousin drove me to Adelaide to commence school.

Unley High School, where I went, along with three other evacuees, was, like Darwin High School, a public high school, but with a much older history and quite different expectations of its students, both academically and in dress standards. I remember commenting on this during a video recording sent to Darwin for my parents. I think one of the service organisations arranged for families who were separated to receive and then send messages to each other during the year following the cyclone. I only recall doing this once, but it was a great way for me to see what was happening to my home in Darwin and to see my parents and how they were faring, and of course for them to see what I was up to. On reflection, I was very fortunate to have been able to stay with two families in Adelaide, to whom I owe an incredible gratitude for their generosity in taking me in and their tolerance of me. The experience of being able to live in another city and attend a different school taught me a lot, and in many ways I am grateful to have been given this opportunity courtesy of Cyclone Tracy.

The government provided airfares back to Darwin during the school holidays, and it was with a sense of trepidation that I returned to see what had happened to my home, and Darwin in general. By June 2015 my parents had been given a caravan to lease by the government. This was an upgrade from initially sleeping in the back of the cars, to being lent a campervan by one of my father's work colleagues, Jack Tracey. All living was done out of the brick tool shed underneath the old house. My mother cooked on a two-burner gas stove, and they watched the resurrected (courtesy of the Navy) television that had blown out of the house and was now set up in the corner of the shed with a coat hanger as its aerial. Occasionally a frill-necked lizard would also join them. The old table under which we had sheltered sat outside, and friends would pop by after work to talk and have a beer or two, or have dinner and play cards around this table.

This remained the status quo until about mid 1976,

when we finally moved into our new home, built in front of the remnants of the original house. I returned at the beginning of 1976, and resumed my schooling at Darwin High School. Many of my friends had also gone to school elsewhere the previous year, and it was great to resume friendships and make new friends, with whom I still maintain contact today.

Eleanor Graves.

Photograph by Ramon Williams

CHAPTER 34 - RAMON WILLIAMS

Time marches on, but memories linger.

By Ramon Williams, photographer and journalist with Worldwide Photos.

"Uncle Ray, I can't reach mum and dad," said Joy Pattemore. This was the statement that alerted us to the fact that we could become involved with the situation in Darwin, Christmas Day, 1974.

Joy was the daughter of the Pattemore family at the Retta Dixon Children's Home. She was in Sydney for nursing training. Being a niece of my wife, Dorothy (née Pattemore), Joy was having Christmas Day with us.

I tried the phone and heard a ringing sound, but no answering. I later found out that this was normal for when phone lines are not active.

By now, reports were coming through of Cyclone Tracy hitting Darwin.

Communications were cut, and the world was becoming aware that something had happened, but the situation was unclear.

Throughout Boxing Day, media reports were increasing. Medical evacuees were arriving at airports. It was obvious that something severe had happened

More attempts at phoning Darwin, by us, were useless. What had happened to Joy's family?

As a member of the Australian Religious Press Association, I phoned the executive members later on Boxing Day, to request permission to be the representative in Darwin. Permission was granted.

I realised there were no commercial flights, so I phoned the RAAF Richmond Airbase and spoke to the Public Relations officer. Was there any flight into Darwin with a spare seat, for a religious media representative?

I was surprised to be told, "yes, there is a spare seat on a flight leaving tomorrow morning, at 06.00 from Richmond. We can fit you on, but you will have to bring your own food and supplies, with sleeping gear, and it all has to fit in your camera bag! We don't have any extra space."

I picked the biggest camera bag I had. We filled every available bottle with water, selected tinned food, films and threw in some clothing and packed the bag. The four cameras would be placed around my neck.

As I was about to board the RAAF Hercules, the briefing officer told us to prepare for the worst scenes imaginable. "If you have read Orwell's 1984, that will give you an idea of what to expect."

(Nineteen Eighty-Four, often published as 1984, is a novel by English author George Orwell published in 1949. All of the world lives in poverty; hunger, disease and filth are the norms. Ruined cities and towns are commonplace.)

"Oh, by the way, are your injections up to date, for typhoid and cholera?" he asked.

Six months before, I had been on assignment in Singapore, so all injections were up to date. I was the only one who could claim that all was OK.

The 'plane was jammed full with a team of power workers from Lithgow, their trucks and their gear, as they had volunteered to help restore power in Darwin. They had driven overnight to join the flight.

Below: Commissioner Margarite Warren. Photo by Ramon Williams.

It was a seven hour flight, and when we landed the earlier description of "the worst scenes imaginable" was correct.

Five months before, I had been in Darwin covering a series of meetings with the CWCI (Christian Women Communicating Internationally).

The terminal was a shambles.

Teams of Salvation Army volunteers were obvious, serving the people wanting to leave on the evacuation flights.

Commissioner Margarite Warren was comforting a crying youngster, while nearby ladies were making sandwiches and the men were serving cold cordial. Wherever did they find bread, water and cordial?

Amongst the queues of women and children lining up to leave Darwin, I noticed some ladies I had met previously. I had been in their houses, eaten meals with them and enjoyed their hospitality.

I greeted them as they walked past. They did not even recognise me. They were just staring ahead, with glazed looks. They were in shock.

What was going on? What had they been through?

Buses were transporting evacuees to the airport and returning empty to the city. I spoke to one driver, asking if he could give me a lift to near the Retta Dixon Home. "No problem, mate. Come on board."

As I arrived, Mervyn greeted me with: "Where did you come from?" Of course I could stay with them, although it would mean roughing it a bit. They had lost some of their raised house on stilts, bedrooms and accommodation.

Photograph by Ramon Williams

Saturday morning, December 28, 1974, I was given the use of Joy's car. Then I could travel around and see what had happened to the city but primarily, the churches and missions.

I was able to find churches associated with every denomination, and heard stories from missionaries. The Reverend Alan Hoskin, of the BCA (Bush Church Aid) had crouched on the floor as the cyclone had ripped his house apart. He felt as if he had been sand-blasted by the wind and soil.

He only had his pair of shorts, so pinned a small clergy cross to them. He was still on active duty.

Nearby was the CMS (Church Missionary Society) where folk were checking buildings still standing.

In the city, I found Christ Church Cathedral, or rather the shell of what had been the cathedral. A sign out the front mentioned a combined church service the following morning, at 8.00 a.m., in the United Church, on Smith Street.

As I travelled the city streets, photographing the devastation as I went, I realised I needed to record the general scenes as well as the churches.

Smith Street – where the debris had been swept aside to provide a thoroughfare; the post office; the parks; little known side streets; dazed people sitting in doorways; smashed cars, still standing where they had been parked; a father carrying his child on his shoulders; children playing with salvaged toys. The Roman Catholic cathedral still had its cross standing tall on its tower, even though some of the brick walls had fallen.

Photograph by Ramon Williams

The United Church in Smith Street even had leaves impregnated into glass windows!

The following morning, at the combined church service, communion was served, using Sao biscuits and cordial the Reverend Fred Mackay had brought with him.

He had managed to travel to Darwin to see for himself what the situation was and to support those in need.

Reverend Max Griffith gave me a guided tour of what had been the manse. He had found a billy to boil for a cup of tea, and there was plenty of shattered timber around to light a fire!

The Reverend Graeme Bence drove me, in his air-conditioned car (the first I had ever ridden in) to show me his area of destroyed houses and streets. His own house was one of the worst hit.

The photo of him finding his way through the remains was used by the Red Cross in Sydney, as they appealed for funds.

Betty Watcham was on the initial Red Cross Emergency Team to arrive in Darwin. She came from the church we attended, Gymea Baptist, but her family had not heard from her.

I searched for the Red Cross headquarters and found her amongst a team of worn-out workers. When I enquired about the work they were doing, I realised that here was yet another story that should be told.

I obtained permission to accompany Betty throughout Sunday, as she and her team went about their activities. They were notified of old men, living by themselves, in need of assistance. One had moved on, but another was found, in a filthy condition, transported back to the Red Cross centre, cleaned up by a couple of nurses who had volunteered to help and then evacuated from the airport.

Out at "Check Point Charlie", on the main highway South, vehicles were being checked by the Police for roadworthiness, while the Red Cross workers were trying to register family names, so that relatives and officials could be informed. It was surprising how many drivers gave their names as "Donald Duck" or "John Smith". I didn't realise there were that many Smiths living in Darwin!

A phone call was achieved, via the supervisor at the telephone exchange, and I was able to broadcast a report on the situation for all the denominations over Radio 2CH in Sydney. That report was repeated several times that Sunday. Listeners in Sydney knew what was happening to an unreported series of buildings, the churches of Darwin.

On Tuesday, December 31, I was able to obtain seats for myself and four Pattemore children, to Sydney on the final RAAF Hercules evacuation flight.

At Mascot Airport, a hangar was named "Hangar 96", which coincided with a popular TV series at the time. The actors portrayed a wide variety of personalities, all with different ways of life and needs. This seemed to cover those arriving from cyclone-damaged Darwin.

There were the Red Cross and Salvation Army workers on the job. Each had a job to do, and in later catastrophes, all had designated areas of operation to attend to.

Out of the rubble, communications and co-ordinations had been established for future disasters.

Photograph by Ramon Williams

Other cyclones followed, in different areas of the world, but few as devastating as Cyclone Tracy.

Yes, time has moved on, but memories linger.
Ramon Williams.

Below: Ramon Williams.

Photograph by Ramon Williams

CHAPTER 35 - BETTY WATCHAM

DARWIN DISASTER RED CROSS DISASTER EMERGENCIES TEAMS.

Like so many people, I heard on the 7.30 a.m. news broadcast that approximately 20 houses had been unroofed during Cyclone Tracy, which struck Darwin on Christmas Day. It didn't sound very serious, therefore I didn't listen to any subsequent broadcasts during the day, and I spent the rest of the day in our happy family atmosphere.

By fate, a member of my family broke the house rule by turning on the television set, only to hear that the Red Cross was engaged in dispatching blankets and other urgent requirements to what was thought to be a devastated city, but nobody really knew. All communications had been cut. I was preparing our Christmas tea at the time, so asked my son to make contact with Headquarters for me, to see if further help was required. The first reaction: "they were coping".

The General Secretary, the Assistant General Secretary and the Director of Branches were packing the required items, which were to be sent immediately to Richmond Airbase. The request had been made by the Natural Disasters Committee in Canberra.

Later on Christmas evening I received a second phone call, asking me to report for work very early on Boxing Day. Since the evening news broadcast, things were beginning to 'hot up' at Headquarters. The phones were beginning to run constantly with people seeking information as to what had happened, and anxious for news of relatives. It was obvious that extra staff would be needed. A further phone call, late at night, from Canberra, requested a Red Cross team of 20 personnel to be flown immediately to Darwin.

A telephone call at two o'clock in the morning of Boxing Day found me rushing madly to sort a quick change of underwear and pack for an indefinite stay in the cyclone-devastated city of Darwin. We had to report to Naval Flight Facilities by 7 a.m. Twenty Red Cross workers and three press reporters boarded the plane for a journey virtually into the unknown. One hundred units of blood and plasma were placed on board ready for immediate delivery to the Darwin hospital. The crew of the naval plane, normally based at Jervis Bay, were extremely kind and helpful. Supplying the team with hot drinks proved quite a task, the only available facilities restricting to three the number of drinks made at any one time. Refuelling was at Longreach.

The radio operator had sent a message ahead asking for sandwiches to be ready at the airport; these were eaten in the shade of the airport building. Descending from the plane, we were overwhelmed by the heat and were grateful when the plane was ready for take-off.

Silence befell the team as the second stage of the journey got underway; some dozed and others were lost in thought. The silence enabled me to close my eyes and pray, asking God to give me strength and courage for whatever lay ahead.

Radio contact was maintained with the Naval Base for as long as possible, and then silence. It wasn't until Darwin Airport came into view that it was possible to make contact with the ground.

The control tower had been rendered useless, and the talk-down was from an army truck situated on the edge of the airfield.

Back in Sydney, 'action' was the word. After seeing the team off at Mascot, the General Secretary, with two teenagers (our son Andrew and daughter Sue) and the wife of one of the members of the team, returned to Headquarters to begin a mammoth task. The only thing that could be done in the first instance was to answer the phones.

Offers of help poured in. Accommodation, offers of food (one man offered 2,000 dozen tins of meat). "Yes, volunteers were needed, money was urgently required". Offers of clothing were referred to the Smith Family or Salvation Army. Above all, people were anxious for news of their loved ones. Volunteers came in off the street offering their services. High school students, uni students, housewives, office clerks, people from all walks of life.

Branch members just turned up, some staying for several days, and the VAs had their equal part to play.

By ten o'clock a small volunteer force was working from a comparatively small area; they extended to a further section of the sixth floor, until the decision was made to use the third floor of Red Cross House. This became known as the "Darwin Disaster Area". The operation could not have been undertaken in the old building. Anyone who had considered that the third floor was an unnecessary luxury was proved wrong. The P. M. G. installed 38 extra phones and gave us a new priority phone number.

Staff members were assisted from Boxing Day until the 9th January by 2,700 volunteers. Several staff members worked non-stop for 72 hours. Volunteers who were asked to go home and rest worked round the clock.

With such a volume of volunteers, it was obvious that rosters would be necessary, and people were asked if they had any special qualifications. A large typing pool was necessary, and people were needed to answer the phones round the clock. Help was needed with catering for the large workforce, and a large number of workers were needed to assist the search; tracing names and whereabouts of people. 35,000 people had left Darwin - where were they? Twenty-four hours a day the enquiries poured in, mainly from Australia during the daytime, and from numerous countries around the world at night. The task of rostering the volunteers was undertaken by two people. It was their responsibility to ensure that every post was manned, either for a full 24 hours, or at least 16 hours. For some, their only sustenance for several days was sandwiches and tea or coffee. Their first hot meal was baked beans on toast with a piece of bacon.

On Boxing Day, people who had been trying to phone Headquarters without success were coming into the building for news of relatives. For several days the only available and unofficial list was that compiled very hastily at the airport by the Divisional Commandant of the VASC, as she spoke to the evacuees. This rough list was handed to the Headquarters personnel, and from that, anxious relatives were able to search for a familiar name.

As both the Publicity Officer and Public Relations Officer were with the team in Darwin, a member of the Divisional Council was asked to take charge of Public Relations. Enquires of many kinds were received, people seeking advice on how to contact various groups, people asking how to apply for insurance and the like. The Council of Social Services undertook the task, and set themselves up as an Information Bureau, operating from the third floor of Red Cross Headquarters.

The VAs trained basically in first aid and nursing were on duty from ten o'clock on Boxing morning, when the first plane arrived carrying eighteen stretcher cases. To meet the plane, there was one ambulance, Commonwealth Police, R.A.A.F. transport and two VAs. The patients were transferred to the R.A.A.F. bus, which had been especially converted to take stretchers. Two other VAs had arrived by the time the transport departed for the Prince of Wales Hospital (later some of the patients were transferred to Prince Henry). The VAs could do nothing medically for the patients, they were, however, able to take messages, and later contact relatives if they were in Sydney.

One lady who was a paraplegic, and whose children were also injured, asked that a message be sent to her in-laws living in Maroubra. She just wanted to let them know that they had arrived in Sydney. The first question asked of the VA was, "How is our son?" She didn't know at the time, but he had been killed during the Cyclone.

The VAs, like other Red Cross personnel, worked around the clock meeting planes, many carrying the injured passengers and aiding women with their children. The VAs carried the babies and took charge of the children while their mothers were attending to formalities.

Hangar 96 at the domestic terminal was used as a receiving and distribution centre. The Jumbos could only land at the international terminal, nevertheless they were still met by VAs from Hangar 96. As the news spread, more VAs reported for duty, until there were sufficient numbers available for a roster system. Eventually the Health Department sent a team of two doctors and two nursing sisters to deal with the cases requiring immediate attention; otherwise the injured were transferred to hospital.

Where did all the thousands of evacuees go?

Some were lucky enough to have relatives in Sydney. Those less fortunate went to a Commonwealth hostel, but in the first instance, some were sent to North Head, escorted by VAs, only to find their arrival was rather premature, and nothing was ready for the shocked, tired, hungry evacuees. Not even milk to make a cup of tea! The VAs soon rectified the situation, but not before a feeling of complete despair had overcome many of the women.

Others went to South Head Army Barracks, and eventually everyone was sent to Callan Park before being taken to temporary accommodation.

The Welfare Services of the Red Cross swung into action. Staff were augmented by 32 social worker volunteers, and social work students volunteered, again working around the clock. From the Saturday afternoon, and for the next eight days, $43,250 was handed to 3,425 persons at the airport. Activities ceased at the airport on the 6th January at 2.00 a.m. People still seeking assistance could be helped either at Headquarters or a Regional office. From the 6th January to the 24th January, a further $11,000 was given to 1,074 persons. Daily, people from Darwin were seeking aid, financial help, advice, clothing; a constant flow of people were looking to the Red Cross for assistance. Why do people approach Red Cross? Reasons vary, the main categories being:-

Cash
Bond money
Connection of electricity & gas
Payment of rental
Payment of rental to commonwealth hostels (refused!)
Clothing
Advice on employment
Accommodation
Transfer to Darwin
Purchase of caravans for Darwin
Tracing enquiries for relatives
Furniture

Help with travel requirements

Payment for spectacles

Payment for dentures

Car repairs

Tools of trade

Destitution

Funeral expenses

School fees

Psychological problems (isolation, separation, loneliness, relationship breakdowns, lack of feeling of identity)

Health problems

Children's problems.

Cash requirements:-

A prevailing problem of lack of income. People had come to us because:-

(a) they had not received Social Security and/or Red Cross money at the airport

(b) they had failed to receive the second Social Security payment, which was a cheque payment.

(c) they needed money to look for employment or housing

(d) they needed cash for small requirements on journeys to other States

(e) they had difficulty in cashing cheques from Social Security without sufficient identification, or lack of any bank account in Sydney.

(f) they needed cash for specific clothing requirements.

CONTINUING PROBLEMS.

1. Lack of clear direction as to Government policy on many individual matters – e.g. funeral costs, tools of trade.

2. Lack of clarity as to the number of evacuees in N.S.W., (Social Security said on 30/1/75 that there were in excess of 8,000)

3. Continuing income inadequacies, placing additional strains on family relationships.

4. Even when the Government has an official policy, the continuing difficulties facing evacuees when they strive to avail themselves of assistance – e. g.

(a) Commonwealth Employment Service will not pay fares to people looking for work – but there is a wait of up to four hours, and the job is filled before the evacuees arrive.

(b) Total unreality of ceiling amount of $100 on car repairs when car is in southern city.

5. There is still no Government policy regarding payment of renewal of tools of trade (even a bankrupt is allowed to keep his tools).

6. Doubt about people's ability to continue to pay high rentals.

7. Pervasive unemployment problems in a time of acute shortage of jobs.

This work with the Darwin evacuees has taken place

against a background of work responsibilities to our normal caseload.

Although there wasn't an appeal for clothing, literally tons of clothing and linen was donated. As always, approximately half could be used. The only items that the Red Cross were anxious to receive were baby goods. The layettes received from branches in particular were beautiful – nearly all new, hand-sewn or hand-knitted. There was also a considerable amount of new clothing donated for adults, and these articles have been greatly appreciated. (Men must wear their clothes until the garments fall from their backs, as we never have sufficient men's clothing to give to those in need).

One distasteful job in any disaster is the unenviable task of sorting the donated clothing. Again, one person was responsible for this work. Occasionally volunteers assisted – however the bulk of the work was done by one person working from very early in the morning until late at night, seven days a week. This task didn't end when the immediate emergency ceased; it went on for weeks. On leaving Red Cross House, our helper would return home, only to start making up layettes. Even now, almost at the end of February, the demand for clothing is constant, and daily, Darwin people are seeking warmer clothing. Time is spent selecting suitable attire – frequently a family will enter the door as another is leaving, and the process of selection begins all over again. Staff members, with the help of volunteers, have given up their weekends in an attempt to clear piles of donated clothing. The laborious task is lightened from time to time, when a box contains new handmade children's wear.

That winter there was going to be a desperate shortage of new winter woollies, and it would be the Darwin people who would particularly feel the cold.

What caused these problems? We return to Darwin.

Arrangements were quickly made for units of blood to be transported to the hospital, after which we were taken to the R.A.A.F. Headquarters Operations Room, our role still uncertain.

Debris lay scattered around the airfield, and it wasn't until we reached the Operations building that we became aware of the excessive damage. A very large uprooted tree lay resting against the side of the building. It must have been blown some distance, as there was no sign of a hole in the immediate area from where it could have been uprooted. An old war-time bomber had been blown along like a piece of paper, coming to rest in an unusual position. Dozens of light aircraft lay upside down or completely crumpled.

People appeared stunned, some with suitcases, others with their salvaged belongings wrapped in blankets. They sat waiting until their names were called for boarding planes. There was no panic, and I doubt if there had been any. Shock, accompanied by disbelief that such a catastrophe could have happened, anaesthetised people into being patient and subdued.

It was decided that Red Cross House would be our headquarters. Three male members of the team went on ahead to start preparing the building for occupation. About twenty young bank employees came to our rescue with transport, after receiving a meal at the Mess on the R.A.A.F. base. I was the first female member of the team to be taken to Red Cross Headquarters. The men were still mopping out water, the roof and windows having disappeared during the cyclone. Being a housewife, I realised that mops weren't going to be sufficient, so after a search we found sponges, towels and a few buckets. After sweeping out as much of the glass as possible, it was a case of getting down on our hands and knees and soaking up the excess water.

Within an hour we were able to start treating the overflow of casualties from the Darwin hospital, which is situated on the opposite side of the road from Red Cross Headquarters. The only medical equipment immediately available was my own first-aid bag and the equipment we salvaged from the Blood Bank. However, the R.A.A.F. gave us a variety of requisites, and more were eventually procured from the hospital. The majority of injuries were caused by flying iron sheeting, glass and nails.

Our team of twenty joined the four members from the Western Australian Division, who had arrived a few hours earlier. Everyone seemed to find their own niche. One member of the team took charge of the cooking, and cooked almost nonstop for two days. Men were deployed at the road blocks with the police – this was on a twenty four hour roster basis – whilst in camp there was wood to be chopped, water to be boiled for drinking purposes and repairs carried out to the building to make it waterproof.

Youngsters (most being bank employees) volunteered their services, and worked almost round the clock. They did a fantastic job, and were terribly upset when told they would have to be evacuated, as the banks could not be responsible for them.

I don't know where the lamps and gaslights appeared from, but by dark we had sufficient light to work by, and once people realised that there was life at the Blood Bank, young men came in droves to offer blood. Unfortunately we had to refuse, as there were no facilities to take or store blood, but in the midst of their own suffering they had stopped and thought of others. The flow of people offering to give blood continued until we left.

We arrived in Darwin with nothing – by the end of the first day the larder was stocked with plenty of canned drinks, tinned food of all kinds and boxes of fruit – not only for ourselves but for the hundreds that passed through our doors in the days that followed. The army supplied the green hats to which the Red Cross Volunteer badges were attached. The main shortage was of matches.

The first night we were rostered two hours' rest. The interior of the building was far too wet to stay in, so the majority of the team slept, or rather lay, on the concrete surrounding the building. It was the strangest experience of my life. Everything appeared dead – the trees had been completely stripped of leaves, there were no birds or insects. This was so for three days, then we were woken one morning by a cockatoo calling "Charlie," and later that day a budgie landed on someone's head at the airport. Slowly the flies started reappearing, but there were very few insects. The trees would remain barren for a long time.

A young man brought his pregnant wife to us for

treatment. She had dysentery, and was frightened of losing the baby. The risk of contamination was so great that she had to be nursed in the doorway, and later moved into the open air away from other patients. She was medivacced the next day. In gratitude, the husband returned after his wife had been flown out, with a large carton of frozen chickens, which were eventually barbecued.

A couple celebrated their 28th wedding anniversary on 27 December by lying in each other's arms all night, after two blood donor couches had been pushed together. The wife had a fractured arm, and broken fingers on the other hand, and her husband had the muscle of one arm almost torn away, and both feet badly injured. They had no material possessions left, but they had each other, and so had everything.

An elderly lady had only a hospital gown, her walking sticks and her deaf aid; she was suffering from exposure and shock. She had no one to whom she could go, as her only friends were in Darwin, but it was necessary for her to be evacuated. Like so many others, she was placed on a plane heading south.

On the morning of the second day, our pattern of involvement became clear. We were to be the clearing station for walking or sitting patients; also compassionate cases were sent to us from the hospital. The massive influx came when the obstetric ward was emptied. Day-old babies, post-natal cases, pre-natal cases, some of the latter within a day of confinement. Four babies came straight from humidicribs; they were wrapped in foil and then in bunny rugs. My job was to take charge of the babies, mums and mums-to-be. My main concern was the premie babies, but nature is wonderful, for as the day progressed, the little babies' colour and general condition improved.

Nappies, at first a problem, soon started to appear, and fortunately they were the disposable kind. When I was asked where to place soiled towelling nappies, a look of disbelief and almost horror appeared on the face on one helper, when I said <u>all</u> had to be burnt. There were no washing facilities, and under such conditions it was necessary to burn everything that was soiled.

The buses that should have arrived early in the day were delayed. The hours slipped by, and it wasn't until late in the afternoon that they finally arrived. However, it had been decided that the four premie babies with their mothers and other relatives (mainly children) plus two West Irian twins, should be returned to the hospital. They were all evacuated during the night, on board a plane with a full medical team. The West Irian identical twin girls were five weeks old. Their mother had returned home and they were awaiting passports. They were beautiful babies, but when it came to feeding time, they made their demands simultaneously, and they made sure everyone knew that they each had a healthy set of lungs.

With the exception of those who were returned to hospital, all who came to us were evacuated by five o'clock that day; then we started all over again.

On the Friday, a Darwin Blood Bank Sister and her husband arrived. This wonderful couple, whom we all befriended, were an inspiration to many. He was a minister with the United Free Church of Darwin. His church at

Nightcliff and the manse next to the church were completely demolished. In between helping the remaining members of his congregation by conducting burial services, he assisted the Red Cross in numerous ways. As we were leaving Darwin he said, "I'm going to have 48 hours' rest, move into a flat that is habitable and then start all over again. The church and congregation will be rebuilt".

We take for granted flowing water on tap, sanitation, and above all electricity. These necessities of daily living were temporarily destroyed. Feeding over two hundred people a day without the usual facilities was a mammoth task. One Red Cross member of the N.S.W. team made herself responsible for this unenviable work. Standing over two make-shift bush stoves in scorching temperatures, with excessively high humidity, took tremendous stamina. The fires were lit at first light, and were still smoldering well into the night. The first five days brought an unending flow of people – all grateful for a meal, a cup of tea, a cold drink and a comforting word.

Temporary toilets built in the grounds of the rear of the Red Cross Headquarters soon collapsed during the first heavy storm. This meant that the toilets inside the building had to be used. Notices were placed in the toilets read "Three quarters of a bucket of water with disinfectant to be flushed down the toilet after use". In theory this should have worked, but with continuous use, the toilets soon became blocked, and the men in the team had the unpleasant task of clearing them. The task had just been completed when the Fire Brigade arrived, and with their high-pressure hoses, completely flushed the toilets. The firemen supplied fresh drinking water daily, but even this had to be boiled.

With the medical evacuations, we were advised of the expected arrival times of planes. At a given time the patients, with their relatives and few possessions, would board the bus for transportation to the airport. If the plane hadn't arrived we had to wait. However, the patients were allowed to board the landed planes before other evacuees waiting at the airport terminal.

Where did the transport come from? People gave the Red Cross keys to a variety of vehicles, saying, "I'm off and don't know when I'll be back, you can have these."

The system was that people were asked to register for evacuation at the various reception centres, return to their place of shelter (if any), listen for their names to be read over the radio and report back to the centre with any belongings they might have. They were transported to the airport by a fleet of damaged buses, and there they would wait for hour after hour until there was sufficient room for them in the shelter of the ruined International Terminal. Again, there would be another long, tiring vigil before boarding a plane. First Aid posts were set up at the terminal, and the Salvation Army, assisted by Commonwealth Police, supplied drinks and sandwiches nonstop to those waiting evacuation.

One day rolled into another, and we were oblivious to days or dates. A daily pattern emerged. The members of the team involved in tracing left early in the morning for the office they occupied in the city. The men rostered on the 24 hour road block came and went. The team members involved with reception set up the front entrance daily, and everyone available gave a hand with the tidying-up, sweeping and mopping of floors.

The walls of the Blood Bank and Activities Section were made of brick, and withstood the force of the storm, however the building used for storage and Red Cross work was made of fibro and weather board, and was extensively damaged. The building had been mainly used for storage of used clothing, most of which still hung on the rails dripping with water, days after. Unfortunately most of these articles were completely useless and ruined. Some of the male members of the team cleared the rooms, and eventually new clothing was stored there, but not before the roof had been secured. The first consignment of new clothing was delivered by the police after being rescued from a warehouse in the city centre. Red Cross relief parcels arrived, many containing new clothing and very welcome toiletries. However, some of the cartons contained very thick winter clothing, which of course was useless. Men's working trousers and solid footwear were in very short supply and in great demand, not only with local people but with members of the Commonwealth Police Force. They had arrived wearing uniforms suitable only for duties in the southern states.

The individual stories are numerous, but some stand out very clearly in my mind.

One of our early patients owned a motel. He had several injuries, the worst being a cut on the head, and for several days he appeared for fresh dressings. He was determined to stick it out and rebuild his motel. His wounds wouldn't heal, he contracted dysentery and finally he came in one morning with his bag, "Could we arrange for his evacuation?" As with so many, depression was starting to develop.

The first casualty to walk into the Darwin Hospital was a young naval rating who had been gashed right across the stomach. He was a sitting patient; we were asked to evacuate him and found his only possession was a pair of shortie pyjama trousers. He was eventually fitted out with a pair of jeans that didn't meet in the middle and a tight-fitting T-shirt. He didn't complain.

I was asked to collect two elderly gentlemen from a home and take them to Headquarters to await evacuation. Entering the room of the first, the stench knocked me back – the man hadn't washed, shaved or emptied the urinals since the day of the Cyclone, four days before. He was lying on the bed and greeting me with, "Are you married?" "I'm not," I replied. "It's alright, Pop, I am married and have been nursing for many years". The poor old chap was suffering from bronchial asthma, and found it difficult to breathe every time he moved. Added to the difficulties of getting him to his feet was the fact that he was wearing only an over-large pair of shorts. Every time I tried to stand him up his trousers slipped.

He eventually made it to the kombi van with me hanging onto his trousers! We then collected the second gentleman. He was able to help himself a little more, to my relief. We collected his scattered belongings and placed them in a battered bag. Looking round the room to ensure that we had taken everything of value, I saw his false teeth staring from inside a drinking glass. I said, "We can't leave these behind," whereupon he produced a hanky, wrapped them up and put them in his pocket. Returning to Headquarters, the gentlemen were left in the care of two nursing sisters, who shaved them, soaped them all over then lightly turned the hoses on them, after which they were given new clothing.

Whilst this was going on, I was sent to collect another gentleman, who supposedly didn't have any legs. We found the correct address, and in spite of a thorough search of the ruins could see no sign of him. We never did hear of his whereabouts.

A member of the hospital staff asked if we could arrange for her children and those of another family to be flown to Scotland. They had no relatives in Australia, and the mother had been struggling to bring the children up on her own. The mother was going to remain in Darwin for the time being. It was easy to undertake this assignment. Whilst waiting for the arrival of the planes, the children were fitted out and given new clothing and toiletries. When we arrived there was a long delay, as the planes were held up. Whilst waiting we were approached by a television crew to interview some of the patients. As some were under sedation it was not advisable, but we said they could talk to the children. The interview completed, I asked on which channel the film would be shown, and was told that the film was being made for I.T.N. London. The interview could not have been more appropriate.

A little girl of six was travelling to Sydney on her own. Her mother was a nursing sister at Darwin Hospital, and intended staying there for a while. The little girl was the happiest kiddy I met during my stay. She had a delightful smile, and was so excited at the thought of going on an aeroplane. The first plane to arrive was a Jumbo. My six charges (five going to Scotland and one for Sydney) were so excited, especially as they were allowed to board the plane first. On arrival in Sydney, the five for Scotland were met by Division C Commandant, who took charge of them until arrangements were made for their care. They eventually left for Scotland in the care of a young Scottish couple.

On another trip to the airport, I was talking to a mother who told me it was her little boy's birthday. I related the news to a policeman whom I knew fairly well. Five minutes later he arrived with a large carton of lollies. As the box was handed to him we gathered round and sang "Happy Birthday"

While I was escorting the mother of a 10 day old baby, she said "I phoned my mother last night. My mother could not believe that I had lost everything. She kept saying 'you must have something.'" The young mother had only been discharged from hospital on Christmas Eve to be home for Christmas. Little did she realise that two days later she would be back in hospital with broken ribs.

Two injured policemen cried because they didn't want to be evacuated. They felt they were deserting their mates. One had severe lacerations to his feet, and he sat in the corridor of the hospital crying whilst his mates stood round him. The Red Cross worker who had gone to the hospital to collect him said, "Come on, let's wipe those tears." Instead of producing a hankie from her pocket, she pulled out a pair of ladies' briefs. "Never mind, these will do just as well". The other policeman not wanting to leave had a spinal injury, and did not realize the seriousness of the injuries.

A garage employee with a complicated fracture of the hand served petrol continuously from late on Christmas Day. I was asked to call and dress the cuts on his legs and re-strap the hand. I advised him to go to the hospital to have it set, but he was too busy and said he would try and get along to the hospital that afternoon. I told him that I would call again the next day, and that if he hadn't been to the hospital I would personally take him. By my next visit he still hadn't been, so I said, "You might be over six feet, but you're going to the hospital." I informed his boss, who was filling other vehicles with petrol, and took my patient to the hospital. On viewing the Xrays the doctors couldn't believe that the man had worked with his hand in such a condition. He had to be given a general anesthetic and kept in hospital overnight. I reported his condition to his wife, who was very relieved that something had been done, and also advised his boss. That evening I called into the Ward to see him. "I suppose you feel like hitting me with the plaster," I said. "Yes," he replied, "but I will be grateful to you one day." After being discharged the next morning he returned to the service station, and the last time I saw him he was still serving petrol.

Patients with serious mental disorders were evacuated on special flights, as were alcoholics. Somehow five alcoholics were not evacuated on the early flight, and as they were 'sitting cases', we were asked to arrange for their evacuation. They had been hospitalized for various reasons, some with medical problems, others with withdrawal symptoms. I think I had more sympathy for them than most. Others would start life anew, but I wondered what would happen to them, and if they would be sent from one place to another.

Depression and psychological effects would be long-term. Depression was beginning to set in by the sixth day. One severe case was obvious in a boilerman from the hospital. He came in asking if we could 'get him out'. I said I was sure it could be arranged, but he would have to come back in the morning. He had worked practically nonstop since the cyclone; he even brought his time sheets to prove it. He went away shouting that nobody cared. Five minutes later he returned to apologise. He had been a loner all his life with no family. He sat crying and talking, saying that a man should not cry. I said he shouldn't be ashamed to show his emotions. He returned the next morning with his few belongings, saying he was very grateful for our kindness.

A mother of a large family brought her children in for clothing. While they were being issued with the required articles, we noticed infected sores on the little boy, and asked if we could treat them. While we were attending to him there was a sudden loud bang. He grabbed someone's hand and said, "The roof isn't going to blow off, is it?" It made me realize that such an experience as the children had been through could have long-term effects.

How did we survive without the so-called essentials of today's living – running water, electricity and sanitation? For the first couple of days we didn't shower, deodorant being the thing to use. We didn't have time to join the hundreds of night bathers along the Stuart Highway. Hoses had been attached to the main water pipe lines, and at dusk people would go along and shower by the roadside.

When water was turned on in the Nurses' Home and we were allowed to use the facilities, the first cold shower was wonderful. The second night three of us arrived at the Nurses Home just as someone shouted, "Anyone for hot showers?" We couldn't believe our ears – we would be in that! We were taken to a container ship which had docked the previous day. It was like walking into a first class hotel; carpet, electric lighting, air conditioning – the smell of clean air. A peep into the dining room revealed tables set with white cloths, shining cutlery and glassware. We were shown to the Radio Officer's cabin and enjoyed the luxury of hot water and a chance to wash our hair, even if it was with soap. After cleaning ourselves we were invited to the bar for drinks. It was like being in another world. The officers were spic and span. Those that didn't favour beards were clean-shaven. It was relaxing to sit for a short time. I found myself sitting next to the President of the Northern Territory Division of the Red Cross. Her husband was the harbour master, therefore they had to stay in Darwin. She wanted to assist the Red Cross, but couldn't until her teenage daughters were evacuated. She would be an asset to the Red Cross personnel, all of whom were from other states, as her local knowledge would be invaluable, and I suggested that she should bring her daughters along to Red Cross Headquarters early the following morning and arrangements would be made for their immediate evacuation.

The necessary arrangements were made, and the girls were on their way to Sydney by the middle of the following day

Our hour of luxury was tremendous: it lifted our morale and we returned 'home' with renewed stamina and strength. The next luxury came in the form of an additional generator. The first one we acquired was being used for the running of the fridges, although there was constant supply of cold drinks from about the second day. The Ice Works was one of the buildings which had escaped serious damage, and as soon as the plant was operational, ice was being produced. Queues up to a mile long could be seen daily. One of our local volunteers used a little influence and was served immediately. We did need cold drinks for the continuous stream of patients and those seeking help. We had managed with candles, torches and gas lamps, and therefore an overall vote was a preference for the second generator to be used for air-conditioning in the mixed dormitory. The mattresses supplied earlier were placed side by side so that twelve people were able to enjoy the sheer luxury of sleeping in a cool room.

As we were an Emergency Service, the PMG gave us priority in reconnecting the lines, and contact with the outside world was re-established. The first night the line was open the phone rang continually, with calls coming in from all over the world. Relatives were anxious for news of their loved ones. All we could do was to take the necessary details and pass on the enquiry. Whilst being driven round the completely devastated suburbs of Nightcliff, Casuarina and Ludmilla, I couldn't help noticing the signs people had erected - many with a tone of humour. The outstanding one to my mind was a notice on the board of the Darwin High School: "Book of the Month, GONE WITH THE WIND."

The police, who were given mammoth tasks, stayed calm and extremely helpful to everyone, provided those they came into contact with stayed on the right side of the law. They, too, managed to retain a sense of humour. Whilst sitting on the tarmac for the planes one day, I asked if one of the policemen had a piece of string. No, he could only find a length of plastic which needed cutting –if someone had a pair of scissors. I produced the scissors, and upon completing the task they took it in turns to have a manicure. Talking with a policeman one morning, I asked how things were going. He said, "We've been told to smarten ourselves up and go back to wearing blue and navy blue. I look alright, don't I?" He was wearing navy shorts, a T-shirt, duty boots with a bright pair of football socks, plus a green army hat with his badge on the front.

The members of the team gradually returned to Sydney to allow new personnel into Darwin from other states. The relief teams started to arrive, firstly from South Australia, then from Western Australia. The first twenty-four Red Cross personnel never considered themselves two separate teams; they worked tirelessly to help others as a united, happy coordinated body. After watching and helping some of the members to board the Hercules bound for Sydney, I only hoped that we would be lucky enough to return on a commercial plane. Luck was with us, and the final eight to return to Sydney travelled by TAA, who lived up to their slogan and were extremely friendly. On coming in to land at Brisbane, the delightful hostess who was sitting behind me leant forward, saying, "Would you like some perfume?" Laughing, I replied, "I'm not quite sure how to take that?"

"A girl does like to smell nice," she said. I accepted the offer of the perfume, but declined the offer of nail polish. Whether or not I needed to change my deodorant I wasn't quite sure, as I had completely lost my sense of smell during my stay in Darwin. I was told that the streets smelt unpleasant and I didn't query the comment, as I was sure the stench was pretty high. My family greeted me at the airport with, "Aren't you a mess!" and the embraces were quickly over. I realised that a shower with plenty of soap was a priority.

Back in Sydney, on returning to Headquarters on the Monday morning, I quickly became involved in assisting with tracing. By this time a system had been well established, but numerous difficulties were still being encountered due to lack of information from relatives. Anxious, almost desperate phone calls and telexes were being received from Darwin. "A husband is almost demented – he has not heard from his wife." The available manifests were vague, and it wasn't until the end of the week of the 10th January that the tracing people were able really to answer that mountain of queries. The Department of Social Services released the names of all who had received benefits. Lists of people accommodated at the Commonwealth hostels were made available, and so after long searches and many anxious days, news was passed on as to the whereabouts of families.

Thanks have come in many ways, such as a biro from a lady at Darwin Airport, given me when I needed it. Her son had drowned in the cyclone – another son had drowned some years earlier. Many said "Thank you". It was the thanks from the average Darwin people that made our involvement so worthwhile. Several people who returned to have their wounds re-dressed at the Red Cross Headquarters in Darwin said "The hospital staff are very good – but at Red Cross we receive TENDER LOVING CARE."

BETTY WATCHAM. Member of the 1st NSW DIVISION RED CROSS DISASTER EMERGENCIES TEAM.

25th February 1975.

Photograph by Ramon Williams

Photograph by Ramon Williams

dri·tot

SIZE

DARWIN PUBLIC LIBRARY

Photograph by Ramon Williams

Photograph by Ramon Williams

Photograph by Ramon Williams

CITY OF DARWIN

CENTENARY 1969

WOOLWORTHS

Photograph by Ramon Williams

Photograph by Ramon Williams

Photograph by Ramon Williams

Photograph by Ramon Williams

Photograph by Ramon Williams

Photograph by Ranson Williams

Photograph by Ramon Williams

Photograph by Ramon Williams

Photograph by Ramon Williams

In 1974, the most destructive tropical cyclone recorded in Australia's history devastated Darwin on Christmas Eve, turning the city into a war zone. This book is a collection of survivor stories.

When I first began putting this book together, I had no idea how gut-wrenchingly sad it would be. While working on the formatting of this book, and reading a few passages here and there, I found myself crying as the words on the page opened old wounds and memories I'd thought long healed and long forgotten. How wrong I was. It was then that I began to realise just how traumatic it must have been, too, for those retelling their stories from that terrible night so long ago.

Some penned stories of innocent lives lost, others of how beloved family pets had been torn from their arms, then shot to prevent the spread of disease. All remembered the demonic sound of the wind as invisible hands snatched loved ones away, while the walls, ceilings and eventually the floorboards vanished from beneath their feet. Many tell of the dystopian, war-like devastation that greeted them as they crawled out from beneath the rubble as the sun rose on that fateful Christmas morning, grateful still to be alive.

How it was that so many survived that brutal, unforgiving night will forever remain a mystery to me, and to the thousands of other souls who survived the night from hell with Tracy.

Patti Roberts. Author/Publisher.

To all those who supplied photographs and took the time to write down their stories before they were lost forever.

THANK YOU.

Cyclone Tracy photos online
http://bit.ly/CycloneTracypicsonline

Printed in Great Britain
by Amazon

78463385R00226